Brothers

Brothers

A Memoir of Love, Loss, and Race

Nico Slate

 TEMPLE UNIVERSITY PRESS
Philadelphia / Rome / Tokyo

TEMPLE UNIVERSITY PRESS
Philadelphia, Pennsylvania 19122
tupress.temple.edu

Design by Kate Nichols

Library of Congress Cataloging-in-Publication Data

Names: Slate, Nico, author.
Title: Brothers : a memoir of love, loss, and race / Nico Slate.
Description: Philadelphia : Temple University Press, 2023. | Includes
    bibliographical references. | Summary: "A story of love and loss across
    the color line, Brothers is a historian's quest to make sense of the
    life and death of his older brother, a mixed-race hip-hop artist and
    screenwriter, who was the victim of a racially charged attack"—
    Provided by publisher.
Identifiers: LCCN 2022042454 (print) | LCCN 2022042455 (ebook) | ISBN
    9781439923825 (cloth) | ISBN 9781439923849 (pdf)
Subjects: LCSH: Slate, Peter, 1972–2003. | XL the 1I, 1972–2003. | Slate,
    Nico—Family. | Brothers—Biography. | Rap musicians—United
    States—Biography. | Screenwriters—United States—Biography. | Racially
    mixed families—Biography. | United States—Race relations—Biography. |
    LCGFT: Biographies.
Classification: LCC HQ759.96 .S58 2023 (print) | LCC HQ759.96 (ebook) |
    DDC 306.850973—dc23/eng/20221227
LC record available at https://lccn.loc.gov/2022042454
LC ebook record available at https://lccn.loc.gov/2022042455

Printed in the United States of America

9 8 7 6 5 4 3 2 1

FOR KAREN SLATE—

Age cannot wither her,

nor custom stale her infinite variety.

—WILLIAM SHAKESPEARE,
  Antony and Cleopatra

Contents

Brothers

The Joshua Tree

T HE NIGHT MY GRANDFATHER DIED and my brother lost his right eye, I slept with all the windows open. Spring had come to the Mojave. The air smelled of sagebrush and rain, and tiny gold flowers speckled the dark basalt hills. The desert, for all its austerity, knows how to be grateful. Seeing the first buds of spring, our mother would quote Kahlil Gibran: "The deeper that sorrow carves into your being, the more joy you can contain." Maybe that's why she moved us to the middle of the Mojave, two miles off the paved road, between the dunes and the cracked clay of the dry lake. Our mother found beauty in survival.

She let me sleep through the first call. Her father had been sick a long time; his death brought tears but also relief. The second call brought only terror. My brother, Peter Slate, had been assaulted at a nightclub in Los Angeles. He was a large Black man dancing with a young White woman, and a group of skinheads attacked him—at least, that's how I understood it then. Years later, I found a more complicated story in the police report. My brother left the dance floor to put his beer down on a table. He exchanged words with a man sitting at the table. Both had been drinking, and their argument escalated. The man at the table was White, as was the other man who came from behind and smashed a bottle into my brother's right eye, pushing glass up toward his brain. My family saw the attack as a hate crime, but what role did race play that night?

The security guards let the attackers go and grabbed my brother instead. They twisted his arm behind his back and shoved him into an alley. The police found him barely conscious, slumped on the pavement, his shirt soaked in blood. When our mother got the call, the doctors did not know whether he had brain damage. He had lost the eye, but they didn't tell her that. She had slept one hour after grieving her father, and now she faced losing a son. She woke me by yelling my name.

My brother and I had the same mother, but different fathers. His was from Nigeria. Having a White mother and a White brother complicated his Blackness, but it did not change how he was seen by strangers as he walked down the street—or danced in a club with a White woman. He was Black. I was White, and so were the men who attacked him.

The drive to the hospital was strangely reassuring. We had driven into LA so many times that the road had become an extension of home. It was only three hours through Barstow, Victorville, Palmdale. Most of the ride was sand and sagebrush. Nothing disturbed the desert, not the occasional clump of gas stations and fast-food shacks, not the outlet mall where my friends sold cheap luggage to tourists on their way to Vegas. We considered taking the Cajon Pass, a route I associated with fierce winds that toppled trailer trucks, but decided on the 138, a winding two-lane road known as the Deathtrap Highway. Every week, some exhausted driver would swerve into oncoming traffic. Normally, we found a big truck and stayed behind it, like a running back with a blocker. That morning, desperate for speed, we careened around every car on the road.

The sun had yet to rise, but the night was already lifting, a vague blue shadow slouching toward the hills. I watched my mother's face, afraid to ask how she was feeling. Her mouth was clenched tight. Her long dark hair flapped in the wind. I looked out at the desert. The air was painfully clear. My brother was hurt. My mother was driving us to the hospital. There was nothing to keep my mind from her face or his.

Then came the Joshua trees. In school, I learned that Mormon pioneers had coined the name. The towering yucca, its branches twisting upward, reminded them of Joshua reaching his hands up in prayer. The first time my brother and I drove that road, he stopped the car next to a thick grove. Without explanation, he slid out of the driver's seat, crossed in front of the car, and walked twenty feet off the road to the base of a towering tree. I figured he was going to pee, but he waved me toward him. I climbed out and pulled on a baseball cap. It was hot, and I could smell the highway roasting in the sun. He placed his big hands on the jagged spines of the tree, turned to me, and smiled: "They're softer than they look."

Speeding toward the hospital, I thought about his hands on that Joshua tree. He was always doing that kind of thing, putting his hands in a river or on a rock, finding new ways to touch the world. I thought about his hands and tried not to think about his face, what they had done to his face.

I was fourteen. My brother, seven years older, was my best friend and the closest thing I had to a father. When I was seven and we still lived in the city, the Domino's Pizza guy was mugged outside our home. We had iron bars over our windows, but I was still too scared to sleep. My brother sat by my bed, held my hand, and told me that there was only one tool that could cut through those iron bars. It had a diamond blade that cost thousands of dollars. Even with that special saw, it would still take robbers more than three hours to cut through one bar, and the high-pitched squeal of the saw would wake everyone in the neighborhood. I slept deeply from then on.

The sun had risen by the time we reached the hospital, yet the hallways were strangely silent. We met the doctor in a tiny room—too bright, too clean—crowded with white plastic chairs. I have no memory of what he said, perhaps because I was overwhelmed by what came next: my brother in the hospital bed, his face covered in white bandages, dark blood seeping through the gauze. The air smelled of antiseptic. He forced a grin, of course, always trying to make us happy. When we were in the room with him, I believed that everything would be fine, but when I stepped into the hall, a shadow washed over my eyes, and I woke up on the floor. I had passed out. Worried about a concussion, the doctors put me in the room next door. Our poor mother—her father gone, and now both her sons in the hospital.

I wish I could have shown her that it would be OK, that we would be OK, at least for a while. I wish I could have brought her forward six years to that night in San Francisco when my brother opened the

Fillmore, wearing that black patch that would become his trademark, the patch that hid more than one secret where his eye had once been.

THE CROWD WAS PULSING like a vein. The lights dimmed. The bass rumbled. Smoke filled the air. Everyone screamed when he ran onto the stage. His arms cut through the smoke like the wings of a giant bird. As the spotlight lit up his face, bags of pot rained down on the stage. He picked one up, held it in the air, and screamed into the mic: "You ready to rock the Fillmore?!"

I looked around the crowd and thought, none of these people know what this means to him. They had not seen him perform Michael Jackson routines in the supermarket line. They had never woken to him belting, again and again, the same ten-second clip from George Michael: *If you love me, say you love me, but if you don't, just le-et me go-o-o!* Unless they knew Peter Slate the man as well as XL the rapper—how could they know that this was his dream?

He was onstage at the Fillmore. One of the pillars of 1960s counterculture, the Fillmore hosted almost every major performer of the era: the Doors, Jefferson Airplane, Jimi Hendrix, Santana, the Who, Led Zeppelin, Pink Floyd. The Grateful Dead played the venue more than fifty times, cementing its reputation as the mecca of the counterculture. My brother was not the first person to wave a bag of weed from that stage. In *Fear and Loathing in Las Vegas*, Hunter S. Thompson remembers spending night after night "half-crazy" at the Fillmore, steeped in wild music and drug-induced euphoria. Now, it was Cypress Hill rocking the room, and my brother hyping the crowd.

XL the 1I. The name fit. He was always a big guy and had gained weight in his twenties. The reference to his eye made sense too. The patch suggested a certain toughness, a street-hardened authenticity that couldn't hurt an aspiring rapper, especially someone who had not grown up in Compton or the Bronx, someone with a White little brother tagging along. Cypress Hill was of the street in a way Peter Slate was not. The patch bridged that gap, but not as a mask or a disguise. Sure, it helped him look hard, but what was it—that black flag across his face—if not a sign of his own mortality?

I don't know how my brother joined the Cypress Hill family. Everyone told me he'd always been around. Maybe that was true in a way. XL was born through his ties to Cypress Hill. But Peter Slate definitely wasn't there at the beginning. He was still crooning teenage love songs with his boy band, Up N' Comin, when two Cuban American brothers, Senen Reyes (Sen Dog) and Ulpiano Sergio Reyes (Mellow Man Ace) became the nucleus of a new rap group. The year was 1988, after the Sugarhill Gang and KRS-One, before Tupac and Snoop Dogg and Biggie Smalls. Hip-hop had gained mainstream attention but was only just becoming an industry of its own. Cypress Hill helped define hip-hop by stretching its boundaries—musically, personally, and racially. The Reyes brothers partnered with an Italian American DJ, Lawrence Muggerud (DJ Muggs), and Louis Freese (B-Real), the son of a Cuban mother and a Mexican father. It doesn't surprise me that my brother, a mixed-race man, would find his musical home with Cypress Hill. Like him, they lived across racial borders. But their bond was growing up on the wrong side of the tracks, and we were from the Valley! Was it the patch? Did that glass bottle that shattered his eye open the door to hip-hop stardom?

Let's call him Steven—the one who started the fight, not the one who hit my brother with the bottle. I found his real name and phone number in the police report, and now I'm sitting on my front porch in a camping chair, working up the courage to make the call. It's a bright fall day in Pittsburgh in October 2014. The air smells of leaves and wood smoke. It's been more than twenty years, but many people keep the same number, and I have to be prepared for Steven to answer the phone. I practice my introduction:

> My name is Nico Slate. I'm a historian writing a book about my brother, Peter Slate. He was involved in an incident in the Renaissance Club in Santa Monica on March 22, 1994, an incident you might be able to help me understand.

An incident. A fight. An attack. A crime. My words matter. I need to make clear that I'm not interested in vengeance or even justice. I want only the truth.

Do I want only the truth? I'm fooling myself if I think that I can approach this as a historian and not as a brother. I'm curious, but also angry and confused. I don't know what I want from this man who bears responsibility for my brother losing his eye, but it's more than the truth.

A shrill whine erupts across the street. Our compulsive neighbor is cleaning her stairs again. I'm annoyed by her leaf blower and fumble for my headphones. Then, I remember my purpose: I'm calling Steven. My mouth is dry, and I reach for a can of cheap soda water. It's empty. I consider going inside to make the call. It's daytime, and I don't want to use my cell phone minutes. I can use the house phone instead. Strange, how you can think so small and so big in the same moment. Cell phone minutes, soda can, glass bottle smashed across his face, his bright green eye.

It wasn't a fight, really. According to the police report and all the witnesses I tracked down, my brother and Steven had only a few seconds of tense confrontation before another man entered from the side with a beer bottle. The police never identified that man. When I spoke with the police sergeant, he used a phrase that I thought was reserved for the movies: "The file is cold."

The file is cold. The sergeant's voice sounded defensive. He knew that he had nothing to tell me that I wanted to hear. "It isn't like today," he explained, "where there would be a hundred cameras recording everything." The idea lingers. If only I could see that moment from a hundred angles, like the Buddhist goddess of compassion, Guanyin, whose thousand arms stretch out to comfort the suffering. Even if I get through to Steven, all he can offer are his own biased memories. If I had footage, even just one grainy recording, I would pore over it, searching for clues. Instead, I go back to the police report:

W1 [witness 1] said she had been dancing with Slate near the edge of the dance floor when Slate appeared to ask S2 [suspect 2], who was standing near the dance floor, to take Slate's beer bottle and put it down for him. An argument ensued between Slate and S2 and suddenly S1 [suspect 1] came from the side, in W1's peripheral vision, and swung at Slate's face with a bottle. WI did not see S1 because it happened so fast. As we were talking S2 walked out and was standing by the rear door of Renaissance when W1 pointed him out as being the one who Slate had been arguing with immediately before the incident.

S2 is Steven. He is White, 5'10", 155 pounds, brown hair, hazel eyes, medium complexion, brown shirt, black cap, twenty-two years old. Now, he would be forty-six. He might have kids. They might be home when I call.

S1 swung the bottle. He's also White, twenty-five to twenty-seven years of age at the time, 5'10", 170 pounds, brown hair, wearing a blue shirt. I don't know his name, only his crime: assault with a deadly weapon. That's what the report says. Nothing about motive. Nothing about the role that race played that night.

Mom remembers the police deeming it a hate crime. Her certainty makes me suspicious. I ask Uncle Dan, expecting him to corroborate my doubts, but he also remembers it as a hate crime and adds that the man who swung the bottle yelled, "We got the n****r."

The police sergeant informs me that the hate-crime law did not exist when my brother was attacked, and so "it couldn't have been reported as a hate crime." That's only partially true. It wasn't until September 1994, six months after the attack, that the Violent Crime Control and Law Enforcement Act heightened the penalties for federal hate crimes. But the first hate-crime statute in California had been passed in 1978, and the Civil Rights Act of 1968 had allowed federal prosecution of anyone who "willingly injures, intimidates or interferes with another person, or attempts to do so, by force because of the other person's race, color, religion or national origin."

I am tempted to play the historian card, to explain to the policeman that there was a hate-crime law in California when my brother was attacked. Instead, I thank him and hang up with most of my questions unanswered. I could blame my fear of conflict, but something bigger constrains me, something that prevents me from calling Steven, something I must confront before I can uncover the truth about the night my brother lost his eye.

WHEN I WAS TEN and he was seventeen, we went camping at a lake ringed by hills. One of the hills pressed up against the lakeshore, its summit reaching out over the water. The older kids jumped off the edge, their wet skin gleaming in the light as they plummeted toward the dark water. The drop couldn't have been more than twenty feet, but when my brother asked whether I wanted to try the leap, I was terrified. We were sprawled on inflatable donuts, our gazes turned up toward the cliff. He had no way of seeing my face, yet he sensed my fear immediately. "You don't need to jump, bro. I get it. It looks like a long way from down here." He paused, and I could tell that he wasn't going to leave it there. I could hear the soft lapping of the waves, interrupted by a loud splash every time someone made the leap. "We can just chill here." He paused again. "I bet the scariest part is right now, just thinking about it. Once you're in the air, it's gonna be fast, and it's gonna be fun." I stayed quiet, staring up at the edge of that cliff. "If you want to stay here, I'll stay with you," he said. "If you want to jump, I'll jump with you." I imagined what it would feel like to leap off the side of that hill with my brother. The other kids wouldn't have seen us as brothers, his dark brown body against my sunburned pink. I didn't care. Wherever I was, my brother would be there with me.

SOMETIMES, I WISH WE COULD demolish the entire edifice of race—crumble it like a mountain of glass and push it all into the sea. Then, I remember that night my brother lost his eye, and I know that the wounds of the past are still with us, that we cannot pretend race does not exist if we are to fight racism. I am a White man writing about a Black man, even if I am writing about my brother. I failed to press that police sergeant for the same reason I'm scared to call Steven: the more I learn about my brother, the more I'm forced to recognize the distance between us. That's what drives me to forget my own place in our divided world. I cannot know my brother if I do not know myself, but knowing myself means accepting that I cannot fully know my brother. Steven and I share more than I want to admit.

I'M STILL SITTING on the porch in my camping chair, gripping my phone with both hands, too scared to make the call. Steven might not be a skinhead or a member of the Klan. Maybe he's just an average White guy who doesn't think much about race. Maybe jealousy explains what happened that night. My brother had a way with women. There was something about him—his boyish face, his green eyes—that made him hard to overlook. It wasn't just that he was 6'6" and 200 pounds. He loved to party, to dance and laugh and sing. Maybe the attackers were jealous.

Maybe they were jealous and drunk. Everyone was drinking. Later, my brother would blame the booze for his own behavior, his failure to protect himself. If Steven and his friends were also drunk, their actions cannot be separated from the effects of alcohol.

One witness offers a third explanation: he says that the girl was overweight and that the attackers were making fun of her. My brother defended her, and that's what sparked the conflict. I like this interpretation; Peter Slate loved being the chivalrous stranger. Yet even if things escalated because he was defending the girl, even if everyone had been drinking, it remains unclear why it was my brother who ended up in that alley, bleeding from what had been his right eye.

All the witnesses said that the men were watching him dance with the girl. Maybe they thought, "That Black guy deserves to be taught a lesson." Maybe they used the N-word, as Uncle Dan remembers being told. Maybe they didn't. I try to put myself at that table, another White guy drinking beer and watching a tall Black man showing off on the dance floor. I close my eyes and imagine staring at the crowd, the beer loosening my muscles and heating my blood, the pulse of the music like a tick in my jaw. That tall guy spins and laughs. Who does he think he is? This joker, this clown, this asshole, this . . . somewhere, somehow, I must recognize that he's Black. Even if I never think the word, it hangs in the air like smoke. In Los Angeles in 1994, as in any American city today, a group of White people could not look at a Black stranger and not see him as Black.

Two witnesses said that they heard Steven and a group of friends congratulating each other after the attack. "We got him good," they heard someone say. "We got the n****r" is what Uncle Dan remembers my brother telling him. Why doesn't the police report say anything about the role that race played that night? The report describes the music at the club as "some rap band" and says that "the crowd seemed especially young, 20–21 years." The phrase "some rap band" makes me wonder whether the police saw the violence as somehow inevitable. These were the days of Ice-T's "Cop Killer," of mass hysteria about gangster rap. I wonder whether that influenced how the police responded to the attack, why they didn't make any arrests, perhaps even why the security guards let the attacker slip away and instead grabbed my brother and threw him bleeding into the alley. He looked dangerous. He wasn't a rapper yet, but his skin color already linked him to the violence that many White people associated with hip-hop.

Steven told the police that he was working as a promoter for one of the bands playing that night. The manager of the club denied that Steven had been hired as a promoter. Steven claimed that he was not involved in the fight, that he had been standing far away when the commotion began, yet both police officers noted a splatter of blood on Steven's right pant leg. That is how they describe it in the report: "a splatter of blood." My brother's blood. Blood from what was his eye, dried on the pants of this man I am about to call on the phone. To say what? "Hello, my name is Nico Slate. I am a historian writing a book about my brother, Peter Slate. Do you have blood on your hands?"

I lean back into the camping chair, watch a fat white cloud float across the sky, and try to picture Steven. I have no idea what he looks like, but somehow I try to imagine his face. What about the other man, the one who swung the bottle—what is he doing now? Strange, that the hand that brought that sharp glass against my brother's face might be caressing a child or a dog. Strange, how easy it is to put myself at that table, to look across the color line the way those men looked at my brother. That man is different from me. That Black man is different from me—and from that difference, the bottle swings.

I'm wasting time. I take a deep breath and dial the number. It rings twice and then: "The number you have dialed is disconnected or no longer in service." I breathe out, let my head sag into the chair, and a memory returns.

I'm seven years old, sitting in a dark movie theater, straining to see over the seat in front of me. It's my birthday, and my brother has brought me to see *The Three Amigos*. He folds his puffy jacket and slides it under my butt. He's only fourteen, but there is nothing but confidence in his face. His high cheeks, his strong jaw, his smooth brown

I always looked up to my brother. (Author's collection.)

skin—all of him lit up by that magical flickering movie-screen light. He tells me to sit up as tall as possible and tilt my baseball cap upward. The idea is that no one will sit behind us. Just as the movie starts, we move one row back, leaving two open seats in front of us. I don't remember whether the trick worked, whether those seats remained empty, but I can still feel the thrill of sitting next to my brother, straining my body up toward his glowing face.

ON AUGUST 31, 1997, the day after Peter Slate turned twenty-five, and three years after he lost his right eye, a Mercedes-Benz W140 collided with a concrete pillar in the Pont de l'Alma tunnel in Paris. The car's most famous passenger, Princess Diana, died a few hours later. Also killed were the driver, Henri Paul, and Diana's boyfriend, Dodi Fayed. The son of an Egyptian billionaire, Fayed was a film producer whose credits included *Chariots of Fire*, *Hook*, and *The Scarlet Letter*. He had purchased the rights to one of my brother's screenplays but hadn't come through with the money.

I was entering college that fall; that's my excuse for not knowing more about my brother's relationship to Fayed. I didn't realize it then, but going to college would begin a long period of distance between us. He knew that my going to college would strain our connection, just as he knew that I was more nervous about college than I would admit. Maybe that's why he insisted on dropping me off at campus for my first semester, why he never mentioned Fayed on that long drive up the Central Valley. He didn't want to confuse my anxieties with his own.

Ten minutes from campus, he shocked me by stopping at Fry's Electronics to buy me my first computer. It was 1998, and a personal computer was a luxury. It was the kind of thing he had done throughout my life—surprise me with a gift that showed that he supported my dreams. He knew that I needed his love to survive those first weeks of college. He also knew that I would find my footing, that I would come home a different person.

Years later, Mom told me that just after they left my dorm, my brother pulled over to the side of the road. He felt as if he had forgotten something back at the dorm. It was me—he was missing me. He thought back to all those times he had dropped me off at a friend's house or at school. He would always be back to pick me up. Now, he was saying goodbye for months and, in some ways, forever. The child he was dropping off would never return. He put the car into park and wept.

We talked less and less over the course of that year, and whole episodes of his life passed me by, including his dealings with Fayed. I stored those dealings in the category of "stories I exaggerated as a child"—like that epic ninja battle that turned out to be a couple of teenagers in Halloween costumes. It would be years before I realized my mistake, before I stumbled upon evidence that Fayed did owe my brother money, a lot of money, and that the trouble with Fayed was linked to the night my brother lost his eye.

It's a Tuesday, Election Day, in November 2014. I'm sitting at the kitchen table, eating a banana smeared with peanut butter, trying to decide how to vote in the local Pittsburgh races that never make the news. It's cold, and I'm draped in a red wool blanket. I open my computer to look up a particular candidate but instead google, "Peter Slate Dodi Fayed," and before I can swallow a bite of banana, I'm reading about my brother in *Variety* magazine. The article, "High Price for Payday," describes his screenplay *Rave* as a crime thriller focused on a female cop hunting a serial killer in the "post-punk nightclub scene." Fayed had purchased the script "for low-six figures." Several first-time screenwriters had recently landed lucrative deals, but "perhaps no one deserves the money more than Peter Slate." While "doing research" for the script, the article explains, my brother was "coldcocked on the dance floor of a punk club in Santa Monica . . . stabbed in the face with a broken bottle, and lost his eye." I look up from my laptop, lean back against the cold metal chair, and close my eyes. I can taste the salt of the peanut butter, and I'm crying.

Is the story true? I know that the Renaissance wasn't exactly a "punk club" and that Peter Slate wasn't "doing research" that night, but the description of the screenplay is accurate, and I need to know whether that script is linked to my brother losing his eye. I take another bite of banana, close the *Variety* article, and scroll through the search results. I'm about to close my laptop when a link draws my eye to an Associated Press article that was published in newspapers across the country. Readers learned that my brother had sued Fayed's estate after the car crash with Princess Diana and that the judge dismissed the case when my brother failed to appear in court. It's bizarre that my brother would be mixed up with a figure like Fayed, bizarre that the names Dodi Fayed, Peter Slate, and Princess Diana were lumped together by readers of the *Pantagraph* in Bloomington, Illinois, and the *Kokomo Tribune* in Kokomo, Indiana. I imagine old couples discussing this peculiar anecdote over breakfast. I wonder whether their questions were the same as mine: Why didn't he show up in court? Was the script ever turned into a movie?

My brother wrote more than a dozen screenplays, fourteen by my count. He loved unfolding a story. Often, in the middle of a conversation, he would stumble upon a new idea for a script and whip out a mini-recorder: "The scene is the Mall of America. A legion of demons breaks through the glass windows and descends upon the terrified shoppers. Our hero looks up and smiles." That mini-recorder went everywhere with him. Later, I would find boxes filled with tiny tapes, each one packed with ideas for scripts, songs, stories, even jokes (he tried stand-up for a while). One of his scripts made it to video, but he knew that it was nearly impossible to get one onto the big screen. Still, he kept writing, even after his hip-hop career began to heat up and he landed a radio gig on Power 106. He kept writing because he loved to write and because he coped with failure by digging deeper into his dreams.

A few months after he lost his eye, we spent a week together in the desert. It was hot, and we slept with the windows open. The spring rains had gone, and the air that trickled in was parched and unsatisfying. One night, I awoke at three in the morning, covered in sweat. I stumbled toward the bathroom to pee and found him sitting on the couch, his computer on his lap, working on a new script. He looked up at me. "This one's really coming together," he said. "My hero is coming to life." His face glowed with computer light. Still half-asleep, I stared at him, then used the bathroom and staggered back toward my bedroom. Something stopped me in the doorway, and I leaned back toward him. "Tell me about him in the morning. Your hero." He looked up and smiled.

I FINISH THE BANANA, put the peanut butter back on the shelf, and stare at the photo of my brother that hangs on our fridge. He's wearing the patch, the black elastic strap snug across his forehead. It looks too tight, and I feel a strange urge to pull it off.

That night, something wakes me at two in the morning. I check to see whether my son is having a bad dream. No, he's sound asleep. I'm too awake to go back to bed and so take my laptop to the bathroom, where I won't disturb my wife, Emily. I open a browser, planning to read the news, but google Steven instead. I know his full name, birth-date, and address in 1994. Nothing works. I try Facebook; too many men share his name. I scroll through their photos until my eyes ache, then close my laptop and stare at its shiny aluminum skin. The bath-room floor is cold against my feet. Suddenly, I remember the friend who offered Steven an alibi that night, the friend who told the police that she was with him in the VIP room while my brother was assaulted on the dance floor. Her name is less common. I open the laptop, and within seconds I am reading her Facebook profile. What am I to do with this person I have never seen, never spoken to, this person who twenty years ago lied to protect the men who took my brother's eye? I ask her to be-come my "friend."

My eyes are aching, my back hurts, and my feet are freezing. I should have put my slippers on. I'm exhausted and want to go back to bed, but I need to explain to this woman why I sent her a "friend" request. I copy and paste the language I had prepared for my phone call with Steven:

> My name is Nico Slate. I am a historian writing a book about my brother, Peter Slate. He was involved in an incident in the Renaissance Club in Santa Monica on March 22, 1994, an inci-dent you might be able to help me understand.

Then, I reconsider. Why does this woman need to know that I'm a historian? Does it make what I'm doing less threatening? In that case, maybe I shouldn't mention that Peter Slate is my brother. I could feign complete objectivity. That would be lying, of course. Maybe I'm already lying to myself, to think that I can write this book as a historian and as a brother and not have to choose, to think that writing about the violence my brother faced as a Black man will somehow bring us closer.

I send the message unchanged and close my eyes. The bathroom smells like lavender. I can hear the sound machine coming from the baby's room, a soft white hiss. My head grows heavy. I rest it on my hands and think back to that long drive through the desert and my brother in his hospital bed trying to make me laugh, half of his face shrouded in white bandages. We called it the "dressing," a strange word that the doctors used and that we adopted without discussion. The nurses changed it once a day, always when we were gone. After the first day, it was easy to forget what was underneath those bandages. But the morning that we arrived at the hospital, a dark shadow stained the dressing where his right eye used to be, a circle of blood we could not ignore. It shifted every time he smiled.

It's HIS FIRST NIGHT HOME from the hospital, and we're in the kitchen. The countertops are cluttered as usual: duct tape, a ruler, a pair of socks, like an open-air junk drawer. He floats an idea: maybe we should remove the dressing. Maybe we should assess the damage. He has not seen the wound, and neither have we.

The dishes from dinner are piled in the sink, half-covered in soapy water. They will sit there all night. The Slate family way of washing dishes—the soak method. Just as piles of clean clothes sit on the couch for weeks, our sink is rarely without dishes. We are good at procrastination, at not seeing the mess in which we live, until the mess becomes too big to ignore.

"Should we take a look?" He points at the square white bandage that covers what was his eye. His "we" is ambiguous. As he and Mom walk through the living room toward the bathroom, I'm not sure whether I should follow. I'm fourteen and have been treated as an adult for longer than is good for me. He would never tell me not to come, but I don't know whether I should, especially given that I had passed out in the hospital. I'm afraid that I will let him down again, but I don't want him to think I can't handle it. I don't want him to think his wound is that bad, as if my being there might prove that it isn't such a big thing after all to lose an eye.

It's a warm night in the desert, and we have the swamp cooler on high. The wet air softens the heat, but only if you're standing within three feet of a vent. Otherwise, the night clings to the skin, hot and dry. I walk over to one of the vents and let the cold air fill my shirt like a balloon. I take a deep breath, then stride toward my brother.

As I enter the bedroom, I hear him call out in pain. It's not a scream but a sharp gasp, followed by my mom's voice, almost a whisper, "I'm sorry." "It's OK," he says. I'm standing two feet from the door of the bathroom, close enough to smell the antiseptic spray we have been given to wash the wound. I wait, unsure whether to go in or to retreat to the kitchen. They are quiet now, and they stay quiet for what feels like a long time. Finally, I force myself to round the corner. I see her first, standing behind him, the bandages in one hand, the other hand resting on his back. They look like a Renaissance fresco, the mother blessing the child.

My brother stares intently in the mirror. His wound is on the other side of his body, but I can see it in the mirror. A gash, pink and purple, cuts across his eyebrow and down his cheek. Where his eye had been, a hole deep and red, "inflamed" the doctors might say, as if it were on fire. I don't want to stare. I don't want him to see me stare, but I cannot look away. So, I stand there, trying to be casual, as if every night after dinner we gather in Mom's bathroom to air our wounds.

TEN YEARS LATER, I'm back in the desert. It's the winter of 2003, and I'm a few months shy of my twenty-fourth birthday. I feel all grown-up in that way that only a kid can feel, as I stand on the back deck, a thin wool blanket pulled over my shoulders, looking out over the wind-swept sage. It's really blowing now, a hard December gale that tears across the dry lake and over the dunes, rocking our mobile home like a ship at sea. I turn my back on the wind and walk into the kitchen, locking the deadbolt to keep the door from blowing open. The kitchen is dusty and cluttered, a pile of dishes in the sink. I pass through the living room, covered with half-packed boxes, and step into Mom's old bedroom. I stop near the spot where I had waited all those years earlier, when the two people I loved most in the world had huddled together with a pack of bandages and a can of antiseptic spray.

The silence is broken by a quiet whistling, as if one of the windows is open. I check them, one by one; they're all shut and locked. The whistling persists. Is there a crack in the roof? I look up just as a strong gust hits the side of the house. It feels like the roof might pull right off, exposing our mess to the sky.

I turn to my left and step into Mom's closet, stuffed with boxes that need sorting. Most of this junk is bound for the dumpster. I pry the lid off an old box and start to rummage through when a large manila envelope catches my eye. It's labeled "Peter" in Mom's handwriting, with a heart drawn carefully around the name. It's the heart that makes me pull the envelope out of the box. As I pry open the metal clasp, a glossy photo slips onto the floor. I look down and then away reflexively, as if pulling my finger back from a flame. It's a photo of my brother's eye socket, shattered and bloodied. It must have been taken at the hospital after the attack. I look back again, but not for long. It's not disgust that makes me look away—more like guilt. I feel guilty seeing my brother's wound without his permission and ashamed by how quickly I look away. I turn the photo over, sit down on the floor, and pull the rest of the papers from the envelope. The wind rocks the house; the windows rattle.

Beneath a stack of terrible photos, each of which I look at as quickly as I can, I find a document I did not know existed, a document that I will study again and again for years: the police report. It's the first time I've seen it. In the months after the attack, I had cycled through the same unanswered questions: What happened? And why? With time, my focus shifted to my brother and his recovery and then, more quickly than I like to admit, back to the petty preoccupations of my own life. In my hands, in this police report, is a chance to return to that night with a new sense of purpose. As I read through the conflicting witness testimonies and official summaries, I begin a quest that will drive me to become a historian and to focus my research on the violence and trauma that shaped my family and this country.

It wasn't the police report that most startled me that day. It was a single sheet of thin, crepelike paper that became the foundational clue in my quest to understand my brother's life, to make sense of his evolution from a shy mixed-race kid to a rapper, screen writer, radio show host, and aspiring reality TV star—XL the 1I, that towering Black man who filled the stage at the Fillmore. It was the historian's favorite kind of find, a document that reveals not only through what it says but also through what it hides, and it startled me even more because I found it pressed amid those horrific images. Our mother, for reasons I still don't understand, had slipped among the carnage of the hospital photos an original copy of my brother's birth certificate.

Sitting on Mom's floor, staring at that birth certificate, I learned something I would come to see again and again as a historian—that the smallest detail can reframe a life, a family, a social movement, or an entire historical era. It was his name. I knew that he hadn't been born Peter Slate. Long before he became XL the 1I, he had left behind his original name, the name his father had given him: Uderulu Osakwe. I don't know why, but sitting on the floor, listening to the wind, and bringing that name to my lips, I saw how my brother embodied the story of a people—a people born, like him, in the space between Africa and America. The wounds he bore on his body were part of a larger history of suffering and struggle. I saw those wounds as if for the first time, and I realized that I would never know my brother if I couldn't explain what had happened to him that night he was attacked, and that I'd never be able to explain that night if I couldn't understand everything that came before.

Should I start at the beginning? His, not mine.

I ask Mom to tell me the story of his birth.

I have two kids now. I wish he knew them.

I ask Mom to tell the story.

I don't tell her that I can't imagine what she has lived through.

I say, "Tell me the story again."

And she does.

Uderulu Osakwe

Karen and Chukwudi

WHEN MY BROTHER WAS BORN, the doctors thought he was sick, but it turned out that he was just Black. Our mom beams telling the story, but I doubt she smiled when the doctor announced that her baby's bluish skin meant that he wasn't getting enough air. Did she panic, or did she see the error immediately? The baby had bluish skin because his father was from Africa. As a child, I liked to imagine my brother's father striding into the room and comforting the poor doctor: "Don't worry, my friend, you could not have known I was Black." The key phrase being "my friend," the word *Black* rendered harmless by the kind-hearted lilt of Chukwudi Osakwe. More than six feet tall and some two hundred pounds of soccer-toned muscle, Chukwudi might have been intimidating if not for his smile. Confronted with such a beaming grin, the doctor could not help but smile too. So do we whenever the story is told, safe in the knowledge that the doctor's error was a small thing, an easy mistake, to assume that if the mother is White, the father must be also.

I doubt that our mother was smiling. In August 1972, when my brother entered the world, she had not yet grown accustomed to being the woman with the African husband. She had not yet grown accustomed to the stares and forced smiles, the way landlords changed their story when Chukwudi appeared. She did not want to become accus-

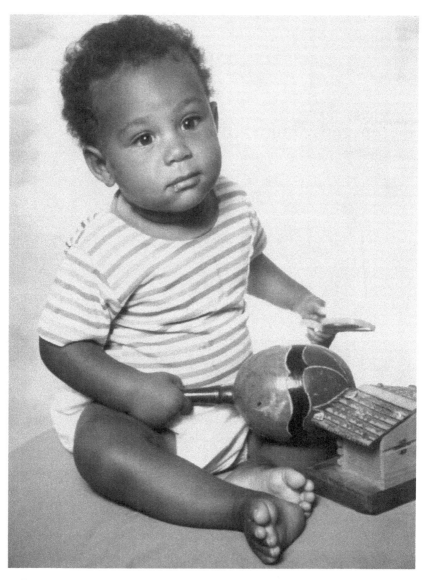

Uderulu Osakwe, already in love with music. (Author's collection.)

tomed to such a world. Karen Slate had been one of the few female physics majors at UCLA and one of the only White students to join the Black Student Union. She didn't mind standing out, but she didn't want her identity to be defined by her husband's skin color.

She wanted to live in a world beyond race. She knew that world did not exist. She knew that her newborn child had entered a country in which his body would be a problem. The doctor assumed the father was

White because he lived in a society where White was standard. Karen grew up in that world. Her freckled face and pale skin meant that her racial identity was never questioned. She had learned to see race, but only as many White liberals come to see race—as a problem to be solved from a distance. Chukwudi made that problem personal. Married to an African, Karen learned the difference between identity and identification, between how she saw herself and how the world saw her. She believed she was marrying the most amazing man she had ever met. The world saw her marrying a Black man.

So did her parents. When I was in middle school, I found a pile of her letters to them in a wicker trunk in her closet. When I opened the trunk, I was trespassing in the land of my mother's memories, but I felt no guilt. I was still too young to understand that her life was distinct from mine, that she might have secrets she wanted to keep her own.

TWENTY YEARS LATER, Mom and I are in Pittsburgh, sitting on her bed talking about my brother's birth, when I remember the wicker trunk, its brittle sides held together by a purple ribbon. Mom has stenosis and arthritis now and finds it hard to sit in a normal chair. She is reclined against a special foam pillow she bought from an AARP catalog. She sits up when I ask whether she remembers writing angry letters to her parents, letters that they must have returned to her and that she stored in that wicker trunk. I feel anxious as I explain.

"I never told you this, but one time, I found that trunk and—"

She interrupts me: "Honey, I knew you went through that stuff more than once. You always forgot to retie the ribbon."

She laughs and I look away, embarrassed. When she stops laughing, I ask, "Where are the letters now?"

"They must be in the basement." That "must be" is not reassuring. It's no use asking where in the basement the letters might be. It's a disaster zone: boxes piled on boxes. It takes hours of sorting through tax forms, electric bills, and old take-out menus before I find that familiar wicker trunk, its ribbon tattered and faded with age.

"Do you want to open it?" I hold the trunk in her direction.

"No, that's behind me now." She pauses. "But I'm glad you're interested."

"Why?"

"Sorry?"

"Why are you glad I'm interested?"

"Because he'd like it, what you're doing. He'd be proud of you."

I open the trunk and remove a stack of thin sheets of lined paper, fragile and stained brown at the edges. They smell like old books. I pick up the first letter and stare at my mother's handwriting, so careful and precise, as if she were practicing to become an elementary school teacher. Reading these letters for the first time, I was shocked by their defiant tone, by the courage with which she challenged her parents. Her boldness still stuns me:

> I love him. I want your support, and I believe you will support me . . . will support us. But we are getting married . . . with your support or without. I love you but I love him too. Why does it matter where he is from . . . the color of his skin?

She loves ellipses. I first noticed it in college, the way her emails flowed from thought to thought. Now I see where it came from, that unwillingness to hazard something as permanent as a period.

"Why does it matter where he is from . . . the color of his skin?" Why should it matter? My grandfather, a proud son of Nashville, Tennessee, had joined the NAACP when few White Southerners dared to support civil rights. My grandmother was from Illinois, the land of Lincoln. They lived in the liberal milieu of upper-class Los Angeles, a world where people accepted *Brown vs. Board of Education* and bemoaned the bigots who were making such a fuss in Alabama and Mississippi.

It was one thing to support integration in the South but something else to countenance their daughter marrying a Black man. Karen challenged her parents to choose between their prejudices and their daughter. I imagine that is not the choice they saw before them: in their eyes, they could allow their daughter to ruin her life, or they could force her to come to her senses.

On August 30, 1972, when my brother, Uderulu Peter Houston Carl Daniel Osakwe, entered the world, our mother's parents chose to stay home. Karen had offered them an olive branch in the middle names she gave her son. Houston: her father. Carl and Daniel: her brothers. "This child is yours too," she told her family. "Just look at his names."

In 1967, one year after Karen met Chukwudi, Spencer Tracy and Katharine Hepburn made famous the liberal White couple confronted with a daughter who had fallen in love with a Black man. But Karen wasn't starring in *Guess Who's Coming to Dinner*, and Chukwudi wasn't Sidney Poitier playing the perfect suitor. He wasn't far from perfection, though, at least in our mom's eyes, and in mine too. I grew up seeing him as the embodiment of cosmopolitan grace. He was the distinguished foreigner, his fate bound up with the destiny of a distant land. My brother saw him that way, too, at least part of the time, but he wanted more from Chukwudi than a glamorous mystery. He wanted a father.

Maybe that's why he never tried to dig up the past, never pursued his father until it was too late. Maybe that's why it fell to me to uncover the story of Chukwudi Osakwe. Sometimes it feels like a betrayal—to learn things my brother should have known, to see his father as he always wanted to see him. It's all I have to keep him with me, this unfinished story that is now ours. It should have been his to tell.

CHUKWUDI WAS BORN on November 5, 1938. The name Chukwudi means "God exists" in Igbo ("ee-bow"), the language of one of Nigeria's largest ethnic communities. The Igbo have their own language, history, and culture—all of which had shaped Chukwudi by the time he arrived in the United States in the summer of 1960.

It was a remarkable year to come from Africa to America, especially as a student. On February 1, four Black college freshmen sat down at the "Whites only" counter of the Woolworth's department store in Greensboro, North Carolina. They sat for hours without being served, but they did not leave their seats. The next day, more than twenty students joined the protest. On the third day, there were more than sixty. By the end of the week, thousands of young people, Black and White, had launched their own sit-ins throughout the country. A revolution had begun.

Chukwudi led his own civil rights protest in a movie theater in upstate New York. A few months after arriving in America, he went to see a film with a group of Black students. Racial segregation is associated with the Jim Crow South, but Northern states were segregated in their own ways. Unlike his fellow students, Chukwudi refused to sit in the balcony, the usual place for Black customers. Instead, he parked his towering frame in the middle of the front row. Imagining him in that front-row seat reminds me of my brother sitting tall as we waited to see *The Three Amigos*. Unlike his father, Peter Slate never faced segregation within a movie theater, but his body had been marked long before he lost his eye.

DESPITE THE OCCASIONAL PROTEST, Chukwudi remained focused on his studies. At a time when most American universities remained overwhelmingly White, he chose to attend Lincoln University, one of the oldest African American colleges in the country. Prominent Lincoln alumni include Thurgood Marshall, Langston Hughes, and the jazz legend Cab Calloway.

I learn these facts from Wikipedia on a sticky summer day in Pittsburgh in July 2017. I'm standing in the kitchen, pasta boiling on the stove, trying to open a jar of marinara from Trader Joe's. My shirt is heavy with sweat. My hands slip over the lid of the jar. I should have taken Emily's advice and ordered pizza. At least the kids are happy: our eighteen-month-old daughter in an inflatable pool on the back deck, her three-year-old brother blowing bubbles. They were yelling at each other a few minutes ago, but now I hear them laughing. I wipe my forehead, stir the pasta, and turn back to my laptop. The name Cab Calloway sticks in my brain. I listen to my children laughing and try to remember why that name is familiar. I stir the pasta again, and suddenly I know.

I am seven years old, and we are watching Calloway sing "Minnie the Moocher" in *The Blues Brothers*. My brother must be fourteen. His arm is around my shoulder, my head on his chest, our bodies warm where they meet. As Calloway struts the stage in his white tuxedo, we lean forward in anticipation. The song is a dark tale of a woman named Minnie who begs for food, becomes addicted to drugs, and then dies. But the film gives us none of the tragedy. We laugh as we scoot to the edge of the brown shag couch and Calloway croons, "Hi-dee-hi-dee-hi-dee-hi!" I cannot hear my brother's laughter in my memory, but I still feel his body next to mine.

AFTER THE KIDS ARE ASLEEP, I reopen my computer and follow a link to the website of the Lincoln University archives. As a historian, I revere such bastions of the raw stuff of history. I know the rules: no bags, no pens, no food or drink. I imagine handing in a request slip, waiting for a cart to appear laden with boxes of old papers. I will open the first box, breathe in the smell of old paper, and gently remove the first folder. If I'm lucky, after hours of searching, I will stumble upon a clue that reveals something new about my brother's father.

I note the opening hours of the archive and am about to close the page when I see a link to "online resources." Thirty seconds later, I am downloading a trove of yearbooks, annual reports, and other official documents. I search for "Osakwe" in the PDF of the 1963 yearbook, and suddenly I'm staring at a photo of a young man whose life I know only through stories, but whose face is my brother's—high cheekbones, sharp jaw, bright restless eyes.

I study a photo of Lincoln's African Student Union: thirty young men in dark suits on the stairs of a brick building. Chukwudi, the president of the union, stands on the far right of the front row, smoking a pipe. Here is a young man with great dreams for himself, for his country, and for Africa. Chukwudi must have admired Lincoln's famous African American alumni—Marshall, Hughes, Calloway—but his decision to enroll was inspired more by the institution's links to Africa itself. Two of modern Africa's most prominent leaders attended Lincoln: the first president of Nigeria, Nnamdi Azikiwe, and the first president of Ghana, Kwame Nkrumah.

Chukwudi arrived at Lincoln at an exhilarating time for Africa. In 1957, Ghana had become the first sub-Saharan country to gain independence from colonial rule. Other African nations followed: Guinea in 1958, then a torrent of countries in 1960—Senegal, Mali, Togo, Congo, Somalia, Ivory Coast, Chad, Central African Republic, and Chukwudi's homeland, Nigeria. All of Africa seemed to be gaining independence. Chukwudi carried the promise of decolonization with him when he traveled to the United States. He came with funding from the African Scholarship Program of American Universities, a program that placed 238 African students at one hundred universities. In exchange for his scholarship, Chukwudi was expected to strengthen ties between the United States and Africa and to return home with the skills to transform his newborn nation.

Even in rural Pennsylvania, Chukwudi maintained his ties to Africa. In 1962, he participated in a panel discussion on "Africa in a Modern World" at the Foreign Policy Association of Harrisburg. I imagine an upbeat speech on the promise of Africa and of Nigeria in particular. At Lincoln, Chukwudi served as the president of the African Student Union and the vice president of the Nigerian Student Association. Most Lincoln students lumped the Nigerians together with the other African students. When they left campus, they all wore colorful dashikis to proclaim their status as foreigners and thus minimize police harassment. Sometimes it worked; racists often made exceptions for those seen as exotic. Most of the time, however, African students found that their national and cultural identities mattered less off campus. In America, they were all seen as Black.

Chukwudi thrived at Lincoln. He played soccer, threw javelin, and was elected president of the freshmen class. He pledged Alpha Phi Alpha and joined the Canterbury Club, a group that aimed "to promote a better understanding of the spiritual aspects of the Episcopalian Church." Chukwudi was known by most friends as George, the English name he had been given as a child. "In his short time at Lincoln," the student newspaper reported, "George has made himself well known. He is an outstanding player on the soccer team, he has been appointed to the influential Personnel Committee and he is known campus-wide as 'the new African with the fancy British accent.'"

Being "the new African" was not easy. Chukwudi's appointment to Lincoln's disciplinary board sparked a controversy that revealed tensions surrounding the large contingent of African students at Lincoln. In a letter to the student newspaper, an African American student questioned whether someone "new to Lincoln and the United States" should be allowed to serve on such an important committee. "What would be the results," the student asked, "if President Kennedy appointed a foreigner just arriving in America, but who plans to live in America for some time, to the Supreme Court?" In the same edition of the newspaper, an article titled "Freshmen Elect African Student" celebrated Chukwudi's election as class president. Even that laudatory piece accentuated his foreignness by noting that his father had four wives and seventeen children.

Did Chukwudi feel like an outsider at Lincoln? The student newspaper reveals how others saw "the new African with the fancy British accent," but how did he view his classmates? I struggle to imagine his experience of that small campus in rural Pennsylvania, his first home in America. I want a diary or a letter home that reveals his impressions of Lincoln and of America. I want to hear his voice.

EMILY AND I are bringing the kids home to Pittsburgh after a week at the beach in Cape May, New Jersey. It's August 2017. We take a detour to visit Emily's grandmother in the suburbs of Philadelphia, then meander through Amish country on the way back to the Turnpike. We stop for sandwiches, and I check the map on my phone. There it is, less than ten minutes away: Lincoln University. While paying for the sandwiches, I raise the possibility of a visit. The kids are tired, and we should keep driving, but Emily is quick to make the call.

"We're too close not to stop. You owe it to yourself to stop."

So, here I am, walking the Lincoln campus like a tourist, herding squirrely kids over manicured lawns, trying to prevent them from picking flowers or running into the road. It's late summer, and the campus is empty. It feels right, the solitude of these lanes. I gaze down a shady path and imagine Chukwudi walking toward me, his arms full of books. My son darts toward a road, and I scoop him into the air, tickle his belly, and return him to the grass. I think of my brother. I wish he could join us here and walk with me and my family through his father's stomping grounds. My children scuttle across the grass, their small bodies growing taller every day, and I try to imagine what their Uncle Peter would say to them.

My son finds a clump of berries: green, orange, red. "My favorite berries," he says with quiet reverence. They're in the nightshade family, these berries, toxic if eaten. He does not eat them, just pulls them off the stem, one by one, and lets them fall, drops of color between blades of grass.

I squat and lean in. "Why are these your favorite?"

He ignores me. It's as if I have said nothing at all. Then he turns and his whole face beams. "Look, Papa, my favorite berries!"

I smile at my child, then look up and am startled to find that we've wandered into the shadow of the Langston Hughes Memorial Library, a sprawling brick building with a shiny glass entryway. I wonder what it looked like when Chukwudi was here. Hughes graduated from Lincoln in 1929, more than thirty years before the young Nigerian student arrived on campus. This place was already full of history when Chukwudi walked these paths. We tend to deny the dead their own place in time, to forget that the past was the present for those who lived it. I cannot know how Chukwudi saw his world, what he felt as he walked across campus, a twenty-three-year-old man, his life an open road ahead of him. It's not just time that divides us. I look at the kids wearing their matching sunhats, their overpriced Keen sandals, and I feel our Whiteness like an insult to this place, a wall between us and my brother's father, between me and my brother. It's not enough that Chukwudi held me on the day I was born or gave me an Igbo name. Time and race push us apart, and the more I learn about his life, the more I see the distance between us.

Does it matter that my brother's love defied such distance? One of my earliest memories is of playing hide-and-seek in our backyard. It was a tiny space, with only one good place to hide: a row of bushes along an old wooden fence. He was around twelve and must have known where I was hiding every time, yet he pretended to search for me all around the yard before—and this is the part I remember so vividly—he would reach his arms, already long like his father's, underneath the hedge. I would press back against the fence, waiting for his hand to find a foot or a leg, and only then, when the warmth of his grasp closed against my skin, would I burst into laughter, emerge from my hiding place, and call out, "Again! Again!"

Now, it's my turn to search for him. I start in the shadows of his father. I don't know whether it's love or grief or denial—denial of our differences—that drives my quest to understand his life and thus also the life of his father. All I know is that I can't stop now. My brother never gave up on me.

CHUKWUDI TOLD THE STUDENT NEWSPAPER that Lincoln had given him the impression of "a small man with an open heart." His emphasis seems

Karen Slate, around 1964.
(Author's collection.)

Chukwudi Osakwe, around 1960.
(Author's collection.)

to have been on the openness, but its smallness must have bothered him. After graduating, he decided to pursue graduate studies in engineering at UCLA, one of the country's largest public universities. At UCLA, Chukwudi maintained his passion for Africa, leading conversations on postcolonial politics in front of the main library. He must have known that he was a dynamic speaker and that his "fancy British accent" made him sound even more sophisticated. I wonder whether he noticed his influence on Karen Slate, that tall, quiet undergrad who listened to him for months without working up the courage to introduce herself.

It's the fall of 1966. Tommy James and the Shondells are at the top of the charts singing, "My baby does the hanky panky." *Batman* is in theaters. Thousands of Marines pour into Vietnam, Martin Luther King Jr. marches in Chicago, and the Black Panthers are founded in Oakland. At UCLA, a White undergrad listens to a group of African students debating politics in front of the library.

She is a twenty-minute drive from her parent's home, yet she moves as if in a distant land, with the curious step of a foreigner. She sees him in the crowd, his dark beard like a black flower in the sun. She walks toward him. He smiles at her, and she grins back. Her long dark hair frames her pale face. He introduces himself. He is moving that day and asks whether she might be free to help. He does not mention that he is moving out of married student housing. He does not mention that he had married just before graduate school, that his marriage had fallen apart only a few weeks earlier. Maybe she sees something behind his broad smile. A glimmer of pain? She agrees to help him move and hands him her phone number.

It's an unlikely match—a rich White girl from Hollywood and a poor African student. But it's 1966, and everything seems to be changing.

IN RETROSPECT, their romance seems inevitable. She was an adventurous young woman, new to the university and eager to explore the world. He was a graduate student from Africa with a talent for storytelling and a broken heart. It's easy to link their attraction to their differences. The young woman and the more experienced man: they fall neatly into their roles. Their racial difference only makes the romance more daring. For most of American history, interracial sex was illegal and profoundly dangerous, at least when a White woman was involved. White men raped women of color with impunity, and not just on Southern plantations. By contrast, it was hazardous for a Black man to even look at a White woman. By the time Chukwudi and Karen met, interracial romance involving a White woman had become less life-threatening, at least in Los Angeles, but it remained taboo. Regardless of how they saw themselves and their love, they were an "interracial" couple in a country divided along racial lines.

One night, in April 1968, they were sprawled on their bed, listening to jazz on the radio, when the music was interrupted: Martin Luther King had been shot and killed on the balcony of a hotel in Memphis, Tennessee. At first, they could not believe the news. As shock gave way to pain, they held each other and cried.

I see them huddled together, Black man and White woman, a testament to the dream for which King lived and died. They didn't see themselves as living that dream, at least not in that moment: they saw King's death as proof of how little their world had changed, how alone they were.

Two months later, Bobby Kennedy came to Los Angeles, and Karen and Chukwudi drove to hear him speak at the Ambassador Hotel. The grand ballroom filled with young people desperate for a reason to believe in the future of their country. That night, Kennedy won the delegates of the State of California. After the victory speech, Karen and Chukwudi walked to their car amid a sea of hopeful people, inspired yet again to believe in America. Only a few blocks from the hotel, they heard on the radio that Kennedy had been shot. At first, they thought that he had been only slightly injured. By the time they reached home, they had learned the truth: Kennedy had been shot at point-blank range while walking through the kitchen of the hotel. They turned off the radio and sat in the car, the engine humming quietly. They held each other again.

What did their love mean amid such loss? I said that they were a testament to Dr. King's dream, but his vision for the future went far beyond the end of racial segregation. Just before his death, King had traveled to Memphis to support sanitation workers on strike against racial discrimination, dangerous work conditions, and abysmal pay. Speaking at a local church, he had connected his personal hopes to the struggles of his people:

Like anybody, I would like to live a long life. Longevity has its place. But I'm not concerned about that now. I just want to do God's will. And He's allowed me to go up to the mountain. And I've looked over. And I've seen the promised land. I may not get there with you. But I want you to know tonight, that we, as a people, will get to the promised land!

I want to believe that Karen and Chukwudi embodied such a hope, that their love was a reflection of the promised land, but King's "we" spoke to the shared destiny of African Americans, not to the fairy tale of a postracial America. His vision of the promised land entailed the elimination of poverty, police brutality, and the many other forms of violence that continue to be directed at Black bodies. So, what does it matter that an African man held a White woman in a car in Los Angeles in the summer of 1968?

What does it matter that their son lived across the racial divide? I began writing this book to pay tribute to my brother, but now I see that

I also harbored a more selfish hope—that telling his story would bring us closer, that our brotherhood could, like the love his parents shared, testify to the promise of a future beyond racism. That future now seems so far away. My brother's life reveals that love can cross the color line, but what if love is not enough?

Since she began dating Chukwudi, Karen had barely spoken to her parents. Her first Nigerian boyfriend, Andrew, deserves some of the blame. Karen had met Andrew while working at UCLA's International Students Center. They had dated for a few months until he became too controlling, and she broke things off. When she started seeing Chukwudi, Andrew tried to win her back. Then, he visited her parents.

The young suitor, his heart broken and his pride bruised, sat down to tea with the parents of his former girlfriend. They huddled in a circle on the patio, passing a platter of salted nuts before diving into the topic at hand: why Chukwudi was bad for Karen. Andrew stressed that Chukwudi was ten years older and could not be trusted. He laced his criticism with stereotypes of the conniving Igbo—Andrew was Yoruba—but his anti-Igbo diatribe missed its target. Karen's parents weren't worried about their daughter dating an Igbo—they were worried about their daughter dating a Black man.

Once Karen made clear that her love for Chukwudi was nonnegotiable, her relationship with her parents went into deep-freeze. She does not recall any dramatic farewell conversation. They just stopped calling her, and she stopped calling them.

Without parental support, Karen was forced to become a part-time student and take a full-time job at the phone company as a long-distance operator. When someone wanted to place a call, she would ask for the number, write it down on a piece of paper, and then put the corresponding plugs into jacks on a giant switchboard. I find it remarkable that our mother played a role in the globalization of the telecommunications system, the interconnected networks of phone lines and fiber-optic cables that would eventually become the World Wide Web, at precisely the moment that her own world was shrinking. Her family had cut her off. Her days revolved more and more around Chukwudi. Yet she could plug a cord into a jack and connect someone in Los Angeles with a friend in New York, London, or Paris.

There is nothing surprising about the disconnect between her role as a cog in a global machine and the smallness of her own social circle. To live in the modern world is to be simultaneously connected and disconnected. Consider Karen's parents. I was shocked to find old photos of their trip to Russia and the safari they took in East Africa. They look so adventurous and cosmopolitan. Where was that openness to the world when Chukwudi came knocking? I shouldn't have been surprised: being a tourist has little to do with being open to the world. I doubt they saw any inconsistency in jetting off to Africa after rejecting their daughter for dating an African man.

Separated from their families, Karen and Chukwudi decided to move in together. First, they had to find a landlord who would rent to a mixed-race couple. In 1963, the California Legislature passed the Rumford Fair Housing Act, which declared that landlords could not deny someone housing because of race or ethnicity. One year later, California voters approved Proposition 14, amending the California constitution to nullify the Rumford Act. Thus, in the same year that the Civil Rights Act outlawed Jim Crow segregation in the South, voters defended housing discrimination in the Golden State. Proposition 14 was declared unconstitutional by the California Supreme Court, but enforcement of fair housing legislation remained lax, and many property owners continued to discriminate.

It happened again and again: one look at Chukwudi and the landlord would develop an excuse for why the apartment was no longer available. Frustrated by their inability to find decent housing, Karen and Chukwudi contacted the local NAACP. Their timing was impeccable: the Rumford Act had just been reinstated by the courts, and the NAACP was seeking test cases to put the law into action. Karen and Chukwudi were the ideal team to expose racism in the housing market. Young, polite, and unquestionably White, Karen was the perfect applicant to gain interest from a landlord. If she arrived alone, the apartment would be shown with eagerness. If the landlord reversed course as soon as Chukwudi arrived, they would report the landlord to the NAACP.

Chukwudi encountered a different kind of racism after he took a job in Oxnard, a farming community north of Los Angeles. He had a graduate degree in engineering but was paid less than his White peers. The young couple had to live in the "bad" part of town, in a row of tiny one-story houses. Karen worked nights as a waitress at a cowboy bar. During the day, she volunteered with the United Farm Workers, the organization led by Cesar Chavez. Mild-mannered but resolute in his cause, Chavez had emerged as the most prominent advocate for the farm workers who toiled in California's fields. Karen worked with the children of those farmworkers through Head Start, a new free preschool program that was part of Lyndon Johnson's war on poverty.

Karen and Chukwudi wanted a child of their own, but they struggled to conceive. After years of failure, they decided to adopt. They saw themselves as committed life partners, but to adopt they needed to be married. They drove up the coast to a small town in Ventura County and were married by a judge on July 3, 1969. Chukwudi was thirty years old; Karen was twenty-one. The marriage license I found online offers these facts, but nothing more. I imagine a sunny day, the courthouse facing the sea, but when I ask my mom for details, her memories are fragmentary. She remembers the drive up the coast, talking with Chukwudi about whether they would adopt a boy or a girl. She does not remember the face of the judge or whether anyone seemed troubled to see a young White woman marrying a Black man.

For their honeymoon, they drove down to San Diego and spent an afternoon strolling through Balboa Park, dreaming of their future amid reflecting pools and Spanish arches. Marriage was a bourgeois ritual out of place in the new world they were creating. Still, it felt like a marker of how far they had come, and it made it possible for them to bring a new person into the family they were building.

Only after getting married did they learn that adoption would be difficult for a couple "of their nature." Interracial couples were not deemed fit to parent children of any race. A Black child would find it "confusing," they were told, and for a White child to be raised by a Black father was unthinkable.

The world kept reminding them of their differences. Every time they went out together, they had to worry about how they would be treated. That perpetual uncertainty added urgency to their desire to create a family of their own, a family in which they would be seen for who they were. With adoption no longer an option, they began to lose hope in their dreams. Karen felt sick for more than a month before she realized that she was pregnant.

She went into labor soon after midnight on August 30, 1972. She waited until four in the morning to wake Chukwudi. The contractions had grown stronger and closer together, but they decided to drive to the beach and watch the sunrise before heading to the hospital. Ten minutes from the beach, the contractions ramped up, and they rerouted to Santa Monica Hospital. Three hours later, Uderulu Osakwe entered the world.

Born Blue

NOW ENTERS THE HAPLESS DOCTOR. The baby's skin is too blue. Is he breathing? Is there something wrong? Chukwudi arrives to resolve the crisis, his dark skin answering the doctor's questions while raising others. The confusion about skin color is not Mom's favorite memory of the birth. At least with me, the moment she relives starts when the nurses move in to take the baby away from her. The foreign doctor—Mom always notes that she was from India—swoops in to declare, "Give that baby back to his mama!" I'm not sure why that moment resonates so strongly with our mother. Maybe because she never felt happier than in that moment, cradling her child in her arms. Maybe because that doctor became her advocate when her family was not there for her.

I ask her how it felt to not have her parents with her when she gave birth to her first child. "I didn't care. I didn't miss them," she tells me. "It was only him. He was the only thing that mattered." The baby. I do not doubt the overwhelming love she felt, holding her first child in her arms. Still, I can't shake the feeling that there was more in her heart that day than love.

We are sitting in my backyard in Pittsburgh on a cold October afternoon. A stiff wind is blowing, and most of the leaves have fallen. I put on my hat, rub my hands together, and lean in toward my mom.

"Did they call?"

"Who?"

"Your parents."

"No."

She is silent, and I wait for her to say more. The few surviving leaves shake in the wind. I watch one fall, then ask, "Did you want them to call? Did you think of calling them?"

"No. They knew what they were missing. It was their choice, to come or not to come. It was their choice."

I assume that her parents struggled with that choice, but she does not seem interested in their struggles. She does not mention that her mother arrived after the delivery to watch the baby through the glass walls of the nursery.

I learn about our grandmother's visit from our mom's best friend, Terri, who had her own experience with the challenges of interracial marriage. Terri also married a Nigerian man, a friend of Chukwudi's named Chuma. Her parents tried to convince Terri to end the relationship, and her father did not attend the wedding. Still, both parents stayed in contact with their daughter. By contrast, Karen's parents retained their wall of silence even after the baby was born. Yes, her mother came to see the baby, but she left without visiting the new mother—her own daughter.

My grandparents were far from outliers in believing that the best way to love their daughter was to force her to marry her own kind. In 1966, the year that Karen and Chukwudi first met, interracial marriage was illegal in seventeen states. Even where the law allowed it, marriage across the color line risked social stigma, family trauma, and violence. For generations, segregationists had attacked "miscegenation" as a way of defending racial segregation more generally. "If you let them sit at the lunch counter," the argument ran, "tomorrow they'll want your daughter." It wasn't just rabid bigots who opposed intermarriage. Most Americans believed that people should marry their own kind. Even in California, interracial marriage was outlawed until 1948, when Sylvester Davis and Andrea Perez demanded the right to marry.

Davis was Black. Perez was of Mexican descent. California law treated Mexican Americans as White, and that is how Perez identified herself on the application for a marriage license. The county clerk, W. G. Sharp, rejected their application on the grounds that the California Civil

Code declared that "no license may be issued authorizing the marriage of a white person with a Negro, mulatto, Mongolian or member of the Malay race." If Perez had been treated as non-White, the courts would have had no reason to prevent her from marrying an African American man. The purpose of the law was not to stop racial mixture *per se* but to protect the supposed purity of "the white race."

Perez and Davis refused to let a racist edict stand in the way of their love. They challenged the law all the way to the California Supreme Court. In 1948, the court issued a groundbreaking decision in the case known as *Perez v. Sharp*. California's ban on interracial marriage was ruled unconstitutional, and Perez and Davis were married.

I didn't know about *Perez v. Sharp* when, some forty-five years later, I asked my brother for his thoughts on interracial marriage. It wasn't deep curiosity that inspired me to raise the topic; it was an assignment for school.

"WILL INTERRACIAL MARRIAGE end racism?"

It's the winter of 1993. I'm thirteen; my brother's twenty. He's in the kitchen, making his favorite snack, a bean and cheese burrito, heavy on the hot sauce. I'm sitting on the couch, the TV on, working on a paper for school. I turn down the volume and repeat my question: "Will inter-racial marriage end racism?"

He laughs. "Why are you asking?"

"We're supposed to write a report on a magazine cover. I chose this one."

As he walks back into the room, I hand over the recent issue of TIME; a woman of indistinct ethnicity smiles above the title: "The New Face of America."

"She's not real," I explain.

"What?"

"The woman—she's not real. She's a computer animation. You know, computer-generated."

"I see." He looks at the cover and reads aloud the subtitle: "She was created by a computer from a mix of several races." He hands the cover back to me, takes a bite of burrito, then asks, "What's your question again?"

"Will interracial marriage end racism? You know, once everyone's all mixed up."

"What do you think?"

I hate when he does this, turns fatherly and makes me answer my own questions. I can't tell whether he wants to know what I think or whether he's hungry and wants to finish his burrito. I can smell the melted cheese.

"I don't know. A part of me thinks that it might be the solution, getting everyone to marry across racial lines."

"A part of you?"

"Yeah, I guess I see both sides."

"What's the other side?"

Man, he's really in father mode now. I try to hide my frustration, but it bubbles over.

"Look, are you going to answer the question or what?"

He smiles, pops the last bite of burrito into his mouth, then grabs the remote and turns off the TV. It's silent while he chews and swallows.

"No, I don't think interracial marriage will end racism."

I wait for more. A strange silence settles on the room. I ask, "Why not?"

"For starters, there's been a lot of interracial sex in this country for a long time. Just think of all those Black women raped by their White owners. Did all those mulatto kids end racism?"

I know the history, but his use of the word *sex* and his reference to rape leave me uncomfortable. Like most of my friends, I'm fascinated by sex and painfully shy about it. He senses my discomfort and puts his hand on my knee.

"I'm glad you're asking these questions. I don't want you to be pessimistic, just realistic. People will always divide into camps. If it's not Black against White, it'll be Christian versus Muslim, or short versus tall. You know what I mean?"

"That sounds pessimistic."

"No, just because you can't end something doesn't mean you can't make things better. Bring it home for a minute."

That's one of his favorite phrases: *bring it home*. It means to stop philosophizing in the abstract and start being practical. He leans in toward me.

"You and I are brothers. We're family, but strangers will never see us that way. They're wrong, right? We have the same mother. We love each other. That makes us brothers. Back in the day, you and I couldn't go to the same school, sit in the same restaurant. Now, we can do all those things. It's not the end of racism, but it's progress."

I look down at the computer-generated woman, then up at my brother's face—his smooth brown skin—and for the first time in my life ponder the fact that my brother is both mixed and Black. How can that be? I feel a new distance between us; his life is complicated in ways mine will never be.

He senses my mood and pulls me in for a hug. "We don't all have to look the same in order to love each other. In the end, it doesn't matter what anyone says: I'll always be your brother."

Four months later, he'll be bleeding in an alley, shards of glass pushing up toward his brain.

IN 1967, almost twenty years after *Perez v. Sharp* and one year after Karen and Chukwudi fell in love, the Supreme Court defended interracial marriage. The case was perfectly named: *Loving v. Virginia*. Mildred Jeter, a Black woman, and Richard Loving, a White man, had been in love since they were teenagers. They were from Virginia, where the law forbade marriage across the color line. So, they drove to Washington, DC, where they were able to marry. Their troubles started in 1958, when they moved back to Virginia and were arrested for illegal cohabitation. The judge in the case explained his position in biblical terms: "Almighty God created the races white, black, yellow, malay and red, and he placed them on separate continents. . . . He did not intend for the races to mix." The judge offered the Lovings a choice: they could spend a year in prison, or they could leave the state for the next twenty-five years. They left. Five years later, they returned to visit family. Late one night, the police raided their home and found the couple asleep in bed. They were arrested. This time, they refused to be forced from their home state. The Lovings proved to be an ideal couple to challenge laws against interracial marriage— and not just because of their name. Childhood sweethearts with multiple children, they embodied the prototypical American family—except, of course, for their color.

Did Karen and Chukwudi celebrate the Supreme Court's decision? Did they feel part of a larger movement to bring love across the color line?

"No, Honey," Mom tells me. "We didn't feel part of a movement. It was more like the whole world was turning in a new way. Our love was the future."

We're heading to Trader Joe's, my mom's walker in the trunk. I switch lanes and notice her hands gripping the seat belt. I reach over and pat her left hand. Her wrinkled skin looks like crumpled paper but feels like silk. She repeats herself quietly: "Our love was the future."

She stopped driving a few months ago: arthritis in her shoulder, stenosis in her back. I glance at her face and think about the fact that my mother lives every day with pain. Her voice brings me back to the conversation: "I still feel that way."

"I'm sorry?" I pull into the parking lot and ask, "Still feel what way?"

"That our love was the future. I still feel that way. Even now."

Even now. Is she thinking of my brother? I pull into an open spot near the shopping carts and wonder what he would say about the future of race in this country. I'm startled when Mom speaks again.

"I know that things have changed. A lot has improved. But we thought ours would be the last generation to struggle against racism, and look where we are now."

I put the car in park and turn toward my mother. She smiles at me, her eyes hidden behind her sunglasses. I stare at those dark ovals and smile back, hoping she can see the love in my eyes. I will never know what it was like to raise a mixed-race kid in 1972. Maybe she had to believe in an end to racism, a world in which love did not respect the color line, a world with space for her son.

WHATEVER DREAMS Karen and Chukwudi nurtured within their tiny family, reality returned when it came time to find a bigger apartment, and they had to confront the profound segregation of their city yet again. After several nasty encounters with bigoted landlords, they found a small place in Signal Hill, an African American neighborhood near Long Beach. Famous for its oil fields, Signal Hill had become increasingly African American over the course of the 1940s and 1950s. The federal government played a key role in shifting the demographics of the neighborhood. On May 4, 1939, an agent of the Home Owners Loan Corporation submitted an official report on the housing stock in the Signal Hill area. A positive report would boost property values, while a negative report would drive the neighborhood toward poverty. The report proved disastrous. The agent warned of a "slow increase of subversive racial elements"—otherwise known as Black people. As a consequence of Signal Hill's Black residents, the agent assigned the area "a medial red grade," one of the worst categories a neighborhood could earn. The practice of "redlining" neighborhoods based on their ethnic makeup created a self-fulfilling prophecy. Communities of color were deemed risky for home loans. Without loans to support new purchases, the value of homes plummeted, thus making loans even harder to secure. Thus, the federal government made many neighborhoods increasingly Black and increasingly poor.

Karen and Chukwudi didn't know the history of their new neighborhood. What mattered to them was that they could find an affordable place to live. I struggle to imagine their life together, not as Black man and White woman, not as African and American, but as Karen and Chukwudi. I know some of the details, those our mom likes to remember. Chukwudi loved Jimmy Smith, the master of the jazz organ. She loved the Stones, and any kind of blues. He did most of the cooking. Every week, he would make a giant pot of chicken peanut stew. They would put the pot on the floor and dig in with balls of fufu. Traditionally made of cassava, Chukwudi's fufu was made with cream of wheat, the best substitute he could find. They used their thumbs to make the balls of fufu into spoons that they dipped in the spicy soup. Chukwudi must have missed home, sharing his improvised fufu with his American wife. He was far from the world of his youth. That distance must have been even harder, given that the society he grew up in no longer existed. It had been destroyed by a war that would leave my brother fatherless and clear the path for me to enter the world.

CHUKWUDI HAD LEFT NIGERIA IN 1960, proud of his country and hopeful for its future, despite the fact that the British had burdened their former colony with a dangerous mixture of poverty, authoritarian rule, and ethnic tensions. *Divide et imperium*, divide and rule, a strategy perfected by the Romans. Chukwudi knew that the British had pitted Nigeria's three largest ethnic groups against each other, but he was still shocked and devastated when civil war erupted in the spring of 1967. The war centered on the fate of Biafra, a new country carved from the southeastern corner of Nigeria. Although the leaders of Biafra strove to present theirs as a multiethnic project, the new nation was an Igbo creation, its territory roughly mapping to areas of Igbo predominance. The Nigerian government responded to Biafra's declaration of independence by launching a series of military assaults and blockading the secessionist region. Medicine and food grew scarce. Children starved, their skeletal limbs and swollen bellies grisly icons of the new Africa. Jimi Hendrix and Joan Baez headlined a relief concert in Manhattan, and an American college student set himself on fire to protest the death of "innocent Biafran babies." Karen sewed a Biafran flag, a rising yellow sun, and joined an Igbo dance troupe that performed at churches and libraries, raising money for relief. Their concerts often ended with a rendition of the Biafran national anthem, "Land of the Rising Sun." Its lyrics came from a poem by Nnamdi Azikiwe, the Lincoln alum who had become the first president of Nigeria.

When the central government won the war in January 1970, many Igbo Americans returned to Nigeria to help with the recovery. Karen and Chukwudi discussed making such a move. It was still two years before Uderulu would be born. Karen had few remaining ties to her family and had grown close to Chukwudi's relatives. They called her *adamma*, meaning "good daughter." Chukwudi's eldest brother gave her an even more affectionate title: *Ezeluagbo*, or "water after a drought." Karen and Chukwudi had little binding them to Los Angeles, but they had good reason to delay a move to Nigeria. Prominent Igbos returning from abroad were seen as threats, and Nigeria's troubles outlasted the war, as the military retained power and corruption became endemic.

As his country fell apart, Chukwudi turned to alcohol to soothe his troubled heart—at least, that's how Mom always explained it. Later, I would learn that Chukwudi had always had a drinking problem; the war just made it worse. Chukwudi lost family and friends. He lost his dream for his country and his continent. He would lose his wife and his son.

She made the deadline clear: he would stop drinking before the boy turned one, or she would leave and the child would go with her. Ude's first birthday came and went, and the drinking did not stop. She did not leave. Ude was sixteen months old when it happened. Chukwudi came home drunk and passed out on the bed. A few hours later, Ude awoke crying. She picked him up and tried to comfort him. He quieted but showed no signs of returning to sleep. She carried him into the kitchen to make tea and put him in a high chair at the kitchen table. While the teapot warmed, he began to cry again. Before she could pick him up, Chukwudi stormed into the room, half-asleep and half-drunk. Without warning, he grabbed her by the throat, lifting and squeezing, and slammed her against the refrigerator. Her toes grazed the white linoleum floor. The baby's whimpering cries became a piercing squeal, and Chukwudi let go. She fell on the floor, gasping for breath. Chukwudi stumbled back to bed. She watched him go, scooped up Ude, and called her brother. Twenty minutes later, they were driving away, the child asleep in her arms.

"YOU TOOK AWAY THE CHILD." Another letter I found in Mom's wicker basket, this one from Chukwudi's sister, whom I will call Ola. The letter was postmarked at the University of Ibadan, Nigeria, and dated February 21, 1977:

> You took away the child. We know that some of you over there are very sentimental over children but you cannot face squarely the knocks that life gives. The child is as much yours as it is his. In my part of the world a woman does not retain a child indefinitely when there is a break up in the family. The child answers the man's surname and invariably goes back to the father.

Thus, Ola claimed her own. As she saw it, Ude belonged in Nigeria, and not just because the child "invariably goes back to the father." The bonds of race were at stake. The call of blood to blood. "I should have thought that you would have the sense," Ola scolded our mother, "to know that a black man's child is black and his and can never become a white."

Karen left Chukwudi in January 1974. They were divorced that May, and Chukwudi returned to Nigeria alone. By the time Ola wrote her letter in February 1977, Karen had spent years raising her son on her own. Ude spoke no Igbo. He knew none of his father's relatives. He would be starting kindergarten that fall. Yet Ola refused to consider that it might be best for the boy to remain in America. "A black man's child is black and his and can never become a white."

I am astonished by Ola's audacity. She sent a letter thousands of miles to tell another woman to give up her five-year-old son—and in the tone of a schoolmarm scolding a wayward child: "I should have thought that you would have the sense." Ola's knowledge of race in America was not inaccurate. According to the "one-drop rule," a Black man's child is Black. He can never become White. Of course, not all mixed-race children are bound by the "one-drop rule." The long history of "passing" produced thousands and thousands of "White" people whose fathers were Black. My brother, however, was not one of them. He could never pass for White. He was a Black man's child, and he was Black—even if, in the racial landscape of LA, he did sometimes confuse those who policed racial lines.

It's the spring of 1990. I am ten, my brother seventeen. He has just picked me up from school when a police officer pulls us over. "Are you Puerto Rican or what?" The policeman's voice is smug and confrontational. Then, he sees me and becomes more careful. We had failed to complete a full stop at a stop sign, but he is going to let us go with a warning. The real warning is clear enough, despite the momentary confusion over what kind of suspect outsider my brother happens to be.

When my brother retold the story, he joked about how he should have responded.

"Are you Puerto Rican or what?"

No, I'm Japanese.

"Are you Puerto Rican or what?"

Your wife asked me the same question!

I don't remember what he actually said, but I'm sure that he used his Whitest accent, that polite, accommodating tone he had honed with our grandparents' friends. He always played it safe when I was involved. I never asked how that made him feel—to have to change his diction to seem less threatening, to be followed through his favorite stores, to be stopped again and again by police officers or security guards demanding to know what he was doing, where he was going, why he wasn't where he belonged. In 1972, the year my brother was born, the Black writer Chester Himes said that "race prejudice in Los Angeles" was a kind of "mental corrosion" that left him "bitter and saturated with hate." I never saw hate in my brother's eyes, but maybe that's because I only paid attention when he was looking at me.

CONJURING UP A LIFETIME of discrimination, Ola prodded our mother to give up her child. She pressed her attack by questioning the cause of the divorce. "If your grounds for divorce were genuine," she wrote, "the least you can do is to sever all relationship with him by making him take and look after his child." Again, the arrogant tone unnerves me: "If your grounds for divorce were genuine." But when Ola turned back to race, I find myself more intrigued than angry. Even if her tone was abhorrent, she had reason to ask, "If you marry another man, perhaps a fellow white, would he harbour the son of a n****r in his house?"

Ola concluded with a peculiar racial justification for the tone of her letter. "If it hurts," she wrote, "remember that I am black and we do not mince words. Think it over and send us the child. I shall pray for God's guidance in all our actions. Bless you and good luck." Ola's recourse to a racial stereotype—that Black people "do not mince words"—fit neatly into the overarching message of her letter: the world was divided into Black and White. Ude was Black. He belonged with other Black people. He belonged in Africa. I find it jarring that Ola's letter came from the University of Ibadan, Nigeria's oldest and most distinguished university. Of course, there is no rule that educated people will be tolerant, but I wish that knowledge would poke holes in the walls we erect between us. Maybe it's our mother's influence that stokes my hope for a world beyond race. I wonder whether Ola knew that Karen, when forced to check a box to identify her race, always marked "other" and wrote in "human."

KAREN KEPT HER CHILD. With Chukwudi in Nigeria, she struggled to create a new life for herself and the boy and decided to move in with her parents. That decision always made sense to me. Her parents had a massive house, a mansion really, with room to spare. Why shouldn't she return home? I didn't know that her parents had practically disowned her. They had not spoken to her for years. Their willingness to house her and her child might be seen as the triumph of a love long suppressed, but it's difficult to tell whether they were moved by love for their daughter or the absence of her Black husband.

Her mother remained distant, but her father became the warm, loving parent Karen had always wanted. We all called him Dad. Especially for my brother, Dad lived up to his name. He became the closest thing Ude would have to a father. Dad wore short-sleeved cotton shirts with collars, a strange combination of formal and informal. His favorite was olive green. When he wore the matching slacks, he looked like a Vietcong guerilla adjusting to life as a wealthy White lawyer. Tufts of white hair poked out from his open collar. He would sit by the pool with a bowl of grapes and a tumbler of ice water and read books about the Second World War. He didn't work as much as he had when Mom was little.

Our grandmother also doted on Ude. She drove him to school in her silver Oldsmobile, taught him how to make Illinois meatloaf, and introduced him to the glories of basketball. The two watched games together in the TV room. If it was close, they would sit on the edge of their seats in a form of prayer, as if perching on the edge of the sofa might tip the game in their favor. My brother called her Momamer (Mom-a-mer), his effort at "Mom's mother," not that she and Mom displayed much affection for each other. At least they shared one thing now: their love for Ude.

By marrying Chukwudi and cutting ties to her family, Karen had slid down the class hierarchy. Now, she was wealthy again. Our grandparents' house occupied a large corner lot in Sherman Oaks, one of the most exclusive neighborhoods in the Valley. We used to watch the TV show *Silver Spoons* and joke about the rich kid who had his own train, but the house next door had just such a train. I don't remember thinking much about our class status or the racial dimensions of that status. Momamer and Dad had a maid who was Black. She was the only non-White person I remember spending time in that house—except my brother.

My grandparents had been stubborn in rejecting Chukwudi, but they proved generous in his absence. Their generosity reveals the Janus-faced nature of racism. The same people who stopped speaking to their daughter when she married an African treasured her mixed-race son. There are many bigots whose hatred knows no bounds, but most Americans are like my grandparents; their prejudices are flexible, contextual, full of exceptions, and thus easier to defend or to ignore.

A prominent bankruptcy attorney, Dad was interviewed on the TV show *60 Minutes*. I find an old copy and watch it one night after the kids are asleep. With his warm Southern drawl, my grandfather defends bankruptcy as an ancient practice of forgiveness. The Bible, he tells us, advises debt forgiveness every seven years. Everyone deserves a second chance. He doesn't mention his own family, but every time he defends forgiveness, I wonder whether he is thinking about his daughter—or himself.

I found the *60 Minutes* interview in the Hobbit Room, so named because anyone under the age of five has to duck to get through the door. A tiny corner of our attic in Pittsburgh, the Hobbit Room has become our go-to storage for anything too precious to keep in our musty basement. The room has a single window that does not open. Its light is obstructed by a heat pump that takes up a third of the room. The eaves cut in sharply from both walls, which means that an adult can only stand in the center of the room. That's where I am, a few days after watching the *60 Minutes* tape, digging for more relics of my family history and trying to stay warm. It's a cold December day. The heat pump is busy heating the rest of the attic, but the Hobbit Room never earned a vent of its own. It must be a few degrees above freezing. I'm dressed for the outdoors, thick coat and wool hat, but I forgot my gloves. I rub my hands together and dig deeper into a box of my brother's things.

A few minutes in and I'm depressed by how little these things connect me to him. Sure, I remember him wearing those puffy blue sweats, but they do nothing to bring him closer. That Pepé Le Pew coffee mug he stuffed with match boxes. The copy of Carl Sagan's *Cosmos* I never saw him read. These things were his, but so what? I'm about to give up when I find a fragment of a script called *Bridge*. The manuscript is only thirty pages long. It's neatly bound with metal ties but is missing the cover page. I begin reading without knowing whether it's his work or something he was editing for a friend, but my breath catches when I discover that one of the characters is named Miss Jim, just like our great-grandmother, whose father named her William James, after the philosopher. This is my brother's work.

The story is set in Anywhere, Tennessee, in 1933. The establishing shot: "Two small boys, one Black and one White, run along the bank of the Anywhere river. The river's flow is less than one third its capacity, as the water streams gently by. The two boys laugh joyously as they wade through the water to a small island in the center of the river." Unbeknownst to the boys, a dam has broken upstream. A torrent of water rushes down upon them. Stranded in the middle of a raging river, the boys cling to the top of a tree and to each other. The Black boy's family gets word first, runs down to the river, and forms a human chain, stretching from the shore through the angry rapids. They are just short of reaching the two children when the White boy's family arrives. If just one of the White men will join the human chain, they will be able to rescue the boys. They balk at such cooperation. One yells, "I ain't trusting my life to a n****r!" Instead, they build their own human chain. Now two lines of desperate men snake through the river, neither long enough to save the terrified boys.

This is a story about sharp divisions between Black and White. Where does my brother fit? I put the script on top of an old suitcase and plunge my hands into my pockets. They've gone from stinging to aching. I stand there in the cold, struggling to imagine my brother writing this story. Like most tales of the Old South, *Bridge* divides sharply on the racial lines my brother's life defied. Maybe that's why he never shared the script with me. Maybe he hadn't found a way to make the story his own.

I open the suitcase and drop the script inside. I am about to close the top when I spot a black laminate backing—my brother's favorite way to bind his scripts. It's another unfinished draft, even shorter than *Bridge*. This one has his name on the cover. I'm halfway through the first page, and already I can see that this story comes closer to his own experience, although in a way I never would have imagined.

The story begins in 1952, as a light-skinned African American teenager, Willy Banks, arrives in a dusty Alabama town. His mother has sent him from Chicago to live with a great-uncle. As Willy wanders into town, I am convinced that this is my brother's take on the murder of Emmett Till, the fourteen-year-old boy who was killed in August 1955 outside Money, Mississippi. Two White men beat Till for hours, shot him in the head, and dumped his body in the Tallahatchie River. His mother refused a closed casket so that everyone could see what had been done to her boy. The crime helped ignite the civil rights movement. This is a story that calls for a powerful film, but it is not the Till story that my brother started writing.

Wandering through town, Willy is approached by the sheriff, who mistakes the fair-skinned teenager for a White boy. With the sheriff's help, Willy is adopted by a prominent White family. He attends the all-White high school, gets a job, and becomes a well-liked member of the community, until a local Klan leader discovers Willy's true identity and threatens to kill the "black boy" pretending to be White. Willy is forced to run for his life. My brother's notes end with a scene between Willy and an old African American sharecropper named Cutter:

> Cutter: You colored, boy? (Willy nods.)
> Willy: Why you laughin'?
> Cutter: What, you don't think this is funny?
> Willy: They gonna kill me!
> Cutter: Probably. But your story gonna live forever. Boy I spent my whole life thinking that white folks had something in 'em that colored folks didn't have. But here comes Willy, who was just as White as any White folks out there, and now he say he is colored like me. You just proved the whole world wrong, Willy!

The old man and the boy are surrounded by a mob. The leader yells at Cutter to bring out the boy or both will be killed. Cutter responds with defiance:

> Cutter: Dumb-ass White boys only watchin' the front. Listen boy and listen good. Through the shed, there's a field. When I tell you to, you run out the back and cross that field. Go straight on through the woods till you reach the river. The river'll take you south enough to where nobody knows who you are, but boy, you gotta promise me you won't stop runnin till you get where you come from.

Willy: I promise.

Cutter: Then get on (Cutter looks back out the window and then back at Willy), and boy, I'm proud that I can call you my own.

Here, we come closer to my brother's predicament, and maybe a resolution. A young man trapped between Black and White is accepted as Black by fighting against racism. He claims his Blackness in struggle. I drop the script back into the suitcase, crouch down, and crawl back through the door into the heat of our finished attic. The warmth relaxes my muscles. I lie down on the soft white carpet, put my frozen hands behind my head, and close my eyes. I imagine my brother sitting on his couch late at night, his laptop lighting up his face, pouring himself into the story of this kid whose Blackness would be redeemed through struggle.

Willy is only mistaken for White. My brother's relationship with Whiteness was more complicated. Maybe that's why he didn't share either script with me. He was still trying to figure out what it meant to write such stories with a White mother and a White brother. He was still trying to figure out what it means to be Black if your family is White.

No Dragons Allowed

I N THE FALL OF 1976, a few weeks after his sixth birthday, Ude asked his mother why he was different. She had known that question would come and had prepared an answer that was honest but reassuring, but she surprised herself by responding with a question of her own.

"Different how?"

"Different from you. From everyone."

They were sitting on the couch, watching *Sesame Street*. She turned toward him, trying to hide her concern behind a loving smile.

"How are you different from me?"

She did not want to pretend they were the same, but in that moment, looking at her son, she wished that she could make it all go away—not their differences, but the way the world made so much of a little melanin, the slight curl of his soft black hair.

The first thing he listed was his hair. So, she cut her hair, dyed it black, and got a perm. Now, her hair was as dark and curly as his. In one of my favorite photos, she is sporting the perm and thick brown-rimmed glasses. She is staring at Ude, who is on her lap. They are both smiling, her teeth showing. His mouth is closed, and his cheeks bulge, as if he has just taken a giant gulp of water and is struggling to keep it in while laughing. Their hair looks nearly identical: black, curly, neither long nor short. They are happy together, mother and child.

Karen Slate and Uderulu Osakwe, mother and son.
(Courtesy of Terri Agbodike.)

She kept the perm until her hair started to fall out. They said it couldn't handle the chemicals. So, she bought Ude a Black doll. She was inspired by the Clarks, Kenneth and Mamie, the psychologists whose work helped convince the Supreme Court to outlaw school segregation in *Brown v. Board of Education.* In the 1940s, the Clarks conducted a series of experiments to measure the impact of segregation on African American children. The experiments revolved around dolls of different colors. The children, who ranged in age between three and seven, were asked which doll they wanted. All the kids were Black, but most wanted the White doll. When asked why, the majority assigned the White doll a variety of positive attributes. When asked which doll they most resembled, the same kids who praised the White doll compared themselves to the Black doll. One little boy from rural Arkansas was asked which doll most resembled him. He pointed to the Black doll. "That's a n****r," he said. "I'm a n****r."

Ude named his Black doll Johnny. He loved Johnny and carried the doll everywhere, like a talisman. Because Johnny did nothing to connect

Ude to his White mother, Karen turned to children's stories to show Ude how to think about their similarities as well as their differences. She bought him books with brown children as the main character. She bought him books that explore what it means to be different. Did being Black mean that he had to be different? Contrast two of the stories she read to Ude: *The Snowy Day*, about an African American boy named Peter who encounters snow for the first time, and *Swimmy*, about a little fish that was born black, unlike the other fish that are red. What made *The Snowy Day* stand out when it was published in 1962—and what made Karen buy it fifteen years later—is not just the quiet beauty of one boy's encounter with snow but the fact that the boy's Blackness is so unremarkable. *The Snowy Day* is a tribute to the irrelevance of race. *Swimmy*, by contrast, celebrates the diversity of color. Swimmy's Blackness makes him different, and that difference matters.

Ude must have been confused by these messages. Race does not matter, but race makes you different. We are all the same, but you are not the same. Now, I read these books to my own son. I can't read *The Snowy Day* without thinking of my brother, and not just because the little boy is named Peter. My son is fascinated by all the ways the boy explores the snow, especially the stick he uses to make tracks, to whack the snow-laden trees. He has no interest in the boy's skin color. There will come a time, I know, when he will see these differences, when he will see another little boy as Black.

Last night, he told me that he was afraid to go to sleep. Dragons might come out of the walls, he said. We made a sign together: NO DRAGONS ALLOWED. It was his idea to draw a scary dragon on the sign. How did he know that the best way to keep dragons away is an even scarier dragon? I watched him lie down in his bed, comforted by that sign, and I thought back to the iron bars on my windows and that diamond saw my brother conjured to ease my fears. I can still hear his voice wrapping me in safety. My son will never know my brother's voice, not as I know it. I watched him fall asleep, his tiny chest rising and falling, and wondered how I could teach him to see a Black man as a Black man and as a brother.

KAREN WANTED UDE to be proud to be Black. She also wanted him to see race as silly. She put her hand against a piece of white construction paper to show that she was not white—she was pink. She put his hand against a piece of black paper and asked him, "Is your hand the same color as the paper?" "No, my hand is brown," he said. "The paper is black." "Yes," she said. "But people will call you black. It's all silly. People aren't like crayons you can put neatly in a box."

Karen knew that she could not fully protect her son from the dangers of being a Black man in a racist country. She bought T-shirts that declared, "One People, One Planet, Please," but she knew that a T-shirt wouldn't change how strangers saw her son. He was a cute little boy who happened to be Black, but he grew bigger every year. Soon, he would be a young Black man, threatening and threatened. Ola's prophecy was coming true: Karen would never be able to give her son what he needed in the White world of her parents. She couldn't make racism go away, but she could help him feel less alone.

She and Ude moved in with Terri and Chuma. The only two White women in a group of Igbo families, Karen and Terri might have felt awkward becoming friends. Did they prefer to keep to their own after all? They did not see it that way, of course. They got along so well that their color ceased to matter, at least to them. Now that Karen needed a place to stay, a place where Ude would not be so racially isolated, it felt natural to bring their families together.

Terri and Chuma had a two-story home on Curson Avenue, between Pico Boulevard and Venice Boulevard, not far from UCLA. The area was mixed ethnically and economically. Now, Ude could walk down the street and see people who looked like him. Even his home was a racial rainbow. Terri and Chuma had two sons, both of whom were more light-skinned than my brother but were, like him, never seen as White. Photos from those years reveal a spectrum of difference in which every color shades imperceptibly into the next, yet strangers had no trouble dividing our household between Black and White. Aunt Terri, Uncle Chuma, and their sons became our family, but the American racial system had no place for us as a family—no place for my brother to be fully at home.

I'M BACK IN THE HOBBIT ROOM, staring at a picture of my brother. I found a stack of photos pressed inside a Tony Robbins self-help book— *Awaken the Giant Within.* Most of the photos are from the first few years after my brother lost his eye. He looks so strong and confident in his patch, as if losing an eye was an opportunity to awaken his inner giant. I find these photos captivating, but it's a childhood shot that I can't put down. He's standing on the sidewalk in front of that house on Curson, the house we shared with Terri and Chuma and their sons. His skateboard lies next to him on the ground. Eight or nine years old, he's a poster child for the 1970s—flared jeans, faded T-shirt, plaid coat. He's looking toward his left, beyond the camera. I wonder what he sees.

Living on Curson, Ude had a family that was mixed like him. His school, by contrast, was predominantly White. An elite private institution perched on a hillside off Mulholland Drive in Bel Air, the mansion-studded paradise made famous by the Fresh Prince, the school embodied the creative, child-driven educational philosophy of John Dewey. Students learned by doing and by questioning. They sang and danced and played without the archaic authoritarianism of the traditional classroom. Karen fell in love with the school during her first visit, but she never could have afforded the tuition. Dad agreed to pay the bill, and not just because he wanted the best for his grandson. There were deeper issues at stake, fears that united our mother and her father on one side of one of the greatest racial scandals of the civil rights era.

In 1961, Mary Ellen Crawford tried to enroll at South Gate High, a large public school in the Los Angeles Unified School District. The closest school to her home, South Gate also happened to be 98 percent White. Crawford was Black. That summer, teams of civil rights activists, Black and White, risked their lives to integrate the buses of the American South. Greeted with firebombs and angry mobs, the Freedom Riders helped make "segregation" an ugly word that evoked the violent hatred of the Deep South. But segregation was equally pervasive in liberal, cosmopolitan cities like Los Angeles. While Freedom Riders sat in Mississippi's infamous Parchman Prison, the Los Angeles Unified School District rejected Crawford's attempt to enroll at South Gate High. Instead, she was sent to Jordan High, a school that was farther from her home and 99 percent Black.

Crawford and her parents challenged the decision in the courts. In 1963, while schoolchildren were attacked by police dogs and fire hoses in Birmingham and Martin Luther King proclaimed his dream in front of the Lincoln Memorial, the ACLU filed a class action lawsuit accusing the Los Angeles Board of Education of actively maintaining racial segregation. The Crawford case became the centerpiece of a protracted legal battle. In 1970, a judge ruled that the city had segregated students by race and ordered the school board to design a desegregation plan. Simply allowing students to attend their local school—all that Crawford had wanted when she tried to enroll at South Gate High—would have little impact in a city that was so divided by race. Only one method could effectively desegregate the schools of such a racially divided city: busing.

Karen was horrified. The busing was to begin in the fall of 1978, the very year in which Ude would be starting elementary school. Karen had planned to send Ude to Dixie Canyon Elementary, one of the strongest schools in the city. The kids at Dixie Canyon were overwhelmingly White. Ude would add some diversity, and Karen had begun meeting with a group of parents who wanted to do more to integrate the school. Suddenly, she was told that Ude would have to sit on a bus for two hours a day to attend a school they had never visited when he could be doing just as much to integrate the district by staying closer to home. Now that I have children of my own, I can understand her opposition, but I still find it hard to imagine our mother, the radical anti-racist, joining forces with the conservative, often blatantly bigoted antibusing movement.

Antibusing activists had gained national attention in Boston in 1974, after a federal judge ordered the city to institute a busing policy to redress generations of overt segregation. Violence erupted when busloads of Black students approached the majority-White South Boston High School. In images reminiscent of the South, armed guards were required to protect the Black students from angry White mobs. An antibusing rally that turned violent at Boston's City Hall was immortalized by the photograph known as *The Soiling of Old Glory*. Toward the right of the image, African American attorney Theodore Landsmark stumbles forward, a victim of the mob's aggression. From the left, a young White man leans in, as if to stab Landsmark with a flagpole. At the center, hanging from the makeshift spear, billows the American flag.

I show this image to my students now. I wish that my brother could be there with me to talk about segregation in our schools, the violence in Boston, what it means to have a flagpole rammed into your chest, a bottle brought down across your face. How can I name a wound I will never know?

I'M UP IN THE HOBBIT ROOM AGAIN, this time wearing gloves. The cold has its own presence, like another person in the room. I want to finish searching my brother's things before the kids wake up. There isn't time to wander, but I find myself drawn to an old Converse shoebox stuffed with love letters from my elementary school girlfriend. My special memory box, I call it. I'm halfway through the love letters when I see a tight roll of laminated paper. I pull it from the box and spread it open.

It's an old class photo, but not mine. I scan the rows of young faces without recognizing anyone. I'm about to give up when I spot him in the corner of the back row, his goofy grin almost a grimace. The light in the Hobbit Room is soft and dim. I glance back over the photo and, without thinking, start to search for other Black faces. There are a few Asian kids, and many who resist easy categorization, but I don't see a single other Black face.

I put the photo in one of my brother's boxes and close the lid. My frozen breath hangs in the air. I should check on the kids. I start to leave the room, but reconsider. I find the photo again and stare at my brother's face. He looks so young. I want to hold him like I hold my son when he's scared, his head tight against my chest. I stare at the photo for what feels like a long time, then roll it up and place it back in my memory box.

IN LOS ANGELES, opposition to busing was less violent, but no less vehement. In 1976, a San Fernando Valley mother named Bobbi Fiedler created an antibusing organization called Bustop. Within weeks, it had thousands of members. Many supported integration in principle, like our mother, but they believed that the right to attend a local school trumped the goal of racial equality. Presenting the neighborhood school as a race-neutral tradition, they overlooked the history that had created segregated neighborhoods. Many antibusing advocates were active in the same homeowners' associations that fought against equal housing. The Sherman Oaks Homeowners Association, the organization that represented my grandparents and their neighbors, became famous for combining anti-tax and antibusing campaigns in what appeared to be a race-neutral movement but was, in practice, an effective defense of racial segregation. Backed by homeowners' groups, Bustop attacked the busing plan in the courts and stalled its implementation. Then, they took the issue to the people.

In 1979, California voters were presented with Proposition 1, a seemingly race-neutral law that would block court-mandated busing. Supporters of the new law were sensitive to the charge that they privileged some kids over others. "We love all kids," boasted one bumper sticker that urged support for Proposition 1. As if the claim was not sufficiently saccharine, the "o" in "love" was rendered as a heart. Antibusing activists did not love all kids equally. On the contrary, the antibusing movement demonstrated the willingness of parents to privilege their own children. That is only natural, you might say, and need not be interpreted as racism. You have to look closely to find racism in the law or its defenders. In May 1969, the Los Angeles City Board of Education publicly stated that it "finds wholly unconvincing the proffered evidence that student achievement is related to the racial composition of the student body." Such a declaration sounds anti-racist or at least racially neutral, but by attacking the idea that segregated schools had negatively affected Black students, the board repudiated the logic that led to the *Brown* decision and concluded that racial integration "is most difficult to execute and has no proven value."

California voters agreed. Proposition 1 was approved by more than two-thirds of voters, and Los Angeles schools would remain profoundly segregated. By the time Proposition 1 was passed, Ude had already left the public schools, along with many middle-class or wealthy kids, most of whom were White. In Boston, Los Angeles, and many American cities, White families moved to the suburbs in a vast migration known as "White flight." Others, like our mom, sent their kids to private school. Busing pitted her concern for Ude against what was best for other children and for society as a whole. Society did not have a chance.

CHUKWUDI'S SISTER, Ola, had asked whether a White man would "harbour the son of a n****r in his house." Our mother met her White man,

Bill, at a party in the fall of 1976. Karen was waiting in line for the bathroom. Bill was standing in front of her. When he turned around, she noticed a thin scar that connected his lip to his jaw line. He had been born with a cleft palate. As a child, he had been teased mercilessly, and he still felt self-conscious whenever his scar was noticed. Karen loved scars. She found them dignified and mysterious. She reached up and caressed the scar, tracing the strange thin line across a face she would soon know better than her own. "It's beautiful," she said, and smiled.

Several months later, Bill took Karen and Ude to see *Star Wars*. The film had just been released, and a long line snaked outside Grauman's Chinese Theatre. They passed the time by reading out the names on the Hollywood stars. Karen had hesitated to introduce the two men in her life. Regardless of Ola's warning, Karen was not concerned about her new lover being a racist who would reject her Black son. She was more anxious about what Ude would make of Bill. She did not want him to become attached. She did not want him to lose another father.

Week by week, Bill and Ude grew closer. They danced to bossa nova. They watched samurai flicks. They went to Seal Beach to fly kites and search for seashells. Our grandfather liked Bill, too. They played chess and talked books. Like Chukwudi, Bill was ten years older than our mom, but he had a stable job as a psychologist, and Karen was older now and already had a child. That's how I always explained Dad's warmth toward Bill when he had been so cold to Chukwudi. Maybe it also mattered that Bill had fair skin and pale blue eyes.

One evening after dinner, with Ude asleep in his room, Bill placed a small square box on the table in front of Karen. She picked up the box and looked up at Bill's blue eyes. He smiled nervously: "Don't worry, it's not a marriage proposal." Bill and Karen had agreed that marriage was unnecessary. They maintained separate apartments, and Karen cherished her independence. She opened the box to find a silver ring, beautiful in its simplicity. "It's just a gift, not a proposal," Bill explained.

Karen valued the freedom Bill gave her, but his shaky commitment was troubling. At one point, he ended the relationship, explaining that he had fallen for a Japanese woman. He added that he had always been fascinated with Japanese culture, as if that would make it easier for Karen. She drove to the beach and threw her silver ring into the sea.

A few weeks later, they were back together, but their relationship remained stormy.

In the end, Mom's worries proved prescient. Ude would lose another father. It saddens me that I never saw it that way growing up. The story of Bill was the story of my loss, but my brother lost someone too. I wonder whether he ever saw it as my fault. After all, it was my unexpected arrival that led Bill to leave.

They had been taking precautions. When Karen became pregnant, Bill assumed that she had been skipping pills on purpose. He accused her of wanting a girl and demanded that she get an abortion. She refused.

In the summer of 1979, Karen and Bill went to dinner at Barone's, an Italian place on Ventura Boulevard. It would be the last time they ever saw each other. Once again, Bill asked Karen to get an abortion. Once again, she refused. He said that he would leave if she had the child. She told him to leave. Her choice always seemed a straightforward expression of love for me—of course, she would choose to keep me. I failed to imagine how hard it must have been to lose another partner, to be a single parent yet again, to watch Ude lose another father.

We went to Barone's at least once a month throughout my youth. Their pizzas were thin and square. The paper placemats featured a map of Italy. I was eleven years old when Mom explained that this was the place where she had last seen my father. I don't remember being troubled by the connection. She managed to paint his leaving as some kind of noble dance. Everyone had a role to play, and they moved in rhythm, as if to music, as their relationship fell apart over a mushroom pizza.

Because Bill and Mom were never married, I was technically the bastard of the family. My brother never teased me about that. Even though Mom and Chukwudi had married, it was my brother whom everyone saw as out of place. When Mom and I were introduced as mother and son, no one blinked. My brother required explanation. He knew what it felt like to be illegitimate.

Mom feared that he would feel left out because the new baby would be White like her. To give him a sense of connection to his baby brother, she let him choose my name. His favorite book at the time was the Richard Scarry classic *I Am a Bunny*. The book begins, "I am a bunny. My name is Nicholas." I was named after a rabbit. It could have been

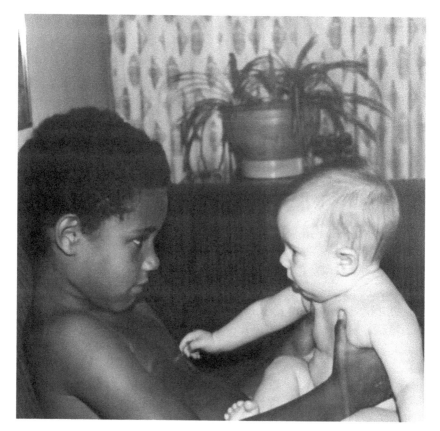

My brother and me in 1980. On the day I was born, he was the first in the family to hold me. (Author's collection.)

worse: Mom had considered naming me "Imagine" after the John Lennon song. I always took pride in the fact that my brother named me. My name became a token of his love. Only now can I see how my birth complicated his place in the world. Suddenly, he was a minority within his own family.

Mom kept finding ways to connect him to me. She took him to all of her prenatal visits and taught him how to listen for the baby's heartbeat. The first time, she warned him that it might take a minute for the nurse to find the right spot on her belly. Still, as the silence stretched on, she began to grow nervous. When the nurse found the heartbeat, she felt like clapping with joy. My brother found a better way to celebrate; he danced to the rhythm of the heartbeat, my heartbeat.

I was born at home. Mom wanted my brother to be as involved as possible, and being at home made it easier to have him close. He watched TV in another room during the labor. As soon as I was born, she asked for him, and he was the first family member to hold me. The midwife even let him cut the umbilical cord. He was seven years old.

My father had left four months earlier, but my brother's father was there to see me born. He'd returned from Nigeria a few years earlier and had become a regular visitor in the months since Bill left. Chukwudi gave me an Igbo name, Obierulu, or "heart of the shrine." Now, my brother and I both had Igbo names. Recalling Chukwudi's presence at my birth always made me feel connected to my brother, but what did it mean for him that his father had returned? Six months before, Bill had been playing the role of father. Now, Chukwudi was back. It must have felt like whiplash.

Chukwudi wanted to rejoin our family. On October 7, 1980, some eight months after I was born, he petitioned for American citizenship. I find the document online, petition no. 451198, and study it for any signs of his plans. What I discover is a glaring absence: our mother. Chukwudi listed two witnesses, neither of whom Mom even remembers. Why didn't he list her?

I show her the document on my laptop. I zoom in to make it easier for her to read, but the margins extend beyond the screen, and she has to scroll across each line to see the full text. It's a hot summer night in Pittsburgh, and the heavy air clings to the skin. I expect her to become frustrated, but her face remains calm, her voice peaceful, as she explains why she didn't serve as a witness for the man she had loved for so long.

"I was worried he would start drinking again. That you would both come to love him and then what? Lose him again?"

"What about you? Did you want him back?"

"Yes, of course, but I was worried for myself too."

Her fears proved justified: Chukwudi returned to drinking and, after a few years of occasional contact, left the country again. I was too young to notice his absence. My brother, by contrast, an awkward tween trying to figure out what it meant to be a Black man in America, must have been devastated by his father's departure. I'm ashamed that I never asked him how he felt. That shame sits like a stone in my chest when, thirty-six years later, I find a diary that promises to reveal how my brother felt when his father left.

It's Christmas night, 2018, and I'm sitting on a balcony in Santa Monica, two blocks from where my brother lost his eye. It's cold and windy. A solitary palm tree, tall and slender, sways through the blue-black sky like an animated postcard of Los Angeles at night. The beauty of the palm is made strange by its own perfection, and I feel as if I've entered a cliché. There's something inauthentic about my being here, trying to learn things I should have long known about my brother and all that he lost, as if uncovering the past can do anything to make things right. The location alone has me feeling unsettled and anxious. Emily and I chose this Airbnb because it's close to the beach and affordable, and it has two bathrooms. It was only after booking the place that I realized how close it is to the club where my brother was attacked.

There is a sharp salt to the air blowing off the sea. I breathe deeply, take a sip of rooibos tea, and look down at the briefcase I took with me onto the balcony, the briefcase full of my brother's things. I didn't expect it to be so big. We're in town to visit family and escape the Pittsburgh winter, and to allow me to talk with my brother's friends and retrieve some of his old papers. I knew that an old friend had a briefcase full of my brother's stuff, but this thing at my feet is more like a suitcase—large and boxy—and it holds more than I expected.

Some part of me must have known what I was doing when I booked this place. There are many beaches in LA, yet I chose an apartment in Santa Monica just two blocks from the promenade. I didn't think about the attack when I made that choice. Maybe it was a decision that had to remain unconscious. Even here on the balcony, I feel uneasy, as if something of that night still clings to the air.

I busy myself with the papers. The first thing I pull out is a small notebook labeled "My Diary." It's dated "Aug 30 1982," the day my brother turned ten. I open the cover and read: "For my Birthday Terry and Chuma got me a Diary. Papa isn't here. I mes him." *I miss him.* I put the book down and look up at the sky. There is a heaviness in my stomach, and my eyes are tired. I close them and think about my kids asleep in their room. What if I left the country and they didn't know whether they would ever see me again?

I turn back to the diary: "Nov 1982. School is going great. On December 3 I'm going to Idilwild. Today I played butts up with my friends, Rodney, Aron, Jonas, Josh. We played volyball at P.E. and saw some films. My favorite books are James and the giant peach, Jonny Tremain, The landing of the pilgrims, chirlie and the choclate factory, which way books and choose your own advanture. My dad still hasn't come back. I hope he will come back soon. I love me."

I expect Mom had something to do with that last line: "I love me." She must have coached him on how to survive his father's absence, how to protect his self-esteem. It would not have been easy. I look out into the night, that lone palm waving in slow motion, and feel the weight of all my brother had lost even before he walked into that club.

EVERY FEW YEARS, we would receive a letter from Chukwudi. I find one from the summer of 1987. A thin crepe of wrinkled airmail, the kind that folds to become its own envelope, it was stuck to the inner lining of the briefcase. I gently pry it loose, rub the delicate waxy paper, then open the letter and read.

"My Dear Loved Ones," Chukwudi begins, "It is JUNE! Already and I owe you a lot!!! So first Happy Thanksgiving '86, Merry Xmas '86, Happy New Year '87, Happy Valentine '87, and Happy Easter '87 all rolled into one!!!! But above all I Love you. It has been a very long time since I wrote last and I am awfully sorry about it." I find his use of *awfully*, like the repeated exclamation marks, to be an empty rhetorical gesture, but I felt differently at age seven. I was thrilled every time we received a letter from Chukwudi. I don't remember feeling sad that the letters came so infrequently. I was still so young, and this was not my father who was writing from a distant land. Chukwudi ended his letter with a note for his son: "Ude Peter, Please don't sulk Great One even if I have given you every reason to. I love you Great One and you must remember that always." I don't know whether my brother remembered his father's love, but I do know that he never stopped craving it.

WE'RE NEARING THE END of our time in Santa Monica. We've been to the promenade at least a dozen times, and I still haven't visited the club. The closest I came was peering down the alley where the security guards dumped him, bleeding and nearly unconscious. I wouldn't have done even that if Emily hadn't pushed me.

"Is this the alley?"

"What?" We're on our way to a pizza place, and I'm focused on holding my daughter's hand. She's almost three and not to be trusted near busy streets.

"Is this the alley where they left your brother that night?"

We had been talking about why I hadn't visited the club, why I didn't think it was "necessary to my research." Emily is a master of gentle nudges. Still, I feel myself getting defensive. I thought that we had left the club behind us, but here we are, crossing a little street—Second Court, it's called—and she's right: this must be the alley. I stop, and my daughter pulls onward, our arms taut between us.

"One second, Louie-bear," I say and stare down the alley. *Empty*, I think to myself. Straight and narrow, with windowless walls on both sides, the alley stretches on without a single car or pedestrian. One street over is the pandemonium of the promenade, and here everything is quiet and still. *Empty.*

"Should you take a picture?"

I turn to Emily. "What?"

"Should you take a picture to remember how it looks?"

I fumble for my phone, snap a few shots, and then start again toward the pizza place. For most of that night, I manage to not think about the club. The kids distract me. My son is obsessed with a street performer we call Robot Man. He is dressed in black leather body armor, with wrap-around sunglasses and a mohawk. He moves like a robot to hard electronic beats, as a gaggle of young kids wait eagerly to give him fist bumps and drop a dollar or two in his tip bucket. My son watches, and it's clear he wants a fist bump too. He's entranced by the Robot Man but also afraid of him, and the first few times we walk away before he finds the courage to reach out his hand. Then, it happens: we are finishing dinner when he says, unprompted, "I want to give the Robot Man a fist bump." We return to the promenade. He walks up to the Robot Man, braces himself as if expecting a blow, and then swiftly touches fists, drops a dollar in the bucket, and runs jubilantly back into my arms.

That night, after the kids are in bed, I visit the club. I know exactly where it is, but I still double-check the police report for the address: 1212 Third Street Promenade, Santa Monica. It used to be called the Renaissance, but now it has a confusing name: 1212. The numbers, nothing else. It's a strange space, cavernous ceilings and long metal tables. It feels like an airplane hangar. I sit at a long table near the center of the room. What am I doing here? I can imagine this space as a club. I can picture him here, dancing in the shadows. What good does that do now? The lights glint off the table, and I feel like crying when the waitress asks whether I want something to drink.

I pay the check, leave the restaurant without turning around, and walk through the bustling promenade, strangely aware of my own silence. Back at the apartment, I peek in at the kids sleeping, then head out to the balcony, my brother's diary in my hand. He must have lost interest after a few days; there are only a few pages of text. I look up at the palm, then start flipping through the empty pages of the diary, as if looking for a hidden message. I try to imagine my brother holding this book, a ten-year-old boy whose father had just left the country, when something else comes into my brain: a memory of the first time my brother talked about becoming a father someday.

WE'RE WALKING IN THE DESERT, the dogs ranging ahead like a forward patrol. It's two hours after sunset, but the moon is up, and we decide not to use our flashlights. We walk in silence, listening to the wind play across the dunes. Thousands of years ago, this whole area was under water. The sand rises and falls like frozen waves. He stops at the peak of a dune, raises his arms toward the sky, and turns to me:

"Someday, we'll bring our kids here."

"Our kids?" I'm thirteen, and producing progeny is not at the forefront of my brain.

"We'll walk with them through this place, and we'll remember when we used to come here. Can you imagine that, bro?"

"Yeah, that's weird."

"Nah, man. It's beautiful. That's what it is. This moment right now will be our past, our history. The desert will still be here, and the moon, and the wind, and you and me, two old men, walking with our kids. Can you imagine that?"

He gets in these poetic moods. I usually find myself swept along with his dreams. This time, I just can't see it. Having kids? He's twenty and doesn't even have a stable girlfriend. I'm tempted to joke about that, his girlfriend, but I can tell that he's not in the mood. I just watch him, his long arms sweeping the horizon as if he's already there, in the future, looking back on it all.

Peter Slate

Suspect

My brother is alone at our grandparents' house when the door-
bell rings. Two policemen ask him to step outside. Later, he'll
learn that they're looking for a 5'5" Black man in his twenties.
He's 6'1" and fourteen years old, but he is Black.

He explains that our grandmother should be home any minute. If
they want, they can wait inside. They tell him to step outside.

He obeys, suddenly aware that neither officer has returned his smile.
He knows to be polite and keeps smiling as the questions begin.

"Do you live here?"

"No, Sir, this is my grandparents' home."

"Your grandparents?"

"Yes, Sir."

"Can you tell us the address?"

"This address, officer?"

"Yes, can you tell us this address?" The policeman seems irritated,
and my brother realizes that the question is a test.

"4106 Longridge." He smiles wider, hoping to have relieved their
doubts, but the next question is obviously a trap.

"And you live here?"

"No, Officer, my grandparents live here. I'm just visiting."

He can tell that they don't believe him. His jaw tightens, sweat starts to run down his neck, and he fights the urge to wipe it away. No sudden movements. Be polite. Be calm.

Then, an idea strikes him. A way to prove he belongs.

"Officers, there's a photo of me on the wall in the entryway. If you step inside, you can see."

They don't move. He can see the photo in his mind: he's at Uncle Dan's wedding, wearing a tuxedo and a frilly white shirt, beaming with pride. Why won't they believe him? He starts to worry they'll notice he's sweating. His hands become clammy, and his legs grow weak.

My grandmother's Oldsmobile pulls into the driveway. She walks over, a bag of groceries in one hand, her purse in the other. All is quickly explained. The officers apologize to her, then leave without once looking at him.

IT'S OPHIR, the smallest of my brother's friends, and one of the most kind, who tells me the story. We're at a pizza joint in Long Beach, the kind of fancy place where they don't cut the pie into slices. Roman style, they call it. I'm not sure whether to cut the thing myself or fold it over and eat it like a burrito.

"They never apologized to him," Ophir says. "Once he was no longer a suspect, it was as if he didn't exist."

I look up at the ceiling and try to imagine my brother standing next to my grandmother as the police drive away. What would he have said to her? What could he have said? I look back at Ophir. I feel safe with him, and I know that my brother did too. I ask:

"Did he cry when he told you the story?"

"No, I wish he had. We were too old for that."

Fourteen-year-old boys pretending to be men—that must have made it harder to process his fear, his anger. At least he told Ophir what happened. Looking across the table, I can still see the scrawny kid who would come over to play Duck Hunt and 10-Yard Fight. He takes a bite of pizza, and I decide to offer my own thoughts:

"It was hard for him to know who he was, right? Half-Black, half-White. Not a kid anymore, but not yet a man. To the police, he was a dangerous Black male, or he was no one. That's why it haunts me, the

This is the image—my brother at our Uncle Dan's wedding—that the police refused to consult when interrogating my brother outside our grandparents' home. (Courtesy of Henry Raynaud.)

fact that he wanted to show them his photo on the wall. He wanted to prove he was somebody, that he belonged."

Ophir nods. "We were all trying to figure out who we were, where we belonged. That's what teenagers do: struggle with all that stuff. He had it the worst, growing up between worlds."

I cut off a bite of pizza and pop it in my mouth. The sauce is sweet and garlicky.

"Did he talk much about race in those days?"

"No, not in junior high. I don't think we really knew how to talk about it." He pauses, then adds, "It wasn't just race. It was his father too. That really confused him."

"His father?"

Ophir pauses, and I can see him working to recover a memory.

"He used to get these letters, long hand-written letters. He would show them to me."

"Was he proud of them?"

"The letters? Yeah, but also sad. It was hard on him."

"Not having a father?"

"Having one so far away."

There it is: another gap between us. My father was never in my life. His came and went.

Ophir is smiling at me. "You know, it was your grandfather who was the closest thing he had to a dad. He really looked up to your grandfather. We all did."

I take another bite of pizza, and a drop of sauce splatters on my pants. I dab it with my napkin, and Ophir continues:

"That's what's so terrible about the police questioning him at your grandparents' place. He was desperate to be rooted, and here he was being told, 'You don't belong.'"

I think again about my brother standing in the doorway, trying to get the police to look at that photo on the wall. I'd heard the story before, but I don't remember ever hearing it from my brother. Strange, that he kept that episode from me. Maybe he knew that I could never really understand.

MY BROTHER BECAME A TEENAGER in the summer of 1985. Ronald Reagan was president; Madonna was singing "Like a Virgin"; and the Slates (my Mom, my brother, and I) were settling into a small one-story condo on Burnet Avenue, just north of Roscoe, between the 405 and Van Nuys Boulevard. Our neighborhood was predominantly Mexican and Salvadoran—and poor—but our place was part of a gated community of sorts. Instead of a gate, we had a giant wall that ran along one side of the property, shielding our grassy lawn, pool, cabana, and tennis courts from the housing projects on the other side. We called it "the wall," as in, "Man, Brandon hit another baseball over the wall." Those were the years when Reagan declared, "Mr. Gorbachev, tear down this wall!" I don't remember making the connection. As to those "projects," I doubt that they were the ill-fated government housing towers that became so infamous in the 1980s and 1990s. Why did we assume that they were crowded and dangerous? Why did we call them "the projects"? The label was, like the wall, a clear sign of the class divide between our condo enclave and the surrounding blocks.

It wasn't a racial divide, at least not in any simple sense. Our condo complex was remarkably diverse when it came to nationality. My brother played Nintendo with a Korean kid. My best friend was half-Greek and half-Peruvian. It was as if the United Nations had set up a middle-class condo in the heart of the Valley.

My brother's school friends were equally diverse. Most were the children of immigrants: from Morocco, Italy, Egypt, Iran. My brother was also the child of an immigrant, but his friends had stronger ties to their homelands. Their parents spoke foreign languages. Their food came from distant lands. He moved effortlessly through their families, eating with his hands, addressing parents with respect. It must have been comforting for him to fit into such families—families that were, like him, struggling to know who they were, where they belonged.

If my brother had come of age in 1960, he would have been proud of his Nigerian heritage. As a wave of African nations gained independence, many African Americans looked on with hope and pride. If he had come of age in 1970, he might have immersed himself in the pan-Africanism that infused the Black Power movement. In 1976, Alex Haley published *Roots*, a sweeping account of his family's history. Released as a TV miniseries in 1977, *Roots* had special meaning for Black Americans eager to celebrate their African ancestry. If my brother had been fourteen rather than four, he might have joined that celebration. But growing up in the 1980s, he came to see Nigeria as a tragic land that embodied the suffering of postcolonial Africa. In 1984, starving African children again became world news, this time in Ethiopia. In December, a group of British and Irish musicians released a song to raise funds for famine victims. Their efforts inspired an even more successful American version, "We Are the World," written by Michael Jackson and Lionel Richie. "We Are the World" sold twenty million copies and raised more than $60 million—but it also reinforced an image of Africa as a disaster zone in need of charity, an image my brother could not avoid, no matter how much he wanted to be proud of his father, no matter how much he needed a land to call his own.

I STARE AT A PHOTO OF US, two boys standing shirtless outside our trailer in the desert. We're both holding spears. Brightly colored hoops dangle from our necks. We're dressed like "noble savages," like Zulu warriors, like "Africans." We knew better than to think that Africa was populated with spear-wielding cannibals, but we didn't know enough to see that stereotype as offensive. It wasn't that we didn't respect African culture. Mom made sure that we knew that Africa is a vast and remarkably diverse continent. Our house was full of West African sculptures and musical instruments, like the mbira, or thumb piano, a little wooden box adorned with thin metal pieces that resonate when plucked. I loved the sound it made, a clean bright twang, but playing it hurt my thumbs, and I never considered taking lessons. My connection to Africa was little more than a source of occasional curiosity, something I could pick up and put down, like the mbira. It was different for him.

I remember one time I visited him in college in the spring of 1991. I must have been eleven. We're walking through an outdoor mall when we stumble upon a few older Black men with dreads and beards, sitting behind a small plastic table, festooned with the red, black, and green flag long associated with Africa. They are selling African-themed jewelry and small fridge magnets in the shape of Africa. I pester my brother into buying one of the magnets but quickly lose interest in my new toy. Something more interesting is unfolding: my brother is changing. As he talks with the older Black men, his diction shifts, his voice deepens, even his hand gestures take on a foreign flare. It may be an act, but it strikes me as grounded in something deep within him, an intimacy he shares with these men, an intimacy I will never know.

It would not be until I entered graduate school that African history became more than a source of curiosity for me. It would take even more years for me to recognize the tragedy of my brother's relationship to Africa and to see that tragedy as a source of distance between us.

Mom still feels guilty for not moving to Nigeria. "Maybe that would have given him greater self-esteem," she tells me. We're sitting in the backyard, watching the kids play with my mom's dog, Sukie, a miniature dachshund that thinks she's a guard dog. Sukie is patrolling our neighbor's fence, and the kids join her in a procession of cuteness. I want to watch them, but I can feel my mom's guilt like a knot in my stomach. I turn toward her.

"You can't blame yourself."

"Why not? I made so many mistakes."

"That's what it means to be a parent. You always tell me that. It's not about being perfect. It's about being good enough."

"Was I good enough?"

Her guilt makes me angry and tired. I take a deep breath and close my eyes. It's early November, and the air smells of wood smoke. The kids are chasing Sukie, laughing as they stumble through the ivy. I want to tell Mom that she shouldn't blame herself. I want to walk over and kiss her on the forehead. Something makes me hesitate—perhaps my exhaustion, perhaps my own guilt. We sit together, saying nothing, listening to my children laughing.

UDERULU OSAKWE started using his middle name, Peter, while living with our grandparents. They found it easier than Ude. By the time we moved to the condo and Peter started middle school, his last name had changed as well. Chukwudi's sister, Ola, deserves some of the credit. Her nasty letter was followed by more menacing messages, some of which contained threats to kidnap Ude and take him back to Nigeria. Karen decided that it would be safest if his last name was hers. Uderulu Osakwe became Peter Osakwe and then Peter Slate.

I called him Bubba. I had trouble with my *R*s and my *TH*s, and so the word *brother* was out of the question. Bubba was close enough. He called me "bro" or "little bro." After a few months of speech therapy, I mastered my *R*s and started to call him "bro" as well. Around middle school, that word began to stick in my throat. It would take years for me to identify the problem: saying "bro" sounded like I was trying to be Black. Eventually, *bro* would become associated with White frat boys, but in the eighties, the word was unmistakably racial. Whereas *dude* called to mind long-haired surfers, *bro* brought forth sneaker-clad Black men with secret handshakes and backward baseball caps. From my brother's mouth, the word sounded right, even when used to describe me. *Bro. Brother. My brother.* These words still stick in my throat. I feel like I'm pretending to be something I'm not. My daughter calls my son "Bubba." She's almost two and can't pronounce *brother.* Sometimes, she'll say it three times in a row—*Bubba, Bubba, Bubba*—like when she wants to get down from eating to go play with him, or if she sees him from a distance. *Bubba, Bubba, Bubba.* Her whole body quivers with joy. She stamps her feet in anticipation. He's coming toward her across the playground. Past the slides, the swings, the sandbox. He comes in close and hugs her, and she tucks her tiny head down into his chest. *Bubba, Bubba, Bubba.* I think of my brother every time she says his name.

I STRUGGLE TO IMAGINE HIM as a kid. Even in my earliest memories, he seems so old. Big brothers often seem older than their years, and mine was forced to grow up too fast.

He was thirteen when he started drinking. He found the booze in our grandfather's home office. A curious kid goofing off with his buddies. It smelled awful, and his friends pretended to vomit after trying their first sips. A noise in the hallway startled them, and he slid the bottle back into the drawer. His friends giggled as they ran into the TV room to watch Mr. T and the rest of the A-Team. The next day, he went back alone.

At first, it was just a game. Then, it became a habit. Our grandfather, my brother's primary father figure, rarely skipped his "stomach medicine." A tumbler of bourbon on the rocks, and his eyes would glaze, his smile begin to droop. I don't blame Dad for my brother's drinking—at least, not entirely. My brother drank to escape his demons; even for a confused teenager, he had a lot of demons.

I'M STANDING IN A PLAYGROUND in Santa Monica, a few days after Christmas 2018, talking with my brother's friend Daneh. She tells me about his drinking, how it became his way of coping with his emotions.

"Did he talk about his emotions in those years?"

"All the time," Daneh tells me. "He used to call me late at night and just cry and cry."

This isn't the tough kid I remember, the one who started lifting weights, taught himself to shave, and bragged about romantic conquests. I'm not surprised; he and Daneh always had a different relationship. Her family was from Iran, and so, like most of his friends, she understood what it meant to not fit into the standard racial boxes. Unlike his other close friends, Daneh was a girl, and he felt safe enough to cry with her.

It's an amazing playground, divided into an older kid's area with a jungle gym and swings and a younger kid's space with a sandbox and a large bouncy rubber mat. We've been coming every morning since we arrived, and the kids now see it as their own. My daughter is barefoot in the sand, digging for imaginary ladybugs with a blue plastic shovel. My son is gathering berries, twigs, and leaves for a magic potion he is preparing. Daneh has three kids of her own and is an elementary school teacher; she's OK with our conversation being continually interrupted by one kid or the other.

"He called you at night," I ask, "in middle school?"

"Yeah, he was so deep, even then. He had so many questions about who he was, why he wasn't happy with himself."

"Was it being mixed that drove that uncertainty? Or his father being gone?"

"It was all of that piled on top of the basic insecurities of that age."

My son yells at us from a nearby bush. "I need more berries, Papa."

I walk toward him and ask, "Can you say it as a question?"

"Please," he replies. "Can you please find more berries?"

I find a small clump of purple berries and hand them to him. He takes them without acknowledgment of any kind, as if my hand exists only to deliver whatever he needs. I should remind him to say thank you. Instead, I turn back to Daneh.

"When did it start, his struggles? Was there some kind of trigger?"

"I don't know. I met him in seventh grade, and he was already so sensitive. Such a smart, deep thinker, with so many doubts about himself."

His middle-school years are the hardest for me to imagine. Mom's memories are patchy and limited by their relationship. Middle schoolers are not known for opening their hearts to their parents. I was too young to pay attention to my brother's inner world. That's why I treasure these conversations with his friends. But the more I learn, the more aware I become of how much I still don't know.

I'm about to pose another question, when Daneh asks me one of her own: "Have you been to the Promenade?" I'm watching my daughter, wondering whether her bare feet are cold. The question startles me, and it takes me a few seconds to reply.

"Oh, yes, they love it there." Another moment of silence. The sun comes out from behind the clouds, and I savor the warmth. Daneh smiles at me with such kindness; I can see why my brother trusted her.

She says, "You know that's where the club is, the place he lost his eye."

"Yes," I respond, "I just went for the first time." I'm not sure what else to say and try to return the conversation to my brother's middle-school years.

"Was he into girls back then, when you first met him?"

"No, not really." She pauses. "He was trying to be the man of the house, to be strong for you and your mom. He was such a sensitive boy. . . . The responsibility weighed on him—wounded him—long before what they did to him that night."

I used to see the attack as a sudden rupture in his life's story; now, it seems more like a culmination. The loss of his father. The challenge of helping my mom. The burden of caring for me. What else did I fail to see?

It's the spring of 1987. He's fourteen; I'm seven. We walk to 7–11, load up with cheese danishes and Coca-Cola Slurpees, and wait for the bus at the corner of Victory and Van Nuys. It's only three miles from my elementary school to our house, but it will take an hour by bus and foot. All the way home, I will talk. I am quiet at school but not with my brother. I will spill out everything that happened that day in a torrent of words broken only by the occasional sip of Slurpee or bite of danish. Most days, my brother seems to enjoy my rambling monologue. Today, he surprises me:

"Bro, let's ride home in silence."

"You mean not talk at all?"

"Yeah, just for today."

"Why? Is something wrong?"

"Nothing's wrong."

I have a thousand things to share, as usual, but I can tell that this silence thing is important. I keep my mouth shut as we wait at the bus stop. Two old women are speaking in Spanish behind us, and I listen to see whether I can pick out any words. On the bus, I can hear hip-hop coming from the headphones of a skinny teenager, and I lean in to identify the song. When we reach our stop, I fly down the rear stairs, eager to break my silence. A last puff of AC blows against my back as the doors of the bus close, and I look up at my brother.

"Could you hear the music coming from that guy's headphones? What song was that?"

"Not sure. Sounded like Run-DMC to me."

"Is that why you had us be silent?"

"Why's that?"

"So that we could hear everything?"

"What do you think? Did you like it?"

"Yeah, it was weird, but I liked it."

We turn to face the Panorama City mall, a low-budget shopping center that looks abandoned. The air feels strangely calm, and I wonder whether we will walk home in silence. I still have so much to share with my brother—my near-triumph in capture the flag, what Colin told Scott about Brandi—and before the bus drives away, I've already begun my monologue. He listens, and I feel heard and loved. I never wonder what he would be thinking if I were not here to demand his attention, if his mind were free to process his own day, to reflect on his own life or the city that pulsed and sprawled around us, the city I ignored as I yammered on and on, safe in the knowledge that my brother was at my side.

PANORAMA CITY was designed for soldiers returning home from World War II. Most of the homes were sold with racial covenants that prevented them from being owned by anyone who was not White. Just to be safe, officials also filed a document with the county recorder, declaring that no home in Panorama City could be "used or occupied by any person whose blood is not entirely that of the white or Caucasian race." Such discriminatory agreements were used in many housing developments in the postwar era, despite the fact that the Supreme Court had ruled in 1948 that restrictive covenants were unconstitutional. The lawyer in that case was none other than Thurgood Marshall, later the first African American Supreme Court Justice. Marshall's victory did not prevent many developers from continuing to use restrictive covenants. It wasn't just bigotry that was at play; a lot of money was at stake too.

My brother saw the connection between racism and greed. I resisted that lesson and clung for most of my life to a vision of racism as irrational bigotry, a sickness of the heart rather than of society, policy, or economics. I should have known better. The truth was all around me. But to see it, I had to see myself as a White kid from a wealthy family who lived in a middle-class condo in the middle of a poor neighborhood. I had to see all the divisions that shaped my life, some of which cut between me and the man I loved more than any other.

AFTER EXITING THE BUS at the mall, we would snag a shopping cart from the parking lot. I would get in, and my brother would push me all the way home. Mom was working as an office manager and wasn't around much. My brother became my primary parent. We cooked mac and cheese, frozen pizza, or fish sticks. One time, he burned a pot of rice. The smoke filled the apartment, forcing us to sit in the front yard and watch TV through the window.

The best part of our routine was the ride home in that shopping cart. If we were late for *Magnum, P.I.*, my brother would run, and as we hurtled down the sidewalk, I would yell out the names of each street we passed. Tobias. Cedros. Willis. Kestor. I would lean back and stare at the clouds rush by, as his slim brown body strained to push my weight, the body I loved like my own, the body that had been branded in ways I am only beginning to see.

HE TAKES THE JUMP ROPE and his new platform shoes and walks outside. It's a chilly January evening, and I follow him into the cold blue air with a basketball in one hand and a half-eaten fish stick in the other. I haven't finished dinner, but I'm curious to see these new shoes in action. With weighted discs attached to the front of the sole, they look like a cross between a sneaker and a flying saucer. He saw them advertised in a sports magazine—"add six inches to your vertical!"—and convinced Mom to buy him a pair. I study the shoes as he laces up and begins to jump. I listen to the rope slice the air and slap the ground—whap, whap, whap—like a helicopter in slow motion. I watch the sweat run down his face and pool at the neckline of his sweatshirt. Finally, I work up the courage to ask, "Will those things make you dunk?"

He frowns at me.

"Be quiet and start dribbling. Let me see what your left hand can do."

I start dribbling but mutter, "They better make you dunk because they sure are ugly."

My brother wanted to be good at sports, especially basketball, but he was slow and uncoordinated and had almost no vertical leap. He was nowhere near dunking. I was blind to his limitations. He was my role model, and I assumed that he was a future Olympian. I told my friends that his father was a famous African soccer player. I never had to describe my father's athletic abilities; the fact that he was White was sufficient to explain my shortcomings. My brother couldn't fall back on the "White men can't jump" thing. Thus, the platform shoes.

Every night after dinner, he jumped rope in those shoes while I worked on dribbling. Right hand, left hand, head up, eyes up, I moved in figure eights around my brother, as he leapt toward the myth that every Black man was good at basketball. There were enough White players—the Larry Birds and John Stocktons—that neither of us saw basketball as a Black man's sport. Every Black man was supposed to be able to play, but it was fine if a White man had skills too. Watching him jump rope in those platform shoes, his breath quick and heavy, inspired me to pursue my own hoop dreams. Only now can I see that his commitment to the sport came, in part, from a sense of obligation—to live up to what our society believed a Black man should be able to do, to live up to the expectations of his friends, his coaches, and that pesky kid who followed him everywhere, blind to his burdens, blind to the fact that he was just a kid too.

GAME FOUR of the 1987 NBA championships. The Lakers are playing the reigning champions, our perennial adversaries, the Boston Celtics. We are in the car, Mom is driving, and Chick Hearn is calling the game over the radio. His folksy voice is familiar and reassuring, even as the Celtics take an early lead. The Lakers refuse to give up and are down just one point, 103–102, with thirty seconds left to play. Through a forest of giants, Magic finds Kareem, and the Lakers take the lead. My brother is in the backseat with me so that I can hold his hand when the game is tense. I turn to see his face and find him watching me. Bird hits a devastating three-pointer from the corner to put the Celtics up by two, 106–104, with only twelve seconds remaining. With the clock ticking, Kareem is fouled and sinks his first free throw. He misses the second, but the ball is knocked out of bounds by the Celtics. Lakers' ball, down by one. The car rolls to a stop. We're home.

Without a word, we leap from the car and sprint toward the house. He yanks open the door. We bound inside, jump onto the couch, and switch on the TV just in time to see the ball inbounded to Magic. He dribbles, hesitates, then drives toward the basket. Halfway across the key, he launches a hook shot over the outstretched arms of two of the lankiest guys in the game: Kevin McHale and Robert Parrish. It's good! The Lakers take the lead with two seconds left on the clock. We leap in the air and pound high-fives with all our strength. I can still feel my hand burning.

WHEN I TURNED TEN, he took me to a Lakers game to see Magic in person. We sat in the nosebleeds. It was strangely quiet up there, especially for someone accustomed to watching the game on TV. I didn't miss the play-by-play, and I didn't care that we were so far from the court. I was with my brother. During half-time, he told an usher that it was my birthday (which had been a few weeks earlier) and talked our way down to the expensive seats. From there, it was only about thirty rows to the floor. He gripped my hand and smiled as we strolled down the stairs, affecting ease, as if we always sat on the floor next to Jack Nicholson. I was thrilled and terrified. We had almost made it to the floor when another usher approached and asked to see our tickets. Without pause, my brother offered a handshake and explained that I had turned ten that very day. It worked again, and we were able to squeeze behind the floor seats to position ourselves near the tunnel where the players would return to the floor. The bright lights of the arena were dazzling so close to the floor, and I felt dizzy. I looked at my feet to regain my balance and might have missed Magic jogging out, had my brother not hoisted me into the air. I leaned my hand over the metal railing just in time to get a high-five from my hero. I vowed to never wash my hand again; I wanted to preserve Magic's touch forever. Now it's my brother's hands I feel holding me up toward the lights.

My only problem that night was the bathroom. I was a shy kid and struggled to pee when I sensed that others were waiting for my spot. I tried to make it through the game without having to go. Eventually, the pressure grew too strong, and I asked my brother to take me to the bathroom. The line was long, and by the time I made it to a urinal, I felt a tight pain in my stomach. I'd held it too long and couldn't relax enough to complete my mission. I pretended to pee for ten seconds and then walked toward the door, unrelieved and in pain. He was waiting for me at the door. He dropped to one knee and looked into my eyes. "Was it hard to go with so many people in line?" I was so relieved that he understood, I almost peed in my pants. I started to mumble an explanation, but he cut me off:

"I've been there, bro. It's hard to let it out when the line is that long and you've got people standing on both sides of you. Are you nervous they're watching?"

"Yeah, I guess."

"I used to worry about that too. Then, I learned a trick. When you get to the urinal, don't focus on trying to pee. Just stare at your shoes and count to five, then imagine that you're holding a lightsaber and are about to spin around to defend yourself against a wave of stormtroopers."

"How is that going to help?"

"Just try it. Come on, I'll wait in line with you."

While we waited, he asked me questions about the game. How did AC grab so many rebounds? Was Byron fouled on that three from the baseline? By the time, we made it to the front of the line, and a urinal opened up, I had almost forgotten that I had to pee. I only had to count to three before my lightsaber found its target.

OUR GRANDMOTHER was obsessed with basketball. The daughter of taciturn German dairy farmers, Gail Slate was not known for her passion. But when it came to basketball, her love was intense and contagious. Our grandfather, by contrast, was completely uninterested in sports. In 1980, when my brother was seven, he sent our grandfather a handwritten apology: "Dad, I am sorry I watched the Basketball on your Birthday. I hope we can go on a walk soon. From Peter. PS I am sorry because you are more important than Basketball." I expect that the note was our mom's idea. Our grandmother would never have approved of anything being more important than basketball.

Had his father not returned to Nigeria, perhaps Peter would have turned to soccer. Chukwudi was a soccer star, and most boys idolize their father, at least for a time. Without his father to steer him toward his feet, Peter followed our grandmother toward the hoop. It helped that he was tall and that he was Black. Because he towered above his classmates and was one of the few Black kids in his school, everyone assumed that he would play basketball.

His commitment to the game came from our grandmother, but his skills came from John Wooden. In the world of basketball, Wooden is a hero. In our family, he was a god. He built the most impressive college basketball program in history. His UCLA teams won ten national championships in twelve years. Wooden believed in fundamentals. To learn those fundamentals, my brother went to Wooden's basketball camp. We still have the picture, my brother next to Coach Wooden. Looking at that photo now, what strikes me is the gentleness in both of their faces. Perhaps a stranger would see a Black athlete standing next to the White coach, but I want to believe that the kindness I see in Wooden's eyes defied such divisions. In 1946, Wooden coached the Indiana State Sycamores into the National Association of Intercollegiate Athletics (NAIA) tournament, but the league refused to allow one of his players, Clarence Walker, to take the court. Walker was Black, and the tournament was for White players only. Walker was not a starter, but Wooden refused to take his team unless Walker was included.

By the time I was a kid, the Lakers were starting five Black players. The majority of fans were White. Most of those fans idolized their favorite players without thinking much, if at all, about the fact that they were Black. If a White kid grows up wanting to be like Snoop Dogg, he might be teased for wanting to be Black. When the same kid wants to be Michael Jordan, race need not be considered. The NBA is raced, but not in the same way as hip-hop. Most players embody racial identities only occasionally, as when LeBron James protested the death of Eric Garner by wearing a T-shirt that read "I can't breathe." As soon as that T-shirt was removed, LeBron's racial identity faded from the spotlight, replaced by his spin move and average points per game.

Basketball could render a superstar raceless or help a teenage boy claim his Blackness; either way, the gaze of others defined the borders of race. My brother could decide to play basketball, but he couldn't decide what was considered "Black" in Los Angeles in 1988. Throughout his life, he had to navigate social expectations to manage his Blackness. When he was a child, Mom was his ally. She bought him his Black doll, Johnny. She introduced him to the music of Nina Simone and Muddy Waters. She got that perm so that their hair would be more alike. Everything changed when my brother became a teenager. Mom helped open the door to Blackness; now, she was an obstacle, and so was I. Not many Black kids had White moms or White brothers.

Styles Ville

He rocked the flattop like Kid from Kid 'N Play, but shorter, and so smooth you could land a plane on the top of his head. He had abstract shapes buzzed into the sides: a Nike swoosh inverted like the arc of a rainbow, triangles within triangles. I wanted the same cut. My hair, blond and straight as hay, was buzzed short. Mom did the buzzing in our bathroom. She used to cut his hair, too, but he didn't trust her to carve the designs, and neither did I. So, we went to Styles Ville.

My earliest memory of being a minority: the smell of the barbershop. Hair oil and aftershave, the sharp spice of incense. Too nervous to make eye contact, I study the photos on the walls, mostly black-and-white portraits from the fifties. All the faces are Black. I am ten years old. More than most White kids my age, I am used to being around Black people, but being the only White person in the room is new for me, and I'm nervous—and guilty for being nervous. I don't know what I'm supposed to feel in such a place, but I'm not supposed to feel anxious. There's no reason to worry. Yet here I am, that unmistakable churn in my stomach, cold sweat on the back of my neck.

Freddie Carter, the man who has owned Styles Ville for decades, reaches out his hand and smiles. I am reassured by his warm eyes and gentle grasp. Carter is old and thin, but he doesn't seem fragile. His

Peter Slate sporting the flattop. (Author's collection.)

long arms are strong. His clothes are simple and neat, black trousers and a gray polo. His gold watch stands out against his dark brown skin. He is clearly in charge and at ease in his kingdom, cracking jokes and laughing even as his hands move smoothly across my head. He doesn't mind my being here.

I am amazed by the sharp designs he cuts into my flaxen mop. They are perfectly formed, as if he shears White boys every day. After he finishes my hair, I sit in an old leather chair and flip through copies of *Ebony* and *Jet* while my brother has his flattop shaped and trimmed. I pretend to read while stealing furtive glances at the other men in the barbershop. They range in age from twenty to seventy, but they all seem to be having a good time. I look back at my brother. He seems calm and happy, laughing at jokes I don't understand. Why am I still so nervous?

A few weeks earlier, I had surprised my elementary school sweetheart with a silver necklace for her birthday. I picked a red rose from my grandmother's garden and took the flower and the necklace to the house of my "girlfriend" to surprise her on the morning of her birthday. I knew that she was having a sleepover with her friends, but I was still unprepared when her father opened the door and ushered me into a room full of girls in pajamas. I blushed so hard my nose tingled, but I delivered the gifts and managed to make it back to the car, sweating and smiling. My brother had parked around the block so that I could pretend I had come on my own. I was nervous, but I was supposed to be nervous. To a ten-year-old boy, nothing is more terrifying than a room full of ten-year-old girls.

In Styles Ville, I had no cause to be nervous. I felt betrayed by my sweaty hands, my hot cheeks. Was my brother nervous too? I doubt that he felt secure in his Blackness with his White brother in tow. His hair was already different, a little too loose, more silk than wool. He brought me anyway, maybe because he loved me, maybe because he didn't want to be Black if he couldn't be himself.

Styles Ville was the oldest Black barbershop in the oldest Black neighborhood in the San Fernando Valley. When Styles Ville opened in 1958, Pacoima was pretty much the only place a Black family could buy a home in the Valley. Back when the area was full of orange groves, real estate developers worked with organizations like the White Home Owners Protective Association to maintain racial homogeneity. Pacoima was the exception that proved the rule. It was a Black and Japanese neighborhood until World War II. After Pearl Harbor, Japanese residents were rounded up and taken to detention camps. It didn't matter that the majority were American citizens. While Pacoima's Japanese community was devastated, African Americans were drawn into the neighborhood, attracted by job opportunities at nearby factories. By the 1960s, Pacoima had become home to 98 percent of the Valley's twenty-five thousand African Americans. It never became entirely Black; some Japanese families returned after the war, and there was always a significant Mexican American community, a community that included the singer Ritchie Valens, famous for his hit single "La Bamba." Pacoima embodied the racial cosmopolitanism forced on non-White people throughout California. The color line divided not White from Black but White from non-White.

In the late 1950s, Emory Holmes, a Black veteran of the Second World War, dared to move his family to the only White part of Pacoima. When the Holmes family arrived, their new neighbors responded by throwing rocks through windows, vandalizing the family car, making phone calls at all hours of the night, burning a cross, and sending a hearse to pick up "the deceased." The Holmes family was not intimidated. They sued, and their case led to what the local Black newspaper called "the first successful anti-discrimination housing suit in California State history."

Most Black residents of Pacoima were unable to move. Instead, they created vibrant neighborhood institutions, such as Styles Ville. Over the course of the 1990s, as Pacoima became less Black and more Spanish-speaking, those institutions began to close. Asked in 1999 about the surge in newcomers from Mexico and Central America, Carter told a reporter, "I look at them as my new friends. It's a cycle, that's all. . . . Hispanics were here, then we came in, now the blacks have sold almost all the businesses." The shifting demography of Pacoima threatened the future of Carter's business, and I am amazed that he could look at the change with such equanimity. His tolerance should not surprise me. He had been just as welcoming to me.

The second time we visited Styles Ville, Carter welcomed us with a smile and a warm handshake, and I was up in the barber chair almost instantly. At first, I felt calm and happy as my hair disappeared in the mirror, but the more I watched Carter, his smooth hands shaping my hair, the more I realized that I had no idea what he made of me. I had no reason to doubt his warmth. I never felt a hint of animosity from him. Still, there was a palpable distance between us, a cloud between our faces. I started to wonder what he thought of my Whiteness. Maybe it didn't matter to him at all. Maybe I was projecting my own social awkwardness onto the racial dynamics of the situation. I was a shy kid who never felt comfortable with strangers, even strangers as kind as Carter. Maybe it would have been the same even if I were Black or he were White. I can't know, just as I can't know what role race played the night my brother was attacked. That's what makes racism such an insidious force: it's bound up with all the ways our world is not what it should be, all the ways we are not who we want to be. I wish I could have sat in that barber chair, joyful and relaxed, as if it were just my brother and me, as if I were the man he always believed I would be.

We lived about fifteen minutes from Pacoima, but I remember going to Styles Ville only twice. Maybe my brother sensed my anxiety and spared me another journey. Maybe I outgrew the idea of having geometric shapes buzzed onto my head. By fifth grade, I had joined the head-banging crowd. I was more into Jimi Hendrix and the Red Hot Chili Peppers than Metallica or Black Sabbath, but long hair was still mandatory. At the time, I did not consider my failure to return to Styles Ville a lost opportunity. Only later would I realize what it meant for my brother to take me to Styles Ville, and what it meant that we only went twice.

"WANT TO SEE SOMETHING COOL?" He grins as we arrive at his new school, Ulysses S. Grant High. We're fifteen minutes early for basketball tryouts. "Sure," I reply hesitantly, nervous he'll be late. He's always pushing the limits. I follow him across the parking lot, up a small ridge, and through a wall of cypress trees. We squeeze through the trees and press our bodies against a chain-link fence. Below us lies a massive concrete ravine. It's an aqueduct, a branch of the Los Angeles River, but I won't know that until later. What strikes me then, and what my brother knew would grab my attention, is the giant mural that sprawls along one side of the ravine. The Great Wall of Los Angeles examines the history of California from prehistoric times to the 1950s, but he doesn't know the name of the mural or its history. He only knows that it's something I will find interesting. He points at two Native American people, one woman and one man, flanking a round wheel-like mandala, with two dolphins swimming in the center next to a pair of lightning bolts. These were the Chumash people, but we do not know their name. "It's weird," he says, "that the river has concrete walls, but it's painted with images of nature. What do you think the river was like when those people lived here?" I imagine the river free of its concrete husk, muddy banks with reeds waving in the light. Before I can say something, he pats my shoulder. "Come on. We'll be late."

The website of the Great Wall tells me this: "The peaceful early history of the region ends with a White hand rising from the sea, symbol of the destruction of Native American life by White settlers." I don't remember that part of the mural. It's easy to celebrate diversity and to forget oppression, to praise the Chumash in their absence as if we are not living on their land, as if this city has not been built on forgotten bones.

"IMAGINE LA LIKE A SERIES OF CIRCLES, one inside the next." We're up on Mulholland Drive, parked in one of those empty lots where teenagers make out. It's early Sunday morning, and we're on our way to Uncle Dan's church, scarfing down Egg McMuffins before the service begins. He passes me some hash browns and gestures over his shoulder. "In the inner circle, the hood, Black people. To the East, the Barrio." He points to the horizon ahead of us. "In the outer circle, the suburbs, grassy lawns and swimming pools pushing into the desert." He sips his OJ and grins:

> In between the ghetto and the suburbs, it gets messy. The Valley is a middle ground. The richest people, the Whitest people, cluster against these hills. In the middle of the Valley, at the bottom of the bowl, neighborhoods like ours fill with our Latino brothers and sisters.

He is in one of those moods where he likes to talk. Sometimes they annoy me, his spontaneous lectures. Not this morning: I'm sleepy, and it's nice to hear his voice so warm and full of confidence. Still, I wonder why he cares so much, why he's so careful to make clear that he has no animus against "our Latino brothers and sisters."

When Antonio Villaraigosa became mayor in 2005, he was hailed as "LA's first Latino mayor." That's true, but only if you look at the last hundred years. If you had visited LA in 1868, some twenty years after California had been taken from Mexico by force, you would have found Cristóbal Aguilar serving as the mayor. Aguilar could not speak English but was still deemed "a good and acceptable Mayor" by one nineteenth-century historian of LA, "because of the general familiarity of citizens of all nationalities then residing here[] with the Spanish tongue." Whenever anti-immigrant radicals decry the "re-conquest" of California, I think about Mayor Aguilar, and I think about my best friend, Alex.

Alex lived next door to us. His mother was from Peru, his father from Greece. That made him mixed, like my brother, although I never saw it that way. Unlike Karen and Chukwudi, Alex's parents could move through the city without being seen as an anomaly. They spoke other languages and ate strange foods, yet Alex's identity was never an issue in the way my brother's was. Being mixed is one thing, but being White and Black is something different.

"It's a series of circles, this city," my brother continues, "but not everyone fits neatly in place." We've finished the McMuffins and the hash browns, and it's time for church, but he doesn't seem ready to end the conversation. I watch him surveying this city we've always called home. His face is inscrutable: somewhere between wistful and restless. I decide to ask a question: "Do you want to live here forever?" He smiles down at me.

"What made you ask a question like that?"

"I don't know." I start to blush. "I just—"

He cuts in, "It's a good question. I don't know where I'll be, but let's make a promise, OK?" I look up, curious. "Let's promise to live in the same city. This world's divided enough. Let's keep our family together."

A FEW WEEKS LATER, we're playing basketball in the driveway when Mom comes home with groceries. An old couple is walking by, and they strike up a conversation. I'm not especially interested in the conversation until the woman asks Mom, "Your boy, was he adopted from Africa?" It's hot, and I'm sweating. My purple Lakers cap shields my eyes from the sun as I look up at Mom's face. She looks tired; this is not the first time she's had to field that question. I turn to my brother. I expect to see him angry, but his face angles down toward his feet. He looks away as he walks past me, picks up a few bags of groceries, and carries them inside.

Strangers often doubted my brother's parentage. Many gave him that long second glance, the racial double take, that made clear they were searching for White blood—only when he was around me or Mom, of course. We complicated his racial identity in a way he never did ours.

For Alex and me—a brown kid and a White kid—to be friends in Los Angeles in the 1980s wasn't a big deal. A White kid and a Black kid as brothers? That was more unusual. My brother was my brother. I never felt confused about his relationship to me, but the fact he was my brother meant that I was constantly reminded that he was mixed, that he was Black, that we were different. By contrast, Alex was raceless to me. It's not that I saw him as White; it's that I didn't see him as raced at all. That's part of what it means to be White, to be seen as beyond race—at least by other White people.

MY BROTHER TRIES TO HIDE his frustration when he asks the question, "Are you White?" We're on the way home from the park. I stink of sweat and seethe with anger and shame. I had let him get to me, the old pudgy guy with the hook shot and the oversized mouth, the guy who liked to call me "White boy." I had started making sloppy mistakes, dribbling off my foot, shooting air balls from the top of the key. My brother had stepped up his game, becoming more physical, taking out his anger on the poor guy guarding him, but we still lost, and now we're driving home exhausted, both of us stewing. The windows are down, and the air is cool against my wet skin. As we crawl to a stop, he turns on the AC, rolls up the windows, and asks, "Are you White?"

Is this a trick question? I'm not sure whether I'm supposed to reject the label as racist or accept it as a self-evident fact. I keep silent. He asks again, this time quietly, almost gently: "Are you White?"

"Yeah," I say, "I'm White."

"So what's the big deal?"

"No big deal. That guy just gets in my head."

"You let him in your head." He pauses. "I don't blame you. It's hard to be White on that court."

I glance at him, and he keeps talking:

You need to embrace that burden and recognize why it's yours to bear. You know, there was a time when Mom's family wouldn't have been seen as White. Even the Germans were discriminated against when they first started coming over. And the Irish took hell.

I stare out the window as we pass a strip mall. We stop at a light. The mall has a Korean BBQ, a Chinese place, and a Salvadoran market. I roll down my window as the traffic starts to move again, and the air rushes over my face, the skin of my arm. My brother is still talking:

What it means to be White keeps changing. First, the Germans and the Irish were brought into the fold. Then, the Italians, the Polish, the Greeks. Some folks, like the Jews, became White but still have people hating them for who they are.

I look down at my pale, freckled arm and think about what it means that I am White, that Alex is sort of White, that my brother is half-White in some ways but all Black in others. I still don't know what that meant for him or for us.

I played Transformers and hide-and-seek with a group of kids as diverse as our condo complex. We embodied the future Mom imagined for us all: a world beyond race—at least, that's how I used to see it. Now, I watch my own children playing. Their favorite game involves my son standing in the middle of our living room. His sister creeps from behind and pushes on his back. He falls forward onto his belly, and she lies on top of him, a slow-motion tackle. They roll on the floor, giggling and screeching, then leap up, ready to play the game again.

I watch them and see my brother, his beaming face turned toward me as I throw my body on top of his. We loved to wrestle. Afterward, I would lie exhausted, my head on his chest. I wish that I could lie there now and ask him about this story I'm telling, his story and mine. I don't want to let his story recede behind ours, to let our love hide our differences. Although we shared some passions—writing, basketball, dreaming of future glory—there was much we did not share. Even his greatest struggles were hidden from me.

I AM SITTING on the blue couch in our grandparents' TV room, eating cold chocolate pudding from a glass goblet and looking at a photo of my brother and an older relative of ours on a motorbike together. They had gone on vacation, just the two of them. Looking at the photo, the way her arms are wrapped around him, something shifts inside me and leaves me unsettled. My brother walks into the room, carrying another glass of pudding, and I quickly slide the photo under a magazine, nervous and blushing, as if I'd been caught with porn.

I was ten years old. I had felt her strange sexual energy directed at my body. Maybe that explains why I never asked him about that trip, never broached the subject of their relationship. I felt implicated. I, too, had something to hide.

I was also painfully shy about sex in general. My brother's romantic life was mysterious to me. I was intrigued by the fundamentals: what it means to have a girlfriend, to make out, to "be serious." I was intrigued by the details. Who was that short White girl my brother was wrestling on the couch? Obviously, she was no match for him. She didn't even seem to be trying very hard, although she did push him off pretty quickly when she noticed that I had stumbled into the room.

Most of my brother's girlfriends were White. I was never surprised by that fact, although perhaps I should have been. His high school was remarkably diverse, yet my brother was drawn to White girls, especially blondes. I never had the courage to ask him why. When he was chosen prom king, his date was Black. All of his friends seemed to pair off by ethnicity. I remember being startled by the photos, everyone in tuxes and fancy dresses. They all looked so old to me. Even then, I noticed the segregation, couple by couple replaying the divides that cut through his body. At least this wasn't one of those schools where they still have two proms, one White and one Black.

My brother's relationships never lasted long. One survived a few months, but most were flings. Even as a child, I sensed an unhappiness in him, a certain restless unease, when it came to women. Casual dating is such a part of our culture that I doubt that he viewed it as a problem. It would be years before he would start to wonder whether something was wrong with him—and still more years before he remembered.

We ARE SITTING on his back deck, watching his dogs play in the yard, when he says, "I have something to tell you." It's the summer of 2002. I'm twenty-two; he'll be turning thirty in a month. I turn my head toward him, a useless gesture in his blind spot. I stare at his patch as he keeps talking: "I was molested as a child. I kept it a secret all these years because . . . because I was ashamed." He starts to cry at the word *ashamed* but quickly composes himself. "I had buried the memories so deep that I was not sure I could trust them, but I know what I remember, and I need you to hear it."

I want to hold him, to comfort him, but he's staring straight ahead, and I don't want to startle him. We sit together in silence for a long time—too long—before I reach out and take his hand.

How DID IT START? A hand on his thigh? His hand where it did not want to go? I force myself to think about his body because that is the only way to make it real. This happened to his body. The same body that would lose an eye had already been violated, not because he was a Black man in a racist world but because he was a good boy who wanted to please.

He did not offer details, and I never asked. I hate how easily I let this part of his past retreat into abstractions like "molestation" or "abuse." This was an attack on his body, and it left scars just as real and profound as the loss of his eye.

It's JULY 1989, five years before he lost his eye, and we're on the freeway, heading to Universal Studios to catch a matinee. We're late, as usual, and he's driving too fast. The windows are down, hot air rushes in, and George Michael's *Faith*, my brother's favorite album, blasts over the sound of the wind. We merge onto the 170, and the traffic slows to a trickle. We're stuck behind a semi belching smoke and roll up our windows just as the song ends. I expect him to pop in his favorite Otis Redding tape, but instead he hands me a notepad and asks me to jot down a few lines of his own:

Now I'm lost within the silence
That started when I said too much
Now I'm holding on to something
That I never got to touch.

To my nine-year-old ears, my brother's lyrics are miraculous, something precious he pulled from the air like a magician. I put the notepad gently back in the center console but hold onto the pen, hoping that he will ask me to write more.

A few months earlier, he had joined a boy band called Up N' Comin. These were the days of New Edition and New Kids on the Block. Singing about love seemed to be the surest route to adolescent fame. At a time when most boy bands were either all Black or all White, my brother's group included an Afro-Brazilian, a Jewish American, and two African Americans, my brother being one of them. Their ethnic novelty was not enough to win them a record deal. Still, my brother kept singing—in the car, in the shower, in his room with Marvin Gaye cranked up high to camouflage his straining falsetto. He was in love with love songs, listening to them, singing them, writing them. Despite his struggles with women—maybe because of them—he could not stop singing about love.

I find an old VHS tape labeled, "You're not my girl, by Up N' Comin." Our VHS player went out with the garbage years ago, so I take the tape to the only place where I can find a working player—the college library. The video room is small, windowless, and stuffed with cubicles. I find an open desk in the corner and pop the tape into the player. The machine sucks in the tape, and now I'm watching my brother and his friends posing for the camera, trying to look cool while lip-syncing a soulless love song. It's hard to listen to my brother, his voice unnaturally low, spout hollow clichés: "So if you love me, hold me tight. If you love me, stay the night." His father gone, his young body molested—and now he's a pop singer crooning about love.

So what if he's hiding his pain? That's the story of America—generations of pain and struggle welling up through the voices of Black people. Marvin Gaye. Otis Redding. Sam Cooke. Peter Slate. *It's been a long, long time coming.* I want to place him in that lineage, but he's just a seventeen-year-old kid trying to become famous, hiding wounds he doesn't know that he has behind a flashy smile and elusive green eyes. No matter how many times I hit pause, they always look away.

WE'RE AT THE VAN NUYS SHERMAN OAKS PARK, running the track. I'm ten and convinced I'm training for the NBA. My brother is a tough coach—sometimes, I think, too hard. Then, Rahn Coleman shows up.

Within minutes, Rahn has me doing sit-ups off the edge of a hard metal bench. With every repetition, he yells, "Want it! Want it! Want it!" I'm not sure what I should want: the pain or the victory. It doesn't matter. His voice—deep and fierce, like an angry Barry White—pulls me through another round of sit-ups.

The first time I met Rahn, a middle-aged Black man, with a goatee and a slim, muscular body, he was sitting at the piano, waiting to give my brother a singing lesson. Rahn had been Aretha Franklin's keyboard player and had also worked with Gladys Knight, the Temptations, Tina Turner, and Ray Charles. His home felt like a recording studio that had been converted into a Buddhist temple. We entered cautiously, prepared to be humbled. When my brother failed to hit the right note twice in a row, Rahn made him do twenty push-ups, then turned to me and said, "Learning to be a singer means learning to be a man. That's hard work."

My brother did the work—singing every day, writing new songs, pursuing his dreams while working part-time jobs, going to school, and helping raise a shy kid who idolized him, a kid who realized too late that his hero might need a hero too.

WE'RE AT THE GREEK THEATRE to see Bryan Adams. Our plan is to watch the show for free by climbing one of the surrounding hills. First, we need to jump a fence. I hate jumping fences. My feet are too big to fit between the chains, my arms are too weak to pull my awkward body over the top, and I'm afraid of heights. My brother and his friends will have to go without me. I don't mind waiting for them . . . in the dark . . . for three hours. Anything but that fence. He kneels down so that his face is directly across from mine, leans in, and whispers:

After you climb the fence—and you *are* going to climb this fence—I'm going to give you this flashlight so that you can use it to get up the hill. I'll be right behind you. When we get near the top, we'll turn off the flashlights so that we aren't spotted. When it's time to turn off the light, I'll tell you, and we can hold hands. You'll be able to see all the lights of the city. It's the best view you'll ever see. Ready?

How to motivate a scared child: help him see beyond his fear.

We climb the mountain. The lights of the city unfurl below us, and I can smell the eucalyptus groves of Griffith Park. The music starts, and the cheers of the crowd rise up to us. I look up at his face. He smiles down at me and winks, and I feel as if I will never again be afraid.

WHEN I WAS THIRTEEN, I developed a crush on a girl who lived down the street. She had two sisters, one older and one younger. Their names all started with A. All three were very pretty, but it was the quiet middle child whose presence overwhelmed my nerves. I called my brother for moral support.

He told me about a samurai warrior, one of the greatest swordsmen of his era. Hunted by a cruel emperor, the samurai went into hiding in the guise of an itinerant salesman. His customers had no idea they were standing face to face with one of the greatest samurai of all time.

"OK, I get it," I told my brother. "I'm the great samurai warrior, and I have to remember that I'm unique and powerful."

"You are unique and powerful, but you're not the samurai warrior. At least, not the only one. Every kid in our neighborhood is unique and powerful, like you, and every single kid is afraid."

"How does that help?"

"It's easy to be afraid when you're alone. But you're not alone. Everyone is afraid."

I paused to digest my brother's wisdom.

"What am I supposed to do with those girls?"

"This isn't about you. If you approach those girls thinking about whether they will like you, you're done. Game over. But if you go to them with sincere curiosity about who they are, what they like to do, their dreams . . . then. . . ." His voice trailed off, and I could see him smiling. "Then," he said, "we're going to have to start talking about condoms." My face burned, and I changed the subject, but whenever I bumped into those sisters, I thought about that samurai warrior.

Now I know that his boldness with sex hid a deeper unease. It must have started before he had sexual urges. Maybe the touching continued even then. She was pretty, large-breasted, and flirtatious. Maybe he found her attractive. Maybe he hated himself for finding her attractive. Even after his memories returned and he wrote that open letter, he didn't like to talk about it, and I didn't want to push him. There would be time, I thought, to make sense of it all.

THE SUMMER THAT HE TURNED SEVENTEEN, he went door-to-door selling subscriptions to the *LA Times.* He took me along on a warm Saturday morning. The first door was opened by an old woman with a cloud of white hair and fifty bird cages in her living room. The stench of the birds was sharp and unpleasant. After assessing the situation, my brother dropped his standard spiel and honed in on something this woman could understand: nothing lines a birdcage like newspaper. She smiled at him but said nothing, and the silence stretched on long enough for me to wonder whether she spoke any English. We were about to leave when she broke the silence. "Let me get my purse," she said. When she turned her back on us, he looked at me and winked.

That newspaper job taught me something about my brother that I would see again and again—when he sold shoes at the Panorama City Mall, when he delivered pizzas for Maria's Italian Kitchen, when he coached my basketball team, even when he chatted up strangers in the supermarket—he connected to people by meeting them where they were. It was a gift, his empathy, but also a burden, especially when coupled with his desire to make everyone happy, even the most abusive people in his life. I'm thinking of the woman who molested him and of a man I'll call Jack.

EVERYONE HAD BEEN DRINKING when Jack dared my brother to ride on top of the pickup—not in the bed of the truck, but up on the cab above the driver. We had just lit the bonfire, a pyramid of cardboard, newspaper, and the rotted siding of an old mobile home. The air smelled of smoke and beer. I turned from the fire to steal a glance at Jack and then at my brother, hoping someone would back down.

Jack was short, about 5'7", and very strong. He had been in the army and still looked like a soldier: short hair, sharp jaw, tight muscles. His skin was several shades darker than my brother's, and although both were strikingly handsome Black men, it would be hard for anyone to mistake them for father and son. Both wanted that kind of relationship. Even in that moment of tense confrontation, there was something paternal in the way Jack stared at my brother, daring him to prove his manhood.

My brother, seventeen years old, walked onto the red gravel driveway, climbed on top of the truck, and clung to the small crease where the smooth metal of the roof met the slick glass of the windshield. I couldn't see what he had to hold on to there, but I was too scared to say anything. In the macho world of the Mojave, a man had to be fearless, which in practice meant reckless and violent. With my brother perched precariously, Jack started the truck and cruised around the driveway slowly, as if he were taunting a child. Once he made it out to the road, he picked up speed, bouncing down the washboard track that stretched to the dry lake. It was a bumpy road even at a crawl. Jack had decided to teach the boy a lesson. By the time he reached the lake, he must have been going at least thirty miles an hour while my brother clung to the slick metal of the truck, his fingers aching with the strain.

MOM AND I WERE in the drive-through at In-N-Out Burger when she told me that she and Jack had eloped. I didn't really know what it meant to be married, but I knew enough to feel scared by the change. When she asked me what I was thinking, I shrugged and hid behind my chocolate milkshake.

The first time Jack and I were alone together, he bought me a large cookie (my favorite, Grandma's brand chocolate chip cookie, so soft and buttery) and took me to the roof of my grandfather's office building. I was seven, and he held my hand as we approached the edge of the building. The view was stunning and terrifying, and I gripped his hand for safety. Something told me not to trust him, but my excitement overrode my fear as we gazed out at the gleaming skyscrapers.

Jack came into our life at the same time as the desert, both a result of Dad's law firm. Dad received land from a number of his bankruptcy clients. One forty-acre parcel was in the middle of the Mojave, about thirty miles outside the old Mormon town of Barstow. I don't know whose idea it was for Jack to move out to the desert: probably his. A strange idea, really, with Mom still in LA—two people get married, and then one of them moves three hundred miles away?

We purchased a mobile home, dug a well, sunk a septic tank, installed a swamp cooler, and bought a massive propane tank that we hid behind a cheap plastic fence. Jack lived there, and we visited on weekends. Mom packed the house with books and West African sculptures. I dug a series of trenches in the clay outside our back door, filled them with muddy water, and pretended they were the canals of Venice.

Jack had his own dreams. He opened a store decorated like a Wild West saloon, complete with batwing doors and engraved curlicues. Business was OK. It might have been better if Jack had been White (like most folks in town) or if he had been less hot-headed. Like so much about Jack, it's impossible to separate his Blackness from his problems.

He was like my brother in that way: race alone cannot explain why both men cheated on women, or drank too much, or sometimes became violent when they drank. But if Jack had not grown up in poverty shaped by generations of racism, would he have been a better man? If my brother looked like me, would he have walked out of that club with both eyes?

ONE HOT AFTERNOON in April 1991, Jack got in a fight with a friend of his, a White guy with a thick mustache. The police were called, and Jack was arrested. For years, I had saved quarters in a large Sparkletts water cooler bottle. I offered my savings as bail, and Mom made a big deal of my generosity. I was eleven years old and proud to be of help. I remember thinking that it was unfair that they had arrested Jack and not his friend, but I don't remember considering whether Jack's dark skin had contributed to his arrest. Even as I grew older and more aware of his profound anger, I never traced it to the burdens of being a Black man in America, the burdens he and my brother both carried, if in different ways. When they fought, I saw their differences, not their similarities. Maybe I knew, on some level, that what united them was something I could never understand, something that separated me not only from Jack but also from my brother.

WE'RE CRUISING "THE SHORT CUT," a narrow dirt track that winds through the desert. It's just after sunset, and a thin strip of blue clings to the horizon. Jack's driving, Mom's riding shotgun, and my brother and I are in the bed of the truck, perched on either side of my Honda four-wheeler. Above us, the sky brims with stars.

Jack is driving too fast. The short cut twists like a roller coaster through a series of sharp turns and abrupt drops. With every turn, I grip the side of the truck. With every drop, the four-wheeler lurches skyward, and I worry that the thing will land on my leg. My brother notices my fear and bangs on the rear window of the cab. Mom and Jack must hear him, but the truck careens onward. My brother bangs louder. I worry that he will break the glass with his bare hands. *Bang, bang, bang.* Finally, Jack stops. My brother leaps from the back of the truck, and for a moment, I think he's going to hit Jack. They glower at each other, my brother fuming, Jack barely suppressing a smirk. Mom gestures for me to come into the cab to sit next to her. My brother refuses to get in and walks off into the desert. I watch him through the rearview mirror, ashamed by the comfort of the seat, the warmth of the cab.

JACK WAS A STRONG BLACK MAN who might have been the father my brother had always wanted. Jack had parents and siblings and a nephew who was my brother's age. Suddenly, my brother had an entire Black family. It was dysfunctional, but so was ours. I doubt that Jack's love for drinking and drugs was a problem for my brother—he was into those things too. The problem was that Jack lurched between being the wild buddy and the stern father. They argued about curfews and money. They argued about who was protecting Mom. Both believed that the other was causing her worry; both were right.

Most weekends, Mom and I would commute to the desert, leaving LA on a Friday evening and returning at four Monday morning. The drive took between three and four hours, depending on traffic. We would eat breakfast at McDonald's on the way back. My brother would stay at our condo in LA, a seventeen-year-old kid on his own. He must have loved it, at least some of the time. I expect that he also felt abandoned. He and Mom had fought before Jack: normal teenage stuff, made harder by the fact that Mom was a single parent. Those fights became explosive after Jack entered our family.

One argument ended with my brother punching a hole in the wall. He stormed off into the night before Mom could ask whether he had hurt his hand. I waited until she went to her room, then crept over and inspected the hole, surprised there was a hollow space inside our walls, that something so solid could be so easily ruptured.

At school, I made a painting of them holding hands in front of a small house: a triangular roof with a rectangular chimney, smoke rising in careful loops. I used speech bubbles to give them dialogue. My brother: "I love you Mama." Our mom: "I love you Bubba." I always knew that they loved me, but the longer Jack came between them, the more I doubted that they loved each other too.

Jack's impact on our family is featured strangely in one of the rare letters Chukwudi sent from Nigeria. Dated July 31, 1990, the letter is addressed to Ude Peter Osakwe. It had been years since my brother went by Ude or Osakwe. I wonder whether he felt proud when his father addressed him with his Igbo name or whether he saw it as yet another sign of their distance.

"My Dear Great One," the letter begins, "Your mother's change of plans about her life took me by surprise and I'm still trying to make full mental adjustments to it." The fact that he refers to the marriage as a "change of plans" reveals how hard it was for Chukwudi to make "full mental adjustments." Equally telling is his insistence that no one should harbor negative feelings as a result of the marriage. He explains, "First and foremost is that I don't want you and your brother to feel LET DOWN OR ABANDONED OR BETRAYED over the issue. Do you understand me?" His use of all caps strikes me as excessive. "I don't want you, me, or Obi Nico to have ANY NEGATIVE thoughts or feelings whatsoever about the matter. And, Great One, THAT'S AN ORDER THAT STANDS THE REST

OF ALL OUR RESPECTIVE INDIVIDUAL LIFETIMES! Understood?!!!" He seems to be aiming for some kind of light-hearted humor, but I find it more sad than funny. It's been more than sixteen years since he and Mom were divorced, yet he uses four different euphemisms to avoid naming the fact of Mom's remarriage. In addition to her "change of plans" and "the issue," he writes that she "reorganized her life" and that we must all "accommodate and relate positively to her new and happy circumstance." I wonder how my brother felt, torn between an absent father and a volatile stepfather—both of whom were dynamic Black men, both of whom would fail him when he needed them most.

The Briefcase

I find Chukwudi's letter in a brown leather briefcase covered in "primordial dust"—what Mom and I call the mixture of baby powder, dog hair, and garden-variety dirt that coats many of the surfaces in her apartment. She was never a great housekeeper; now, her arthritis and stenosis make it impossible for her to clean. "I'll dust in my next life," she jokes. I'm amazed by her ability to find humor in aging, even after the stenosis becomes so severe that she loses the ability to shower herself, to change her own clothes, to grasp a spoon. She often says, "He who laughs at himself never ceases to be amused," but I knew she was scared when the surgeon said that she needed neck surgery. We were both scared.

It's January 2019, and she's still in the hospital. The surgery was a success, but recovery will be slow. I shuttle back and forth between her hospital room and her apartment, trying to clean up as much as possible in preparation for her return home. That's when I find the briefcase, tucked away on the top shelf of her closet. I wipe off the dust with a wet paper towel, sit on the carpeted floor, and pop the cheap metal latches. My laptop is playing Schubert's Piano Sonata in A Major, and the music rises and falls as I open the briefcase and pick out a thin square of wrinkled airmail paper—the letter from Chukwudi.

What first strikes me in the letter is not Chukwudi's response to Mom's marriage but the advice he offered regarding my brother's college plans. Rather than encourage his son to pursue his dreams and attend the best possible school, Chukwudi wrote that the decision should depend on "how far away you can be, conveniently, from DAD and OBI NICO." Thus, my eighteen-year-old brother was told by his absent father to take care of his younger brother and his aging grandfather. Oblivious to the burdens he is placing on his son, Chukwudi pressed his case: "Now that DAD is getting older and is no longer as strong or as tough as he used to be, I think it would be worthwhile to always remember to factor him and his current condition into decisions of this nature." I am amazed that Chukwudi would lecture anyone on the importance of family responsibilities. To be fair, he expressed regret at the distance that separated him from his son: "Congratulations! on your graduation!!!!! That's another great milestone in your life and mind which I have not been around to share with you. But I know you do understand. Don't you?" As if in solidarity, he added, "Great One I know you brood over my absence because I DO TOO." By lumping together Mom's marriage and questions of college, Chukwudi's letter reveals the range of uncertainties my brother confronted at that moment in his life, a moment full of possibility, but also stress and pain. I hope that my brother shrugged off his father's advice, but I can't stop wondering how much his college choices were shaped by the burden of caring for Dad, for our mom, and for me.

The Schubert ends, and I let the silence stretch on as I place Chukwudi's letter on the carpet, reach back into the suitcase, and pull out a letter to my brother from an administrator at UC Berkeley. "I want to congratulate you on your very fine high school record," the letter begins. I always saw my brother as brilliant—the smartest person I knew—but he didn't try very hard in school, and I thought that he had earned a lot of Cs and Ds. It's odd to me that someone would write this to him: "Because you are an outstanding student, you are probably gathering information on various colleges and universities. I want you to know that Berkeley is very interested in you." There are similar letters from a dozen colleges: Georgetown, the University of Arizona, the University of Oregon. It's the one from Stanford that makes my stomach tighten, my eyes mist. It's dated July 1989 and signed by Jean H. Fetter, the dean of undergraduate admissions. Dean Fetter explained that the school had received my brother's name because of his PSAT/SAT score. Again, I'm surprised. I remember my brother bragging about how he had gone out partying the night before the SAT. I didn't think that he had the grades or the test scores to get into these schools, but I was wrong. *Undermatching:* what the experts call the fact that thousands of talented low-income kids fail to apply to the best colleges. Many suffer impostor syndrome, the sense that they can't possibly be worthy. I fear that's what he thought—that he wasn't good enough for a place like Stanford.

The letter from Stanford is the only one that directly references his Blackness. Dean Fetter noted that "the University has a continuing commitment to attract and enroll academically prepared students from groups that are underrepresented in higher education." I wonder what my brother thought of this reference to race, whether he worried that his classmates would assume that he was at Stanford because he was Black. Dean Fetter anticipated that concern: "I hope you will consider applying to Stanford, not simply because you are Black, but because you have much to contribute to the University and much to gain from an education here." I wish that my brother had seen it that way—not because he couldn't get an outstanding education elsewhere but because I wanted him to believe in himself like he believed in me.

I've only just begun to search the briefcase, and already I feel exhausted and overwhelmed with emotions—excitement to be learning about my brother, sadness that so many of his struggles were hidden from me, and guilt for letting them stay hidden for so long. I need music again, and I know what song to play next: Marvin Gaye's "Piece of Clay," a classic that my brother introduced to me on one of our drives out to the desert. Even then, I saw how perfect the lyrics were for him: "Father stop criticizing your son. . . . Everybody wants somebody to be their own piece of clay."

I pull a thick envelope from the briefcase, the acceptance packet for the school he eventually chose: San Diego State, one of the largest colleges in the country. Many students receive excellent educations there, but what attracted my brother was its reputation as a party school and the fact that most of his friends were going—at least, that's how I had

My brother at his high school graduation in the spring of 1990.
(Author's collection.)

always explained his choice. I ignored another factor in his decision: that he could drive home to check on me.

With Chukwudi in Nigeria and Jack the new head of the house, my brother had to cope with both ends of the bad-parent spectrum: the absent father and the bullying stepfather. At least he had his friends. In the middle of the briefcase, I find a card for his nineteenth birthday, signed by a dozen of his buddies. Most of the notes are silly jokes, but Ophir offers something more meaningful: "19 year old from L.A. writes Oscar winning movie. . . . I can see it happen, but you know whatever happens, I'll be here."

I put the card down and pick up a birthday letter from one of his girlfriends. It's full of platitudes like my own teenage love letters, but certain passages strike me as earnest: "You have always been there for me. You were always the person I went to if I needed to talk or a shoulder to cry on. You taught me a lot Peter. You taught me to believe in myself." She ends, "I know we have been through a lot of shit but you always stuck by me even when you thought there wasn't much hope."

Marvin Gaye's voice has gone silent, and I need something more energetic. I choose one of Mom's favorites, "Sympathy for the Devil," by the Rolling Stones.

Beneath the birthday note, I find a stack of letters from me, all handwritten in awkward cursive on lined yellow paper embossed with my name three times in a row: "Nico, Nico, Nico." It touches me that he kept these. "Peter," one begins, "I'm writing you to ask you to write twice a month and tell me how good you are doing in the world. I would like to know this information because I love you, miss you and hope to see you soon. Yet I think it was good that you left home and entered the world of adults. Love, Your bro Nico." In another one, I tell my brother that I miss him "alot, alot alot alot!!!!" I sign "Respectfully," then cross that out and write "Love," then cross that out and add "Like you," then cross that out and finish "You're O.K." I smile at my awkward jokes, then it strikes me: these letters must have felt heavy to him—especially given how much he worried about my being alone with Jack.

I turn off the Stones and think in silence. Jack had threatened to hurt me. I don't know when that threat was made, just that my brother knew that Jack was cheating on our mom, that Jack had gotten into drugs and offered some to my brother, and that Jack used me as a pawn to keep the truth from Mom. I was twenty-one when he told me during a walk in the desert.

WE'RE CROSSING THE DRY LAKE toward the mountain we call "the sleeping dragon." It's more of a hill really, a rounded dome of black basalt, with two long ridges spread out like wings across the horizon. We're talking about Jack, whether he'll ever come back, when he slows down and turns toward me: "Jack threatened to hurt you if I told Mom that he was cheating on her."

"He threatened to hurt me?"

It's a dumb question: I know what I heard, but in all the years that my brother and Jack fought, I never saw myself as anything but a bystander. I feel dizzy and suddenly thirsty, as my mind tries to make sense of the fact that I was used to control my brother.

"I couldn't let him hurt you," he says, and looks away. "I didn't know what to do."

I'm silent, and he turns back to face me. He's wearing sunglasses, and for a moment, I'm not sure which is his good eye. Unsure of where to focus my gaze, I stare off across the brittle clay of the lake toward the rolling dunes. I want to tell him that he shouldn't have been forced to carry that burden, that I'm sorry I wasn't older and able to be there for him like he was always there for me, but I feel ashamed and can't think of the right words. I look up at the sleeping dragon. The black rocks sparkle in the sun.

I'M BACK IN MY MOM'S BEDROOM, digging through my brother's briefcase, when I find a birthday card from Jack. My playlist has moved from Marvin Gaye through the Stones to Biz Markie: "Oh baby you, you got what I need, but you say he's just a friend." I lean over and turn off the music, then open the card. The printed text is generic:

> *Memories of birthdays past bring very special joy,*
> *Because they're filled with thoughts of you when you were just*
> *   a boy.*
> *And even greater is the joy your birthdays now provide,*
> *Because the man you are today brings very special pride.*

Jack crosses out "boy," writes "young man," then underlines "man."

In the envelope with Jack's birthday card, my brother had tucked a piece of evidence from one of the more dramatic moments in their relationship. When my brother went to college, Jack made a big show of giving him a used Ford pickup truck. Although it wasn't new, the truck was a major step up from my brother's first car, a huge yellow Chevy Charger that his friends called the Banana Boat. When Jack's business failed and dragged our family into bankruptcy, Jack decided to take the truck back. Rather than explain things, he came down to San Diego and took the truck late at night, leaving the Banana Boat in its place. On the windshield, he left the note that I found tucked in the envelope, dated September 10, 1990: "Peter, Due to unforeseen circumstances. This Reswitch has to be done. Talk to your Mom. . . . Bye J."

WHEN I WAS TWELVE, I visited my brother in San Diego. He took me to a boat party, one of those pseudo-fancy affairs in which college kids dress up, drink too much, and dance to party jams as the boat goes nowhere slowly. I loved the idea of being at a real college party, but one look at the dance floor, and my body stiffened. I was (and am) a painfully shy dancer. He kept his hand on my shoulder and whispered in my ear, "Just be yourself; everyone's too drunk to notice you." The DJ cranked up "Everybody Dance Now" and I found myself jumping and waving my arms, my eyes locked on my brother's face.

It was easy for me to romanticize his college experience. Now, it saddens me how much alcohol defined those years for him. Stories we once laughed about now have a darker edge, like when he got drunk in Tijuana with a group of friends, and they all ended up in jail, or the drinking game known as a "floor rotisserie," in which each room featured a drink like the "upside down margarita" (you tilted your head back while one person poured in tequila and another added sweet and sour mix), and guests traveled from room to room until they threw up or passed out.

I don't remember seeing him drunk very often—he hid that from me—but I also don't remember seeing him study. After a few years, he dropped out of school, returned to LA, got a job waiting tables at Maria's Italian Kitchen, and moved in with our grandparents. Mom and I had just moved out to the desert. I should have been worried about his leaving school. Instead, I celebrated the fact that he was closer to us and had more free time. He started driving up to the desert every month or so, especially after Jack took a job as a long-haul truck driver, then left for a long trip and never came back. The rumor was that he had moved back to the Midwest. I don't know exactly when Mom filed the divorce papers or when she and my brother started rebuilding their relationship. Jack's name would remain taboo, a land mine like that other name we still avoid.

HE COULDN'T AVOID HER: at Christmas, birthday parties, random family gatherings. That is one of the worst parts of being wounded by a family member: you have to keep pretending nothing happened. You have to smile and pass the corn casserole and try not to remember.

He needed help. He needed to confide in someone. His father was gone. His relationship with Mom was still broken. He had his friends, but even Daneh did not know his deepest secrets. I wish that he could have confided in me. I wish that I hadn't needed him to be invulnerable. Yet another disguise he was forced to wear—the hero's mask.

WE'RE PLAYING ONE-ON-ONE at an elementary school a few miles from our home in the desert. The court is a single hoop on a patch of cracked blacktop surrounded by sand and sagebrush. On windy days, scraps of trash and dead brush blow across the empty land. Now, the air is still and cold. Normally, my brother would play me as if he were a guard, pulling up for jump shots or attempting the kind of acrobatic lay-ups neither of us had the dexterity to execute. I'm in eighth grade, and he still goes easy on me most of the time, but not today. Backing in toward the basket, he uses his weight to roll off me toward the rim. I try to hold my ground, but the force of his body knocks me backward onto the cold pavement. The first time it happens, I scream, "Charging!" He replies calmly that I was moving. If anyone had committed a foul, it was me. I want to argue but instead throw him the ball, determined to stand my ground. He knocks me over again. I throw the ball off the court into the desert. It rolls farther than I expect before lodging in a clump of sagebrush. I turn to him, and he closes the gap between us and presses his face into mine: "You're not a kid anymore. That's why I'm not letting you win. You have to learn to get up when you're knocked down." I'm still angry, but I keep my mouth shut as I walk through the desert to retrieve the ball.

Two weeks later, he tells me to break up with my girlfriend so that I can focus more on basketball. We're sitting in the Banana Boat, the engine running to keep the heater going. We've just arrived home after basketball practice. The night is cold. The stars are thick and bright. I peer up at them through my half-fogged window and remember something I learned in school: that by the time starlight reaches our planet, some of those stars have long since died, sucked into black holes or blown apart by their own uncontrollable energy. It's only their light that survives. I'm tempted to get out and walk into the desert, to stare up at those ghostly lights, to tell him to mind his own business. I know that he believes in my dreams, but that's not what keeps me in the car and convinces me to break up with my girlfriend. It's that he loves me for who I am, regardless of whether I make it to the NBA or play college ball or fail to make the JV squad. He will continue to love me and to believe in me regardless of what I achieve or fail to achieve. It's his love that keeps me quiet as we climb out of the Banana Boat, his face lit up by the stars.

ONLY SOME 40 PERCENT of African American students who start college finish within six years; that's roughly 20 percentage points below the national figure for White students. I'm not sure it's fair to explain my brother's dropping out as a result of his race. I doubt that he would. Unlike many African American students, he came from a family of college graduates in which a university degree was expected. Sometimes, he felt like a failure, the college dropout, sleeping in our grandparents' home. Every morning, he walked past that picture of him as a child, the one he couldn't get the policemen to see. After all those years, he still did not belong.

IT'S THE EARLY 1990s, a strange time to grow up—sandwiched between the Cold War and 9/11. Bill Clinton is in the White House. We watch *The Simpsons, Saturday Night Live, The Arsenio Hall Show.* We listen to Boyz II Men and Arrested Development. When I visit LA, we drive across the valley in the Banana Boat. Cruising the 405 late at night, windows down, it seems as if we're men now—and our lives stretch onward, endless and open, like the road. Then, the bottle swings.

Even before that night, March 22, 1994, my brother knew the dangers of being a young Black man in Los Angeles. Our love defied the color line but did not erase it. No matter how much I loved him, I could not protect him, but if I had recognized that he was facing those dangers without me, if I had asked him what it meant that he was Black and I was White, maybe he would have felt less alone.

WE'RE EATING KRAFT MAC AND CHEESE and watching *In Living Color*. A mountain of clothes fresh from the dryer engulfs one end of the couch, forcing me into the middle, where the cushions sag. I take a bite of pasta, the last in my bowl, crunching the chunks of cheese powder I had failed to stir into the mix. The salty pasta makes me thirsty. I put my bowl down, open a Cherry Coke, and lean my head against his shoulder. The show breaks for commercials, and a strange image appears: grainy black-and-white footage of the police beating a man on a highway somewhere in our city. I can feel my brother's body tense, and I sit up, unsure of whether to watch the body of that man writhing on the ground or my brother's face.

Rodney King. We would all learn his name. King became famous, and his fame was telling. Most White Americans were shocked, as if it were a revelation that the police would beat a Black man in the street. It was no secret that the LAPD had a racism problem. In 1978, a retired policeman went on local TV to denounce the racist violence of his former colleagues. He wore a disguise for his own safety. The revelations of the so-called Masked Marvel came only months before Daryl Gates was sworn in as the chief of police. Gates would cling to power for fourteen years. After a string of young Black men were killed by police officers using a chokehold, he remarked, "We may be finding that in some blacks when [the chokehold] is applied, the veins or arteries do not open as fast as they do in normal people." Thus, Gates explained the deaths of Black men by labeling them abnormal.

My brother had his own history with the LAPD. That time he was pulled over near my school. That time the police wanted to arrest him in our grandparents' home. Sitting next to him on that couch, watching Rodney King be beaten and stomped and kicked, I wondered what he was thinking. I did not have the courage to ask. I knew that he had a different relationship with those images, but I never imagined that he could receive such violence. Only now can I see him on the ground, bearing those blows, another Black body on the streets of America.

More than 90 percent of LA residents believed that the police had used excessive force. Even Chief Gates criticized the beating as "very, very extreme." Four officers were quickly charged, and we followed the trial closely. We were troubled when the proceedings were moved to Simi Valley, a White neighborhood known for being the home of many police officers and almost no Black people. We were disgusted when it emerged that one of the officers on trial had made racist comments that night, comparing an interaction with Black civilians to being in the movie *Gorillas in the Mist*. I knew that King had been under the influence, that he had led officers on a high-speed chase, that he had resisted arrest. Still, I assumed that the officers would be convicted. I assumed that justice would triumph.

Looking back, I'm ashamed at how naïve I was—about that trial, and about racism in America. It was easy to denounce the beating, far easier than to engage with the deeper injustices that produced the beating. I was so quick to see the cops as the sole villains without acknowledging the complexity of that violent episode, how everything that happened that night was shaped by an array of forces—from racism to inequality to crime to politics. Rather than confronting the roots of the problem, my narrative ended the conversation, like the story my family told about the night my brother was attacked. Blame it on skinheads and no one has to think about their own complicity. It's not that the complexity of racism can excuse what we all saw on that videotape or that somehow the fact that everyone was drinking the night my brother was attacked absolves the man who swung the bottle. It's that whatever hope exists for a world beyond racism depends on exposing the deeper wrongs. As a brother, I want justice; as a historian, I want the truth. Or is it my love for my brother that makes me keep digging for the truth? He knew—in ways I never did—how painful the truth can be. But there's nothing else I can give him now.

"MONEY," HE SAYS. "That's the root of it. Unemployment, crime, police brutality. It all comes back to money." We're driving the 101 South toward the 405, careening around anything going less than eighty miles per hour. "People of color built the city, their labor cheap and expendable, their bodies crammed into ghettos. And who benefits?" I hear warmth in his voice. He is enjoying this chance to lay the system bare. "Real estate agents. Do you know about blockbusting?" I grin and crack a joke, "No, but I know about Blockbuster." It's a bad joke, and he doesn't laugh. Instead, he pivots his head and stares at me, as if to say, "Aren't you old enough for a serious conversation?" I'm twelve and a smart aleck, but I'm listening, and he knows it:

Blockbusting worked like this. A Realtor shows up in a nice, middle-class White neighborhood and buys up a few properties at market rate. He sells those houses for a profit to Black families desperate to escape the ghetto. Here's where the real game begins. Once those Black families move in, the Realtor goes door to door, warning all the White families that "those people" are coming. Better sell fast. The neighborhood's going down the toilet. And sell they do. Lightning fast. The Realtor pays much less than market rate because those poor White families are desperate to escape before more Black folks arrive. Then, the Realtor turns around and sells those same houses at above market rate to desperate Black folks. Buy low and sell high. That means good money. Racism has always been profitable. Just think of slavery.

We have exited the freeway and are navigating the streets of our neighborhood, strip malls declaring their wares *en Español*, men huddled in parking lots. My brother waves his hand toward the windshield. "Look around. These are the people who make LA work. And what do they get in return? Just another ghetto."

For much of its history, LA was a distant outpost on the edge of civilization: first Spanish, then Mexican, and finally American. Writing in the 1880s, one of the city's most famous boosters, Helen Hunt Jackson, portrayed her town as quaint and peaceful. "If communities, as well as individuals, are happy when history finds nothing to record of them," she wrote, "the city of the Queen of the Angels must have been a happy spot during the first fifty years of its life." Jackson ignored the brutality of the Spanish missions, colonial garrisons in which indigenous peoples were forced to labor. She also overlooked the war that wrested California from Mexico and the racism of the Americans who claimed Los Angeles not just for the United States but as a bastion of a very particular kind of White supremacy. While such Eastern cities as New York and Boston filled with migrants from southern and eastern Europe, Los Angeles was promoted as a haven for "Anglo-Saxons." Joseph Widney, the second president of the University of Southern California, hoped that the city would become the capital of "the Aryan Peoples." *LA Times* editor Charles Fletcher Lummis called his city "a new Eden for the Saxon homemaker."

To protect such a lily-white Eden, the good people of Los Angeles strove to exclude "unwanted races." Asians faced the most virulent opposition. The Asian Exclusion League mobilized to keep out migrants from China, Japan, Korea, and India. Indians were a complicated case, as their ambiguous racial identity sometimes allowed them to be seen as White. In 1924, a professor of chemistry in Los Angeles offered a remarkable description of Indian racial ambiguity: "The Hindu resembles us except that he is black—and we are shocked to see a black white man." "A black white man" . . . the phrase triggers a memory.

I am thirteen and desperate to learn the Roger Rabbit to impress a girl. I ask my brother for help.

"Move your legs, bro. Kick, kick, kick."

We're in the dining room in the desert, blasting "Bust a Move" by Young MC. My arms are flailing back and forth, and I'm trying to move my feet too. I can't get the rhythm right. I know that I'm terrible, and when the song ends, I try to hide my embarrassment behind a bad joke:

"Well, I guess it's true that White guys can't dance."

A new song begins, but he stops the music and turns toward me.

"Man, don't give me that crap. I'm tired of that White guy, Black guy shit."

I'm surprised by his emotion and by the swearing. He doesn't usually talk like that around me. He sees that I'm startled, brings me in for a hug, then holds me by the shoulders at arm's length, staring into my eyes.

"Look, bro. There's nothing wrong with joking about race, but make sure the joke is funny, and don't use it to cover your own fear."

"I'm not afraid. I'm just—"

"You *are* afraid, and that's OK. Being a man isn't about not having fear. It's about doing the right thing despite your fear."

His words read like a cliché, the kind of thing you'd find on a Hallmark card, but staring into my brother's eyes, his hands warm on my shoulders, I took his words as more than the truth. They were an expression of his love. I wish I'd asked him what he feared and why my joke bothered him, but when he turned on the music, I felt my legs loosening, and all I wanted was to dance with my brother.

DID HE EVER SEE HIMSELF as a "black white man"—straddling the racial divide? I doubt it. Like Indian Americans in the early twentieth century, some mixed kids find their racial identity constantly in question. My brother wasn't one of them. He was Black, and in Los Angeles, despite the prominence of certain Hollywood celebrities, Black people have long been seen as an enemy that must be kept out—or kept down.

In the 1920s, the Anti-African Housing association was formed to stymie the movement of African Americans into the city. Black folks who did arrive were forced into ghettos maintained by bigoted real estate agents, racial covenants, and violence. LA's first Black neighborhood was known as Mudtown. Writing in 1931, the Harlem Renaissance author Arna Bontemps offered a vivid portrait of Mudtown. The area had once been a walnut grove, Bontemps explained. Beneath the trees, "crude shacks had been built and vines—morning-glory, gourd, and honeysuckle—had promptly covered them, giving the whole neighborhood an aspect of savage wildness." Over time, LA's Black community grew in size, and a Black middle class took root, but discrimination remained. In the novel *Devil in a Blue Dress*, set in Los Angeles in the 1940s, Ezekiel "Easy" Rawlins explains that African Americans had long dreamed of LA while living in the Jim Crow South, but "the truth wasn't like the dream. Life was still hard in L.A. and if you worked every day you still found yourself on the bottom."

We went to see the film version of *Devil in a Blue Dress* about a year after my brother lost his eye. I sat on his left so that he didn't need to turn his head to see me. We shared a package of York Peppermint Patties, and the sharp cool of the mint lingered in my throat. We both loved Denzel Washington, and I winced when his character is roughed up by racist cops. I turned toward my brother. He noticed my glance and leaned over to whisper, "I'm glad that will never happen to you."

I'M HOLDING A DRAWING made on the back of a napkin. It's my brother: a spare portrait in black ink. His jaw is a cloud of lines. His hair is wild. A thin black stroke cuts across his forehead, and, for a moment, I think that it's a shadow—the elastic strap of the patch.

The drawing was made by Rozzell Sykes, one of the most renowned African American painters of the twentieth century, and one of my brother's adopted fathers. I don't know how he first met Rozzell. He had no interest in visual art, and, unlike how he related to Rahn Coleman, my brother did not approach Rozzell as a student, at least not with regard to painting. I remember being confused by their relationship, baffled by why my brother would drive an hour each way to talk with an old painter when he could be working on his music or writing a screenplay. Then, he took me to meet Rozzell, and everything became clear.

Rozzell bows slightly as he ushers us into his home, an artist's paradise, so filled with paintings and sculptures that I wonder where we will sit. Stools appear, and we cluster in a tight circle, my nervous hands clutching a sheaf of poems scrawled on crumpled sheets of lined paper. I am thirteen and passionate about poetry. I have yet to share my poems with a real artist, and I'm scared that he will not like them, that he will not like me. My hands shake just enough to make it hard to read. I look at my brother, and he smiles at me and nods, as if to say, "Go on, you can do this." I start to read. Rozzell listens, head bowed and eyes closed. He is wearing a wide-brimmed straw hat, and his white beard glistens like frost. After I finish my last poem, he leans forward and says quietly, almost in a whisper, "Young man, I want you to come back here to read more of your poems. Next time, I want you to type them and put them in a binder. If you don't respect your own work, no one will."

Rozzell's home was on the 4800 block of Saint Elmo Drive in midcity Los Angeles. It was an oasis of art in a neighborhood that struggled with joblessness and violence. Throughout the 1970s, busloads of schoolchildren came to Rozzell to complete workshops in painting, sculpture, photography, writing, music, and computer skills. Many of these opportunities came free of charge, subsidized by private donations and a steady stream of tourists drawn by the fame of what came to be known as St. Elmo's Village. The actor Jeff Bridges helped plant a cactus garden. The singer Billy Preston hosted a fund-raising event for the village and wrote a song called "Saint Elmo." Rozzell liked to say, "If you're given a shoebox, make it the best shoebox in the world." His home embodied his commitment to art as a form of self-improvement.

As we drove away, I thought about the vast difference between Rozzell's home and the stereotypes of "the hood" that characterized Black LA for most outsiders. And I thought about my brother. Visiting Rozzell was like heading for a haircut at Styles Ville, but this time, my brother was sharing more than his Black world—he was sharing his Black father figure. I wonder why he brought me—was it another chance for him to be his full self and to be Black, or was it just an expression of his love for me? At times, that love must have felt like a burden: to be a father when he was still searching for his own.

It took five minutes in Rozzell's presence to understand why my brother saw him as a mentor and a surrogate father, but it was not until I found that napkin sketch, many years later, that I understood the depth of their bond. That drawing reveals that Rozzell saw my brother for who he was, saw him in all his vulnerability, as a father might have, and in that seeing, there was more than art. There was love.

Rahn Coleman and Rozzell Sykes were the most important of my brother's surrogate fathers, but he had many male role models—even celebrities we never met. Growing up with a single mom, we both turned our idols into father figures. We revered them, imitated them, and worried about losing them like we had our "real" fathers.

NOVEMBER 7, 1991. I'm in our grandparents' kitchen when my brother runs in from the TV room. Maybe if he had been less shocked, he might have waited to tell me or tried to soften the blow. As it is, he just blurts out, "Magic has AIDS," and wraps me up in his arms.

Magic Johnson was our hero. He embodied all that was graceful and elegant in our world. In 1991, many people still believed that HIV/AIDS only threatened gay men and drug addicts. For us, the shock was not that a straight athlete had this disease; we were devastated that Magic had a disease at all.

Less than a month after Magic's announcement, my brother began writing his first screenplay, *Big Sis*, the story of a young Black man named Clay who returns home to live with his older sister, Martha. A former college basketball star, Clay is running from something; it is only toward the end of the script that we learn that he is HIV positive. No major film had tackled HIV/AIDS in the Black community. This was before Denzel Washington learned to care for a dying Tom Hanks in *Philadelphia*, before *Rent* opened on Broadway. When my brother was thirteen, the first major film to deal with HIV/AIDS, a made-for-TV drama called *An Early Frost*, was released on NBC. The film follows a young White lawyer who returns home to tell his parents that he is gay and living with AIDS. When my brother was seventeen, an ensemble piece called *Longtime Companion* followed the epidemic through the eyes of a group of gay men, almost all White.

"So far as Negroes are concerned," Langston Hughes said, Hollywood "might just as well be controlled by Hitler." By the time my brother wrote *Big Sis*, Hollywood had just begun to diversify. In the summer of 1989, my brother turned seventeen, Chinese tanks attacked pro-democracy students in Tiananmen Square, Nintendo released the Game Boy, and Spike Lee's *Do the Right Thing* changed how we saw the movies. I remember watching my brother imitate Radio Raheem's famous curbside sermon, pretending that he had the golden nameplates, one labeled LOVE and the other HATE, draped like brass knuckles over his large brown hands. It would be years before I was old enough to see the film, to feel the anger my brother must have felt as Radio Raheem is choked to death by the police. It was as if my brother were being throttled, his breath stolen, his massive body writhing in the air.

PETER SLATE BEGAN his screenwriting career two years after *Do the Right Thing*. Could he be the next Spike Lee? A mixed kid from the Valley? In 1991, the same year my brother wrote *Big Sis*, *Boyz n the Hood* gained fame for its portrayal of Black Los Angeles. Not surprisingly, it was set on the other side of the hill, where Black folks were the majority—the *real* hood, or so it seemed to me at the time. Two years later, in 1993, Albert and Allen Hughes released *Menace II Society*, another drama of the ghetto, grittier than *Boyz n the Hood*. The Hughes brothers were mixed, with an African American father and an Armenian mother, but *Menace* avoids such racial complexities.

If the market for Black cinema was small, the market for my brother's story didn't exist. Maybe it still doesn't, even after the Obama years, in a time when Americans are allowed to check more than one box when asked for their race. In 1991, at the age of nineteen, my brother had only just begun to make sense of what it meant to be Black and mixed, raised by a White mother, his own father a mystery. How could he write his own story if he didn't know where to start?

But maybe he *was* writing his own story. I always saw his first script, *Big Sis*, as a testament to his compassion. He was writing about HIV when our culture had only begun to move away from demonizing those who struggled with the disease. But all we know for most of *Big Sis* is that the main character is, like my brother, a Black man with a secret to hide. My brother channeled his own dark memories of being torn apart by something hidden inside. He turned his pain into compassion and his compassion into art. I want to believe that his creativity gave him a path toward healing. I know that the truth is more complicated, that his struggles persisted even after he embraced his identity as an artist. It still matters that he could give voice to those struggles, but I wish that I had done a better job of listening.

WE ARE WATCHING *CITIZEN KANE* in the desert, sprawled on the living room floor, with the couch as our backrest. The film has just begun, but already I've lost patience with its plot, painfully devoid of car crashes, lightsabers, and basketball. I slide down toward napping position. My eyelids sag as I roll onto my side, facing my brother, close enough to smell the Jergens lotion he rubs on his legs. It smells like vanilla pudding. I catch sight of his face. He is riveted, his jaw sharp, his back straight. I wonder what he finds so engaging, but I'm too tired to ask. When I awake, the movie is nearly over. I ask what I missed. He pauses the film and looks down at me with an amused grin.

"The greatest movie of all time."

I smile back and reply, "The boringest movie of all time."

I feel defensive, almost jealous, that he would be awestruck by a story I cannot understand. So I ask, "What makes it so great?"

"It's real. The main character, Charles Foster Kane, has these dreams, incredible dreams, and he achieves them. But it's not enough. He wants more, always more. And that makes him unhappy. He has everything a man could want, but he's still unhappy."

I suggest we finish the film, but he insists that I watch it all the way through. He even offers to start it from the beginning. The opening scene has become a cliché of sorts, that moment when Kane expends his last breath muttering the name of his childhood sled: Rosebud. An old man yearning for his idyllic youth. Things were different for my brother. Even as a child, he sought his roots. Maybe if he'd grown old, he would have invented a rosebud. Maybe he would've stopped searching.

Art was a way to make sense of his troubled soul, but it was also a path toward the material success he craved. Over the course of his teenage years, he became increasingly obsessed with money and fame. Like Charles Foster Kane, he wanted it all. I try to remember when that ambition started, and a memory surfaces.

We're on the couch, shoulder to shoulder, watching *Diff'rent Strokes*. I'm five, maybe six. He's twelve or thirteen. "What you talkin' about, Willis?" I repeat the famous line, hoping to make him laugh. Instead, he turns pensive. "That could be us," he says. "We could do that."

"You mean be on TV?"

"Why not?"

I had never compared their interracial family with our interracial family. The father, Mr. Drummond, wasn't like anyone we knew. He was White and wealthy, like Dad, but far more involved in his kids' lives. The two brothers were like us, at least in their love for each other. I don't remember thinking about the fact that they were both Black and I was White. "Yeah, that could be us," I agree and wait for him to respond. He stays quiet, and when the show goes to commercial, he leaves without saying a word.

I still don't know what drove his hunger for money and fame. There are two easy explanations: our grandfather's ambition and American culture. It's not surprising that a young man raised in Los Angeles in the 1980s and 1990s, a young man with a wealthy workaholic grandfather, would develop grand plans for himself and his material success. There was something beautiful about the scope of his dreams, but there was also an edge to his ambition, a restless unhappiness that was bound up with all the burdens my brother carried inside. The absent father, the ambitious grandfather, that relative and what she did to him: my brother's troubles stacked upon each other, filling him with pain and doubt. Below it all was the need for affirmation that came from being a mixed-race kid who never fit in and the anger that came from being a Black man in America. Soaring ambition atop a well of pain and anger—my brother and the city he loved.

TWO YEARS BEFORE my brother lost his eye, the jury in the Rodney King trial announced their decision. All four officers were acquitted of assault. The decision was announced at 3:15 on the afternoon of April 29, 1992. It only took a few hours for LA to go up in flames.

My brother was out with friends when the trouble started. Mom was terrified that he would end up on the wrong side of the violence. What would that mean for a biracial kid, some of whose friends were White, others Black, and most—like Ophir or Daneh—racially ambiguous? Our city's divisions cut through his circle of friends and through his own body.

We sat at home, Mom and I, and watched aerial footage of flaming buildings and police in riot gear. The city seemed divided between angry crowds and armies of militarized police officers. Where was he?

Later, we would learn the numbers: more than eight hundred buildings burned to the ground, more than two thousand people injured, fifty-four killed. Representative Maxine Waters called it an "insurrection" against police brutality and poverty. In South Central LA, the high-school dropout rate was well over 50 percent. Underfunded schools led to bad jobs that trapped families in poor neighborhoods with the same underfunded schools. The cycle repeated down the generations. Mom and I weren't thinking about the structural causes of the violence—not that night, anyway. We were thinking about a nineteen-year-old Black man in a city divided along racial lines. Mom sat next to the phone and said nothing when I asked whether she was hungry. I saw her tense face and didn't ask again.

When he came home that night, Mom was furious that he hadn't called, but she didn't say anything. Maybe it was her relief that he was

OK. Maybe she saw the glassy distance in his eyes. I caught his glance for a second but could not read his eyes. It was as if he were looking through me. I should have asked him what he had seen, but I said nothing. He went into his bedroom and closed the door.

I FIND THE VHS TAPE in the bottom of my brother's briefcase. It's labeled *The Real World*, and I anticipate a bootlegged copy of that pioneering saga in reality TV: seven young adults living together in a duplex in SoHo for three months in the spring of 1992. It was supposed to be real, but what did reality mean when everyone had a camera in their face? I'm not a fan of reality TV and am tempted to throw the tape in the trash next to the leftover Indian food. What made my brother keep this tape and not others? I go back to the library, to the same cubicle where I watched his boy band's music video. This time, my expectations are low, and I'm unprepared for what emerges when I hit play.

My brother is sitting on a couch, smiling. He still has both eyes, green and innocent. He keeps looking away from the camera, as if he is shy. Five seconds in, I realize what I am watching: an audition for *The Real World*. For the next ten minutes, I watch my brother as a teenager opening his heart to the world. His seeming sincerity is not real; this is an audition. I can tell from his strained smile that he is acting, playing the soft-spoken dreamer type. Still, this is a window on how my brother wants to be seen, and my heart races with every word.

"My whole life always had some problems," he says with a grin, "but I would never trade it for the world. I had a different experience. It was an open window on two different cultures." I wonder whether he means Igbo and American, the two cultures, but that wouldn't make sense; he had no real connection to Igbo culture. He means two different races. "I see what is Black, what is White," he explains before lamenting the "stupidity people put on it," the "it" being race. "Living in LA," he adds, he has the chance to "meet people from all over." He feels "blessed to be mixed," although the blessing is not uncomplicated. He switches into the second person to discuss his feelings of alienation: "People don't want to accept you, people don't want you to feel like you belong." Which people? Is he thinking about specific moments, incidents he does not want to revisit? His tone remains calm, almost wistful. He may have struggled once, but now he has arrived at a better place. "I have White friends, I have Black friends, I have Hispanic friends." And he can be your friend too. I hear Rodney King: "Why can't we all just get along?"

One year later, my brother was attacked. Did he still feel "blessed to be mixed"? Or would those words he offered so casually have stuck in his throat? For me, all these years later, his words carry an unexpected weight: "People don't want to accept you, people don't want you to feel like you belong." People don't want you to dance in a club with a White woman, your eyes closed, your body moving as if nothing can stop you.

MIKE WAS AT THE CLUB the night of the attack. He saw the men who did it and knew more about them than the police. I didn't know that he had been at the club when I suggested that we meet at a restaurant near LAX. He was one of my brother's oldest friends, an important figure in his hip-hop career. It was Mike who took a teenage Peter Slate to a record store in Hollywood to learn about the roots of hip-hop, Mike who introduced XL to the nucleus of what would become his rap group. I knew that I could learn a lot from him, but I didn't expect to learn anything about the men who took my brother's eye.

It's a strange place, the Proud Bird, a restaurant for aviation buffs, with a dozen old planes parked on the front lawn. The "Aviation Museum," the planes are called. To me, it looks more like an airplane graveyard. There's a runway across the road and giant cargo planes fall from the sky, one after another, as if on an aircraft carrier. The noise is deafening, but the buffet is surprisingly good, and here I am, eating mushroom quesadillas and grilled salmon, while Mike challenges everything I know about the night my brother lost his eye.

"Skinheads? No, they weren't skinheads. They were hip-hop wannabes, you know, White boys in baggy jeans and baseball caps turned backwards. I don't want to say that they wanted to be Black, but you know, maybe they did. They definitely weren't skinheads."

"Why did they do it then?"

"I don't know. I left before he was attacked. The story I heard was that it was about a girl. They were teasing this girl, and your brother stood up for her."

He paused.

"And everyone was drinking. Your brother was drinking."

Of course, alcohol played a role. My brother stopped drinking after that night, a clear sign that he blamed his own drunkenness, at least in part. Race must have played a role too. I can't imagine those security guards would have taken a White guy, blood pouring from his eye, and dumped him on the curb, letting a gang of Black men slink off into the night. And the men who attacked him: so what if they liked hip-hop? Does that mean they had no prejudice? Would they have brought that bottle down on a face that looked like theirs, like mine? Still, this isn't the story I thought it was. I thought that he was attacked by the Klan, and it turns out to have been a bunch of Vanilla Ice wannabes.

"I saw them again a few years later." Mike is looking out the window at a plane taking off. "The guys who did it. I was at a restaurant with a few friends and went to the bathroom. I saw them at the bar on the way in. I came back, not knowing what I would do, what I would say, but they were gone."

These men haunt me—not just their mystery, their elusive motive for attacking my brother, but the simple fact that they are still alive, ordinary guys, going to restaurants, sitting at the bar, disappearing when you need them most.

XL the 1I

Depth Perception

A single hoop against the desert sky, the cracked clay of the dry lake, and a basketball—everything we need to assess the damage. It's one week after the attack, and his scar is a bright pink smile spreading from his cheek to his forehead. Raw flesh where his eye had been. He wears a bandage most of the time but has taken to airing the wound at least an hour every day. Seeing the gash still leaves me queasy, but I have gotten better at faking a stoic calm. It helps that his focus has shifted from how things look and feel to the deeper wounds caused by the loss of an eye.

The doctors warned us that eyes work together to create depth perception. Because our eyes are a few inches apart, each sees a slightly different image. The difference between those images tells us what is near and what is far. If you only have one eye, you can compensate by turning your head slightly from side to side, creating a variety of images from which to judge distance. That trick takes time to learn, and even when you have it down, your depth perception is never as good as it would be with two eyes. We knew that he would struggle to tell distance, but how bad would it be?

His first shot is far short and wide to the left. I'm tempted to yell, "Air ball!" Instead, I remain awkwardly silent and take refuge in chasing the ball while our dogs wander off to hunt rabbits. They never catch anything unless the creature is ancient or deathly ill. One time Ami—short for Amigo—came home with a peacock in his mouth. People raise strange things in the desert: ostrich, koi fish, ferrets, peacocks. Ami's bird must have wandered off and gotten lost. It was still alive when we managed to get him to drop it just outside our fence, its bright plumage aflame amid the gray-green sage. We brought it water and watched as the bird died. I find myself thinking back to that peacock, its labored breaths, as my brother misses shot after shot. To break the silence, I joke that he never was much of a shooter. He forces a grin but doesn't laugh. The silence is oppressive, and I'm grateful when our neighbor, Spike, drives up in his old blue pickup.

Spike is a cowboy of sorts: the hat, the boots, the bushy mustache. As he climbs out of the cab, the dogs run toward us, Ami first, Clumsy in the rear. Named at the shelter after he kept tripping over his own tail, Clumsy lives up to his name. He falls down stairs, collides with cacti, and routinely barrels into me like a hairy bowling ball. As we cross the court toward Spike, the thought hits me: I should warn him about the dogs. Before I can act, they're upon him. While Ami jumps up in a friendly greeting, Clumsy just keeps coming. Without slowing down, he plows through Spike. The cowboy hat flies skyward. Spike's boots swing up in front of him so fast and high that I wonder whether he will make a perfect arc and land again on his feet. He doesn't. His body hits the ground with a strange symmetry, head and feet together, as if he had been reclining on a cloud that suddenly dissolved. We stare in shock. Fortunately, Spike happens to be standing over a sandy patch, and he's more startled than hurt. We start giggling as soon as we turn our backs, and before we make it home, the giggles have become full belly laughs, hoots of joy echoing between us, tears rolling down our faces, as Ami and Clumsy dance around us, oblivious to all that has changed.

WHEN IT CAME TO COPING with the loss of an eye, everyone had suggestions. Rahn Coleman took him to a gun range, gave him a .357 Magnum, and told him to shoot. Mom got out the *batakas*, giant foam clubs we played with as kids. Maybe a glorified pillow fight could release some of his anger. An elderly woman we met at the supermarket showed us her aluminum cane: "strong as steel and light as a feather."

She suggested that my brother buy the same brand, as though he'd lost a leg as well as an eye. He smiled at her and said, "Thank you."

One night, a few weeks after he came home from the hospital, he took a long walk in the desert, laid down on a sandy hill, and wept. Clumsy licked his face and sat on his chest to guard him from further harm. He described the scene to me later. I'm not sure why. Maybe so that I would feel more comfortable with my own tears. Crying helped all of us, but true catharsis was elusive. This was more than an emotional wound that needed expression. He had lost an eye. There were practical challenges to face: going up and down stairs, pouring a cup of coffee, shaking hands. He had to learn to lower the pot until it touched the mug, to extend his hand and let the other person complete the shake.

The most urgent challenge was driving. Not being able to hit a three-pointer is frustrating. Not being able to drive is terrifying, especially if you happen to live in Los Angeles. Determined to drive, he worked at improving his depth perception. He started with a tennis ball: lying on his back, he threw the ball into the air and tried to catch it as it came down. Once, I walked into the room with the ball in mid-air. He failed to grab it, and the ball rolled off into a corner. I was not sure whether to retrieve it for him, make a joke, or offer some kind of encouragement. What could I say? As the younger brother, I was unaccustomed to playing the supporter; that was his role. Now, everything had changed. I picked up the fuzzy green ball, placed it in his hand, and laid down at his side.

EVERYTHING WAS DIFFERENT with one eye. One time, alone in my room, I tried it myself: closing one eye, I threw a wad of paper into the trash can. Had I lost the ability to judge distance? No, I had no trouble getting the paper in the can. I tried it with a pair of socks and again found my depth perception unchanged. Only later did I realize my mistake: I had not considered the power of memory. If you are familiar with a room, you don't need two eyes to judge distance. To come closer to what my brother was dealing with, I would have to go to a new location, somewhere I had never been, and I would need to approach that place with my vision obscured so that I would not form memories I could use as visual crutches.

I developed a plan. I would visit a new park with my friend Alex. We would take along a black scarf and a bunch of random stuff. Alex would tie the scarf across my eyes and lead me through the parking lot to an open field. He would place different objects—a football, a trash can, the car's sunshade—at different distances from me. I would close one eye and take off the scarf. Would I see the world as my brother saw it?

I never tried. I could blame adolescent laziness or claim more noble motives: it would have been disrespectful to pretend that I could experience my brother's loss. The truth is that I became accustomed to my brother's disability and stopped asking what it meant for him.

According to one study, people with one eye have seven times more car accidents. The challenge is more than depth perception. Having one eye leads to a 25 percent decrease in the field of vision. He made up for that loss by turning his whole head to check his blind spot on the right side of the car. What if someone swerved into his blind spot just after he checked it?

Six months after he loses the eye, he takes me to Barnes & Noble. The Valley is short on cultural opportunities, and I'm excited to wander among the latest bestsellers. After an hour or so, we lug our new books across the crowded parking lot and slide into the Banana Boat. I still feel strange sitting on his blind side. The car rolls to a stop at the exit to the parking lot. He swivels his head all the way to the right to check his blind spot, then starts to turn left. A boy on a bike appears on the right. My brother slams on the brakes, and the kid swerves safely around the front of the car. We're stunned. I don't know what to say, and neither does he. The car idles quietly. He checks his blind spot again, then pulls into traffic.

Over the next few years, he had at least six close calls caused by his missing eye. Each time, he slammed on the brakes just in time. Each time, he was reminded of what he had lost, what he might still lose.

THE SUMMER AFTER HE LOST HIS EYE, my brother invited me to stay with him in LA for a few weeks. One night, I woke up needing to pee and tiptoed toward the bathroom. The hall floor creaked and groaned, and I struggled to not wake my brother. He was a light sleeper when he hadn't been drinking. I made it across the hall and rounded the doorway of the bathroom only to find him leaning over the sink, examining the wound where his eye had been. He must have just cleaned it. I could smell the bitter mist of the antiseptic spray. I stared at the pink gash until I became ashamed by my curiosity and slunk back toward bed, still needing to pee.

I saw his wound, like him, as a reflection in the mirror, but I had no idea what he was thinking or feeling. No matter how close we were, no matter how much I loved him, I could not be him. I could not know what it was like to be him. Watching him stare at his own scarred face, I became aware of the gulf that separated him from me, the sharp loneliness of being alive in this world, the aloneness of it all. But even then, looking at a wound caused by what I was convinced was a hate crime, I failed to see my brother's racial identity as a barrier between us. I failed to see how far our love had to travel to bring us together.

THREE MONTHS AFTER THE ATTACK, a team of surgeons installs the new eye. That same day, June 17, 1994, the police chase a white Ford Bronco down the 405 freeway. The new eye cannot see, but it has been made to look as "realistic" as possible. Its purpose is not to see but to be seen. The Bronco's only passenger, the football star and actor, Orenthal James Simpson, is wanted for questioning. His former wife, Nicole Brown Simpson, has been murdered, as has a young man named Ronald Goldman. As my brother recovers from the surgery, we watch the white Bronco parade down the 405. The TV hangs from the ceiling in the far corner of the room. It's too small, and we strain to see it. It's even harder for him with just one eye. Strange, that we're back in the hospital, the same hospital where they brought him the night of the attack. Strange, how slowly it moves, that white Bronco, as if it has nowhere to go, as if it will lead that caravan of squad cars forever.

WE CALLED IT THE NEW EYE. It would have been more accurate to call it the fake eye. It was made to pass for an eye, to be mistaken for an eye. I remember thinking of it as the fake eye, but I never called it that. Before the surgery, I imagined a round glass ball, something he could pop out and roll down a pool table to entertain guests, but the new eye was only a thin disk, a crescent moon, more like rubber than glass. It fit inside his eye socket like a contact lens. I assumed that they would attach it permanently, but they never did. He could take it out, and he did from time to time. Once, he took it out at a hotel pool in Arizona and then couldn't find it. We searched for a desperate hour before it turned up in the pocket of his jeans, wrapped in tissue paper.

Sometimes he called it the fake eye. If he looked too sharply to the side, it wouldn't follow all the way, as if it saw something straight ahead it didn't want to miss. The color wasn't right. While his seeing eye changed from amber to hazel to a golden emerald, his new eye remained the same pale green.

Worst of all were the tears—or, to be precise, their absence. His tear duct had been smashed, and the repair was only partial. Rather than the imperceptible flow of tears that keeps a normal eye functioning, his tear duct would leak a yellow-green ooze that pooled in the corner of the new eye or ran down his cheek. Because he could not see on that side, he had no way of knowing when he needed to clean his face. It became a routine task, telling him when he needed to wipe the eye gunk. What if he were in a room full of strangers? Would they tell him?

So, he wore the patch, that black badge that covered his new eye and most of the scar tissue where his eyebrow had been. Sometimes gunk would still leak out, but most of the time, the patch hid such indignities. He experimented with different styles, but they were all more or less the same—triangles of black fabric strapped to his head with a thin elastic band. He would buy boxes of them at the drugstore. I couldn't remember ever seeing someone wear a patch outside a movie, and I had assumed that he would have to get them at the hospital or from a special order catalog. But there they were in Safeway, as if everyone needed an eye patch from time to time.

Children pointed. Most were more intrigued than scared. Patches mean pirates, and pirates are fun. He didn't seem to mind. From time to time, he would greet an especially awestruck toddler with a bit of pirate brogue: "Argh, I see you be liking the high seas, matey!" It must have been hard to be a novelty. For years, he had drawn stares for being good-looking. The girls in my school had loved to tell me, "Your brother is so cute." He still had those sharp jaw bones, that gleaming smile—his father's smile. Even with his wounds, he was a handsome

Peter Slate in Los Angeles in 1994, not long after he lost his eye.
(Author's collection.)

man, but he would never again be "cute." The attack had aged him. The cute teenager had become the man with the patch.

WE TRIED TO LAUGH. Even in the hospital, the day after the attack, one of his oldest friends joked, "Look at One-Eyed Willie over here." It seemed forced, but my brother chuckled and then offered his own effort at humor. He pointed at his eye and repeated, "Peter Pan. Peter Pan." His friends were puzzled. Did he mean Captain Hook? No, my brother loved Peter Pan. He knew that Captain Hook had both his eyes. Later, Mom set them straight: Sandy Duncan, the actress who became famous for playing Peter Pan, had lost sight in one of her eyes. That reference was lost on me, but I found comfort in the collective efforts at light-hearted humor and in my brother's resilience. His ability to smile and trade bad jokes reminded me that he was still my brother, always striving to make us happy. I failed to recognize the burden he carried, his face wrapped in bandages, the only Black person in the room, trying to convince clueless White people that everything would be OK.

By the time the new eye was ready, our shock had subsided, but we hadn't gotten any better at talking about what had happened, at recognizing the depth of my brother's pain and loss, at giving him space to grieve. Instead, we let ourselves be distracted by the O. J. saga. That white Bronco glided down the freeway in a loop all day and night. When we weren't watching the chase or its aftermath, we were discussing how it would all play out. The trial lasted more than eight months, from January to October 1995. It was a circus from the beginning. The live broadcast ran throughout the day. At school, teachers offered updates after lunch. Every night, the news would replay the highlights. It was like the Super Bowl stretched over eight months, with murder as the half-time show. The lawyers became household names: Johnnie Cochran, Robert Kardashian, Marcia Clark. Even the judge became famous: Lance Ito. Jay Leno featured a group of dancers all made up to look like the bearded jurist.

The case appeared daunting for the defense. Running from the police does not prove guilt but is strong cause for suspicion. O. J. had a history of domestic violence and had been arrested for assaulting Nicole. Then, there was the physical evidence. Hair fibers linked O. J. to the victims, as did the blood stains found at his home and on one of his socks. Most damning were the infamous black gloves, one found at the crime scene and the other at O. J.'s home. According to the prosecution, DNA evidence proved that blood from both victims, as well as O. J., was on both gloves. It seemed an easy case to win.

Then came Detective Mark Fuhrman. The man who found the bloody glove at O. J.'s home had something of his own to hide: a history of racist statements. The defense played audio tapes in which the detective used the N-word some forty-one times. By exposing Fuhrman, the defense cast suspicion over the evidence and thus the entire case.

For generations, Black men accused of assaulting White women had been routinely tortured and killed. Lynched. In a city that had only just begun to heal from the beating of Rodney King, a famous Black man had been accused of killing his White wife and her White friend. Regardless of whether the murders had anything to do with skin color, this was bound to become yet another chapter in the long story of race in America.

In October 1995, a Gallup poll found that 78 percent of Black Americans thought that O. J. was innocent, compared with only 43 percent of White Americans. When the jury returned a verdict of "not guilty," there was only one thing everyone agreed upon: If O. J. had been poor, it would have ended differently. Many people believed that O. J. had used his money to get away with murder. Others argued that regardless of whether he was innocent, a poor Black man would never have walked free from that courtroom. Money and fame were the big winners. "It doesn't matter if he's guilty," my brother declared. "It doesn't matter that he's Black. What matters is that he has the money and the lawyers to get off."

There was a part of him that wanted that kind of money, that kind of fame. I used to explain that hunger as a personality trait, something he inherited from our grandfather, but what if O. J.'s story is more relevant to my brother's life than I would like to imagine? Our family perched on the edge of two divides: race and class. Our grandparents were wealthy, but our mother had drifted away from them: first, when she married Chukwudi and then again when she married Jack. We had been through bankruptcy. We had been through years of Mom working nights and weekends at McDonald's while teaching school during the day. Yet we could still visit our grandparents' mansion, swim in their pool, and count on their wealth to keep us from falling into poverty.

Even as a child, I recognized the peculiar breadth of our experience of class in America. What I failed to see is the way my Whiteness allowed me to move effortlessly across the profound inequalities of our society. Whiteness has long served as a bridge across the class divide—a kind of "psychological wage," in the words of W. E. B. Du Bois, that allowed wealthy Whites to keep poor Whites from rebelling. For my brother, the class divide was a chasm that his Blackness made even wider and more consequential. Isn't that what O. J. taught us? The only way to be safe as a Black man in America is to be rich and famous. Of course my brother aspired to such freedom.

I don't want to trace everything in his life back to race. It's easy for White people to express sympathy for the pain and anger of Black people in a way that obscures the diversity of African American communities and caricatures Black people as one-dimensional icons of struggle—as if every Black person in America is always consumed with grief and anger. I don't want my brother's Blackness to flatten his life, to obscure his uniqueness or the many ways he was shaped by his White family. How am I to write about our lives without making too much or too little of his Blackness and my Whiteness? How am I to write, for example, about the eulogy he offered for our grandfather? He made no reference to race in his speech, but I can't ignore the fact that the man we called Dad died on March 22, 1994—the same night my brother lost his eye.

I find a recording of the eulogy in a shoebox full of old cassette tapes. It's as if I have been granted the chance to ask my brother one more question: *What was it like to be raised by your grandfather?*

I never called him Hugh or Houston or Mr. Slate. From the time I could speak, he was Dad. My brother and I grew up without a father, but we had a Dad.

A clever play on our name for our grandfather, but was it true? As if in response, he tells the mourners, "I gained more from Dad than I have from any other man in my entire life." Yes, this is true, but celebrating Dad obscures the absence of his own father, and I feel strangely distant as he concludes, "The greatest gift Dad gave me is that he could go anywhere, anytime, up to anyone and make them smile." So, we could leave it, the touching eulogy of a young man for his grandfather. But this is April 14, 1994, less than a month after a White man crushed a bottle into my brother's face. I wonder how it felt to stand in front of that group of people, his patch still covering a hole where his eye had been, to talk about Dad as if he really were his father, as if Chukwudi had not left for Nigeria years earlier.

Chukwudi had died earlier that year. We heard the news from Uncle Chuma. My brother did not know how to respond, how to grieve the father he never had. Two months later, he was attacked on the same night our grandfather passed away. At twenty-one years old, he had to face the loss of his eye without Dad and without Chukwudi. His father, his grandfather, and his right eye—all gone in the same year. Of course, in many ways, he had lost his father even before he knew his own name. The taking of his eye forced him to grapple with all he had lost, a series of absences that he could not fully measure. That is the tragedy of the absent father: we grieve something we never had and thus never know the full depth of our loss.

A year before Chukwudi died, my brother sent him a letter. I find a draft of the letter, written out by hand, in one of my brother's old notebooks. Song lyrics, notes for a script, a love story, then this:

Dear Papa, It was so wonderful hearing from you! It brought me a tremendous amount of joy to receive your fax. I do miss you dearly. I am doing very well here. I have spoken with both Dr. DVC and Chuma about what has transpired in Nigeria over the years. I want you to understand that I have no resentment or anger toward you. I understand why you returned to Nigeria. It was best for you and although I have missed you, it was what needed to happen. But no longer do we need to be so distant. I am your son and I would like for us to know each other and share with each other.

The note is dated September 30, 1993, one month after my brother's twenty-first birthday. Even after all those years, he could write that he had no resentment or anger toward his absent father. Was that true? He wanted it to be true, just as he wanted his father to respond with genuine love and curiosity, perhaps even a willingness to meet in person. Neither made the journey in time.

"WAKE UP, BRO, LET'S GO." He's sitting near the bed, lacing his white Adidas. I watch him for a moment, then roll over and close my eyes, hoping he will leave me alone. It's the summer of 1994. I'm fourteen.

He's almost twenty-two. We're spending a few months together in our grandparents' house.

"Let's go," he repeats.

"Go where?"

"Malibu."

Malibu. The land of Hollywood mansions and dramatic ocean views also happens to be where Kelly LeBrock lives. LeBrock had become a movie star by playing the perfect woman: in *Weird Science*, she was the sex goddess brought to life by two computer geeks; in *The Woman in Red*, she was the object of Gene Wilder's fantasies. My brother had met her while working on the set of one of her lesser-known films and, a few months after losing his eye, had landed a job as her bodyguard. I had hoped that he would introduce me to her eventually, but I had no idea it would be that morning.

As soon as he says "Malibu," I leap out of bed and am dressed and ready in three minutes. As we drive the winding road into Malibu, my head begins to throb. The Pacific billows like a giant blue flag, but I have to close my eyes. By the time we arrive at LeBrock's home, pain grips my head and throbs down my neck. Fortunately, LeBrock proves to be a skilled nurse as well as a generous host. She feeds me maple yogurt with homemade granola and suggests that I take a nap. When I retell the story to my friends, I make a point of noting that I slept in LeBrock's bed. Now I cringe, recalling my adolescent bragging. Even then, I knew that the amazing thing was not that I had come so close to a supermodel or that I had awakened from my nap without that abominable headache. The amazing thing was that LeBrock continued to be so disarmingly kind. Strolling through her organic vegetable garden, she picked a stalk of lavender and handed it to me. "Smell this," she said. "It might help with your head." After dinner, we lounged in the kitchen, sipping mugs of peppermint tea.

"That's what I want," he tells me as we leave. It's dark now, and the Pacific is a vast blackness. Cool ocean air rushes in through the open windows of the car. "That's what I want," he repeats. At first, I think that he's praising the fancy house, the endless gardens, but he's talking about the way LeBrock lived with such grace and generosity.

Why did he equate that grace with fame? He knew that many famous people were shallow and conceited. He would learn that lesson again and again as he became friends with more celebrities. Yet he clung to the idea that the key to living the good life was to make it big. Money and fame became foundational to a vision of life that wasn't about money or fame. It was about simple pleasures and small acts of kindness. He was already that person, the person who tipped lavishly and made strangers feel seen, the person who lit candles on a Tuesday night and put on *Sketches of Spain.* The closer he came to fame, the harder it became to see himself for who he was. That's the tragedy of my brother's hunger for the spotlight: in the end, all he wanted was to be himself.

All he wanted was to be himself. I say that as if it's easy, as if a mixed-race man who had grown up without a father, whose stepfather had been violently unpredictable, who had been molested as a child, and who had just lost his right eye should be able to lounge about, listening to Miles Davis without wondering about his place in the world. I forget who I am every day. I forget to be patient in the supermarket line. I forget to put my computer away and take a walk with my kids. I forget that I am a middle-class White man buying organic berries at the Whole Foods in my recently gentrified neighborhood. Why should I expect my brother to have been more in touch with himself than I could ever be? It's not a good excuse that I always saw him as superhuman. It's not a good excuse that I still do.

I'M SIXTEEN YEARS OLD and awkward as hell, the lankiest, goofiest boy at a graduation party for the most beautiful girl in the world—at least in my eyes. I met her at a summer camp. Nothing sexual happened, but enough low-grade tension built up to fuel months of overheated letters. She lived in Ventura, a small beach town about an hour up the coast from LA and three hours from our place in the desert. Too far for regular visits, but I couldn't miss her birthday. It was my best chance to keep our romance alive. I asked him to drive me: four hours each way. It was a big favor to ask, but I knew he would say yes.

I'm standing by her, trying desperately to engage her in conversation, but she is perched on the edge of a sofa, and no matter how wide I spread my legs, I still tower above her. She is short to start with, and the couch makes her even shorter. I'm aware of the awkwardness of the

situation, staring down at her as if she were my child, but I need all of
my concentration to stay on top of the conversation—*Yes, that speech
was super boring. . . . So, what are your plans for the summer?*—and
there aren't any chairs nearby. The room is hot and crowded, and I
begin to sweat. I can feel the sticky wetness creeping out from my arm-
pits. Someone starts a Mariah Carey CD, and I am forced to slide my
legs even farther apart to follow the conversation. It must look like I'm
doing splits. My brother spots the problem from across the room and
glides by with a chair in one hand, sliding it behind me without drawing attention. Even I barely notice him as I sit down, suddenly six inches
from the large brown eyes of my beloved.

I still don't understand how my brother could struggle with commitment and yet be so supportive of my geeky uber-romantic *Princess
Bride*-as-you-wish desire to love one woman with all my heart. He never
teased me for writing dozens of love letters and driving four hours to
talk to a girl I had not even kissed. Maybe that's why I like the idea that
he was protecting that girl the night of the attack, the girl his friends
remember being teased by Steven and his friends. The chivalrous gentleman: that's the man we both aspired to be.

HE SUED THE CLUB, the manager, and Steven. The club had the insurance, and the insurance had the most to lose. The legal papers present a
convincing case. The club was "badly overcrowded" and full of under-
age drinkers. The security was "insufficient" and poorly trained. My
brother was manhandled out of the nightclub, blood gushing from his
face, while the men who attacked him were allowed to walk away. How
much is it worth, the loss of an eye? The insurance company did not
want a jury to decide, so it settled.

He gives me the news right after singing the national anthem at one
of my basketball games. It's 1996, and I have just turned sixteen. As
the gym rumbles with applause, he glides over to give me a "bro hug":
hand shake with the right, the left over the shoulder. Instead of a quick
pat on the back, he pulls me in and holds me tight. "We made it," he
whispers. "They settled for half a mil." It takes me a moment to connect
the dots. Then, heat rushes into my body. I can feel the blood in my ears,
my hands. "We made it," he says again. *We made it.*

Half a million dollars. Ever since Mom married Chukwudi, she had known financial uncertainty. When the settlement came through, she was still working at McDonald's. She quit the next day.

It was less clear what the money would mean for my brother. In one of his notebooks, I find a handwritten note:

Dear God, What am I doing? My mind is spinning out of control at like a million miles per second. I want everything to be settled. Once again I learn. No major changes until the money's in the bank. I pray I never forget this time. I pray that I learn from my mistakes and grow from them. I love you God. Everything is fine. I am not upset at all. I must remember at all times that I am on a mission. I must seek to fulfill my dreams and God's every day. I

The note ends with that lonely *I* hanging in the air.

His first big purchase is a cross-country trip, a grand family adventure, just me, Mom, and him. Not a fancy car, not a new wardrobe—a family vacation. He lets me plan the journey, a major mistake, given my optimism and flawed sense of distance. I chart a path from California through the Rockies up to Yellowstone, over to Chicago, around Lake Michigan and up into Canada, back down at Niagara Falls, through Springfield (the Basketball Hall of Fame) to Boston, New York, Philadelphia, DC, and then across the South to New Orleans, and west through the desert parks—Zion, Arches, the Grand Canyon. All in three weeks. I have it plotted out on a giant atlas. He laughs the first time he sees it and tries to deflate my vision. How could we see so much in just three weeks? I hold firm, and, predictably, he agrees to pay for an extra week so that we can do the grand tour without having to drive every day. He never could bear to let me down.

The trip was meant to be a celebration, but it became a reckoning. Only two years after he lost his eye, the journey forced us all to grapple with the new reality he was facing, the new limits on what he could see and how he was seen.

At Yellowstone, the friendly park ranger notices the patch. "Is that permanent?"

"Yes," my brother responds, his voice cool and even.

"Well, if you want, you can sign up for a special disability pass and get a discount on all parks nationwide."

The ranger speaks with such a friendly warmth that I almost miss the trickiness of this terrain: the first time someone has seen my brother as disabled.

"Next time," my brother tells the ranger. He pays the full rate.

Two days later, we pull into a lonely South Dakota town. The roadside café looks uninviting, but we've been driving for hours, and we're hungry. The ATVs parked outside remind me of the desert, but the men loafing around stare at us, and I don't like the attention. These are not friendly faces. Inside, the staff ignores us, although the place is mostly empty. A plastic sign tells us, "Please wait to be seated." After ten minutes, Mom steps in front of a waitress and asks politely if we might be seated. The waitress responds curtly, "Sit where you'd like." We slide into a booth by the window, but the whole process repeats itself. No one appears with menus or water or a list of today's specials. We are not wanted here. We do not discuss why, and we do not make a scene. We are too polite—and scared. We stand up, walk outside, and eat granola bars until we make the next city.

"Was it that you're Black or that you're Black and we're White?" I ask from the back seat. The windows are up, and the rental car's upholstery reeks of plastic. I usually like the new car smell, but this stench is strong and disturbingly sweet. "Would they have been more friendly if we were all Black?"

Mom is driving. He's in the passenger seat. They exchange a knowing glance before he turns to me: "I thought they just didn't like the way you smell." I smile but keep thinking about those men outside the café, the hard face of the waitress. I wonder how often we will be turned away because of the color of our skins—of his skin.

We drive through Minnesota and Wisconsin, spend a night in Chicago, then cut through Michigan into Canada, reentering the United States at Niagara Falls. We spend an hour huddled in the spray of the falls, then jump back in the car. Across New York and Massachusetts to Boston and down the East Coast. Even with an extra week, it's still a tight itinerary, courtesy of my terrible planning—and my brother's commitment to not let me down. Huddled in our rental car, racing across America, we laugh, tell stories, stare out the window, and listen to Stevie Wonder's *Musiquarium* and Cyndi Lauper's *Greatest Hits*. It feels so strong: our love, our family.

We decide to take a ferry from Connecticut to Long Island. We park the rental car in the belly of the ship and head up to the deck. The sea is covered in thick fog. My brother goes inside to buy us hot chocolate, and a stranger with a white beard and a USA baseball cap asks Mom, "Is that big guy with you?" I'm tempted to respond, "Do you mean that big Black guy?" Mom answers first, her tone guarded: "Yes, he's my son." The man smiles and explains, "He looks just like this guy who used to play tight end for the Giants, what's his name, you know who I mean?" We shake our heads, and the man drifts off just as my brother returns with the hot chocolate, a cup for him and one for me and a coffee for Mom. I wonder whether Mom is going to mention the strange man or whether I should. The fog is thick and quiet, and the three of us squeeze together at the front of the ship, Mom wedged in the middle, staring into the gray. The mist is cool, but not cold. My brother's hand on my shoulder is warm. He tells us, "Just because you can't see something doesn't mean it's not there." I'm not sure whether he's talking about our future, all the possibilities that the money has brought into our lives, or whether there is something else that he has not seen but needs to feel. Our love? I sip the steaming hot chocolate, annoyed by the chunks of powder that cling to the Styrofoam cup and that stranger's curiosity, as if my brother is a novelty even among his own family.

WHEN WE RETURN HOME, he goes on a shopping spree. First, a new car, a Peter-sized car, one of his friends calls it: the Expedition, limited version, with leather seats and fancy trim. Next comes a house in Encino, a few blocks into the hills from the 101. The house is small but beautiful: wood floors, white walls, a deck overlooking a massive yard. He buys two huge white dogs, Great Pyrenees, names them Coco and Mac. Peter-sized dogs. He fills the house with new furniture. Peter-sized furniture.

He's haunted by guilt, the guilt of those who believe that they do not deserve their success. Impostor syndrome again. Losing his eye is nothing to be ashamed of, but he is ashamed of the source of his money and starts to tell people that he sold a script. Only his close friends know the

My brother and me in December 1999. I still have the beard I grew in Nepal. Thanks to the beard and my brother's couch, I actually look bigger for once. (Author's collection.)

truth—that the new car and the new house are a result of the lawsuit and, thus, of his injury. Maybe that's why he starts spending less time with them. They see through the story he's telling, the story in which his money is a reflection of his success rather than of his loss.

SIX MONTHS AFTER OUR FAMILY TRIP, I visit his new place. I'm up early, lounging on his couch, when two young women walk into the kitchen. Both are about my age, nineteen or twenty. One is his type, tall and blonde. The other has short dark hair and an athletic build. I like them both immediately and find it hard to keep from staring at the dark-haired girl. Later, I'll learn that he met both women in a strip club in San Francisco. At that moment, I know only that they are shockingly beautiful and apparently hungry.

My brother walks into the kitchen and starts scrambling eggs. I've eaten already but am not going to pass up the chance to join the party.

I pour some vanilla yogurt in a bowl, place a box of granola on the table, and start prepping my specialty: a fruit smoothie. As we cook, my brother chats with the young women. The blonde is inscrutable. She smiles at a joke, but only for a second, before her face returns to a beautiful blankness. The brunette, by contrast, is eager to talk. Her name is Dawn. She's vegetarian like me. We start discussing the virtues of healthy eating, and somehow the conversation turns to philosophy. I mention my love for Nietzsche and immediately regret broaching what I worry will be a conversational dead end. But Dawn seems just as engaged as she had been by the nutritional merits of parsnips and raw ginger.

After breakfast, my brother leaves with both women. Later that afternoon, he returns home alone. I try to pretend I'm uninterested, purposefully waiting five minutes before blurting out the question I had pondered all morning: how did he convince those women to stay with him? Of course, I also want to ask whether he slept with both of them, but that question would be too embarrassing—for me, not for him. We weren't accustomed to talking about sex. It's strange, really, that silence: we talked often about romance but almost never about sex.

"The key is to be real," he says. We're sitting on his back deck, our feet in the sun, looking straight ahead as if in a car. His voice is relaxed and quiet.

"Women are people. You have to care about them as people. Don't pretend you can solve all their problems. Don't come on like you're going to save them. It's more about listening than anything you say."

He pauses, turns to me, and smiles. "Then, you ask for her number."

"Just like that?"

"Just like that."

I ponder his advice, waiting to see whether he will offer more details. It takes me a minute to realize that he's still smiling at me. When I catch his glance, he laughs.

"You want to know if I slept with both of them?"

I blush and look away. "Did you?"

"No, just the blonde. I'm saving the brunette for you!"

I was a seventeen-year-old virgin whose idea of romance was writing long love letters and delivering roses plucked from my grandmother's garden. Yet I never doubted that my brother respected me. He wanted to fall in love someday too. I could see it in the way he talked with Dawn and her friend, as if their conversation might be the beginning of something real. I didn't know that my brother's relationship to women had been stunted years before, that when he struggled to trust women, to let them into his heart, he was grappling with more than the vexed questions of a young man. He was grappling with the pain of a child.

Addiction

We're at the Studio City park, in the middle of an epic horse battle, about six months after he lost his eye. He's pursuing his normal strategy: close shots he knows he can make. The strategy depends on my getting nervous. He knows that the closer the shot and the easier it seems, the more pressure I will feel to make it. That pressure is my undoing. I make the first two shots, but the third comes up short and careens off the front of the rim with a loud clank. I wipe the sweat from my face with my T-shirt and complain, "Why don't you try a jump shot for a change?"

As soon as I ask the question, I feel bad. I used to revel in his incompetence as an outside shooter, but his depth perception is still terrible, and I have become more cautious with my trash talking. He doesn't seem fazed by the comment. He dribbles the ball a few times and smiles.

"You know I wouldn't make a jump shot even if I had both eyes. You've got to play to your own strengths, bro."

It's a bright, flawless morning, and birds sing in the trees surrounding the courts. He makes another three-footer off the backboard, and as he hands me the ball, he says quietly, "That's why I'm not drinking anymore."

"Alcohol?" It's a stupid question, as if he would give up water or orange juice. I prepare to be teased, but he responds earnestly in the same quiet voice.

"Yeah, I'm giving it up. I have to. It's the only way."

He's quiet, and I dribble the ball a few times, unsure of what to say. The silence feels heavy, and I'm relieved when he speaks again.

"I'm going to need help. I'm going to join AA."

I've heard of AA but don't really know what it is. As the little brother, I feel uncomfortable probing and revert to the Slate family stand-by when something needs to be said that's hard to say.

"I love you," I tell him, dribbling the ball from hand to hand.

He smiles at me. "I love you too, bro," he replies. "Now stop stalling and take your shot."

HIS DECISION TO STOP DRINKING became the most important consequence of losing his eye—more important than the money. He found a new community in AA, a community that supported him for who he was—not just who he was trying to be. Every week, more than two million people participate in some sixty-one thousand AA groups worldwide, yet the program remains invisible to most nonalcoholics. That invisibility is vital to the program's success: many members need anonymity to shield them from the stigma of addiction. My brother's regular meeting took place in a single-story building that looked like any boring postwar bungalow, unless you happened to show up during a meeting.

We're sitting in the front row, the cake on my lap. I can smell the vanilla frosting. It's the anniversary of my brother's sobriety—an occasion often celebrated with cakes given by family members or close friends. I have been to enough meetings to treasure the ritual. It makes me feel less like an intruder to see other family members, and holding the cake gives me a sense of purpose and responsibility, as if I belong too. I don't tell anyone that the closest I have come to alcohol was a sip of Manischewitz.

An older man is talking about the death of his wife, how he had been too drunk to visit her in the hospital, how he could not bring himself to visit her grave until he'd been sober for years. He's "taking a cake," like my brother. Others are receiving chips, small round tokens, sometimes known as sobriety coins, that are used to recognize a certain length of time without alcohol, anything from 24 hours (usually a white chip) to a year (blue chip) or more. I look up at my brother's face and recall the small pile of sobriety coins he keeps in the drawer next to his bed. I reach out and squeeze his hand.

He gives a short, quiet speech. Not his usual sermon, these are the words of a man carrying something heavy he is afraid to put down. I don't recall what he said, but I remember how I felt listening to him: troubled that my hero had been humbled. And I remember his voice, at times not much more than a whisper, as if he were speaking to himself.

A key part of AA is believing that a higher power can help. My brother was not a religious man, but he believed in God, in something greater that bound us all together. "It's like a tree," he told me once, the summer after my first year in college. We were lying on his bed, a queen-sized mattress on the floor of his apartment. I had been reading Plato and wanted to show off by talking about the nature of ultimate reality. "It's like a tree," he told me. "We're all leaves connected to the same trunk."

Other key steps in the AA program include making "a searching and fearless moral inventory" of yourself and admitting "to God, to yourself, and to another human being the exact nature of your wrongs." He showed me his list—the "searching and fearless moral inventory" he had made of his own life and of his failings. The first word was *arrogance*. Maybe that's why he's sharing this with me, I thought: to humble himself.

We humbled each other all the time. Dissing, we called it, although it didn't feel like disrespect to me—more like a way to express love. As brothers, the standard "yo mama" jokes were out. Our favorites had to do with each other's girlfriends, even though most of the time neither of us actually had a girlfriend. *Your girlfriend is so ugly, she was herself for Halloween.* I don't remember ever dissing him for something that mattered: his poor grades, his temper, his drinking. I was wholly unprepared to be confronted with a list of his failures. He was a giant in my eyes, and he knew it. Sharing his list with me must have been an act of purposeful humbling. A confession. Normally, you confess to God. Here was my god confessing to me. It took guts to recognize his failings, to write them down in his sharp, angular script, and to share the list with his little brother. "Look at this," he said, "and see if there is anything missing."

WE'RE DRIVING ON VENTURA BOULEVARD, heading home from a meeting, when I ask the question: "How do you ask God to remove your shortcomings?" It's another step in the program: to "ask God to remove your shortcomings." I'm confused: what does it mean to ask God to do something?

He can't see me without his right eye. It isn't until we hit a red light that he turns to me and asks, "Don't you know how to pray?" This is a weird question for at least two reasons. First, he makes it seem as if we'd been raised good Christians who prayed every night before bed. The intonation in his voice presumes that I should know how to pray. Why would I? Second, his question suggests something I would never have guessed: that my brother prays. I return his question with one of my own: "Do you pray?"

"Yes, I pray."

"For what?"

"To keep the demons away."

We hit another red light, and he turns to me again:

> When you've done as many bad things as I have, you need to find a way to understand those things without seeing yourself as fundamentally bad, somehow evil. Sometimes I can feel it, what it's like to be possessed. It's like being in a car, your own car, but the steering wheel is not yours to control.

The light turns green, and we roll forward. I look at him as he turns back to the road, his patch a black spider clinging to his face. I want to reach up and swat it away, to uncover the eye I know is gone, but he keeps talking, and I resist the urge to touch his face:

> You've got your hands on it, the wheel, but you can't turn. The car is going its own way, and it's going faster and faster. You hit the brakes, but nothing happens. The car just keeps going, someone else in control. It's been possessed. It's a terrible feeling, one I hope you never feel, one I hope I never feel again. So, I pray to God to keep the demons away.

I thought his demons came from the bottle, but now I see his drinking as a symptom of older, deeper wounds.

The twelfth step almost saved him: "Bring the message to other alcoholics." He started mentoring others within months of joining AA, long before he'd reached the twelfth step. He couldn't help himself. He was a big brother. Nothing made him feel more himself than helping someone else.

His AA mentees were rich and poor, White and Black. Alcoholism does not discriminate. In 1955, Dr. Jim S., one of the first African American AA members, spoke at the Alcoholics Anonymous International Convention in St. Louis. AA cofounder Bill W. was in the audience and later wrote:

> Deep silence fell as Dr. Jim S., the A.A. speaker, told of his life experience and the serious drinking that led to the crises which had brought about his spiritual awakening. He re-enacted for us his own struggle to start the very first group among Negroes, his own people. Aided by a tireless and eager wife, he had turned his home into a combined hospital and A.A. meeting place, free to all. As he told how early failure had finally been transformed under God's grace into amazing success, we who listened realized that A.A. not only could cross seas and mountains and boundaries of language and nation but could surmount obstacles of race and creed as well.

In 1955, AA remained profoundly segregated. Even in the cities of the North and the West, it was rare to find an integrated meeting. AA's leadership shied away from challenging racial divisions. In the words of Bill W., "We are outcast enough already." Despite such caution, the vision of interracial harmony offered by Dr. Jim S. slowly came to define many AA communities, as the common experience of addiction brought people together across the color line. I have only one memory of attending a meeting that wasn't racially diverse—and that memory speaks less to separation than to inclusion and love.

We're sitting in a storefront church, the kind with the glass front and the low ceiling, row after row of white plastic chairs. It took us an hour

to drive through downtown to attend this meeting in one of LA's oldest
Black neighborhoods. The room is surprisingly long and narrow—and
crowded. I'm the only White person and also the youngest. Nobody
seems to mind. The AC is pumping, and I find myself wishing I had not
worn sandals. My entire wardrobe could use a change. At fifteen, I had
yet to outgrow my love for shorts. For more formal occasions, I had a
special pair of black "silk" shorts (they were made out of rayon) that
I loved to pair with a black-and-white polyester shirt. The shirt made
me feel chic and sophisticated but was paper thin and garishly ugly. My
brother notices me rubbing my bare feet, my frigid arms crossed tight
against my chest. He takes off his leather jacket and drapes it over my
shoulders. The jacket smells of incense. I smile at him, and he squeezes
my hand, as if he is there to support me.

It must have taken courage to out himself again. Maybe he found it
easier than taking me to Styles Ville. What did it matter how he looked,
his little White brother in tow, if he could stand up and say, "Hello, my
name is Peter. I am an alcoholic."

HE DIDN'T CHOOSE to become an alcoholic, but he chose to name his
addiction. He didn't choose to lose his eye, but he chose to wear the
patch. At first, I thought that it was a way to hide his wound, a form
of denial, that triangle of black felt. But maybe it felt healing to take
control of his face, to make his loss vital to his success, like Nietzsche
confronted with that demon.

We are huddled on the front porch, giant storm clouds sweeping the
desert. The air smells of rain.

"Start again from the beginning," he says. "I want to make sure I
got it."

"OK. Nietzsche's demon comes late at night, tells you that you will
relive this life exactly as it has occurred again and again, forever."

"I can't change anything?"

"That's right."

"Not like *Groundhog Day*, where Bill Murray could tweak this or
that?"

"No, not like *Groundhog Day*."

"That's too bad. Bill Murray was at his best in that flick. Maybe if Nietzsche had seen it, he would have tightened up his thought experiment."

It's the summer of 1999. He's twenty-six, and I'm nineteen. The Backstreet Boys are on the radio, everyone's anxious about Y2K, college kids are discovering something called Napster, and we are sitting in the desert, waiting for lightning and talking about Nietzsche. I'm enjoying the role of teacher.

"The whole point is that everything would be exactly the same. That's the demon's message: you can't change anything. You have to live it all again and again, forever. What would it take for you to see Nietzsche's demon as an angel in disguise?"

"What would it take for me to want to relive my life again and again forever? Cindy Crawford naked and a big pot of mac 'n' cheese. Are you hungry?"

"Just answer the question."

"OK. It would mean seeing every part of my life as bound up with everything else. Seeing the whole thing as beautiful."

"Is that possible?"

"Of course it is. That's how I see you, bro. That's how we should always see the people we love—a complete package, perfect just as they are."

A streak of lightning crests the sleeping dragon, and thunder booms. I lean in, and my brother puts his arm around me. I wish that I could feel that safe again.

A FEW YEARS AFTER LOSING HIS EYE, my brother went on *The Marilyn Kagan Show*, a talk show hosted by a therapist. The episode was about "friendships that became something more." The show sent a limo to pick him up at our grandparents' house. When the limo arrived, long and black and shiny, he looked down at me and shrugged, as if to say, "I guess that thing's for me." I could tell that he was nervous. He hoped that he would be identified as someone with talent, and that hope was exhausting. It wasn't easy to be himself in a way that would make him a star.

Peter Slate came to Hollywood early. He went to elementary school with the children of celebrities, including Beau Bridges, Tyne Daly, and Mike Farrell (Captain B. J. Hunnicutt on the TV show *M*A*S*H*). One of his classmates was Drew Barrymore. Growing up in such company, my brother was destined to dream of Hollywood.

When he began to write screenplays, he met with Farrell, who was generous with his time and advice. He became close with Mike Olmos, the son of Edward James Olmos. When our grandparents' front lawn was being used for a Rob Reiner film, my brother managed to talk his way up to the famous director. Two days later, he hand-delivered a script for Reiner at his Beverly Hills office.

Were any of his scripts produced? IMDB tells me that he cowrote a film in 1998 called *Visions of Darkness*. The title does not evoke subtlety. I wonder whether this is the movie he searched for that day he stopped at Blockbuster and mumbled that he had to look for something he'd written. I was shocked.

"You mean one of your scripts was made into a movie?"

"Sort of. I only wrote part of it."

"That's huge. One of your movies is in Blockbuster! Can we watch it?"

"No, not now. I just want to see if it's in the store. You wait here. I'll be right back."

"You want me to wait in the car? Why can't I come in?"

"I'm not sure they have it."

"I can help you look."

"No. You stay here. I'll be right back."

When he returned, I tried a more subtle tactic: asking what the movie was called. He wouldn't say, even after I promised not to tell anyone. Maybe he didn't want me to see something he wasn't proud of.

He cowrote *Visions of Darkness* with a friend, Tony, who now lives in the Cayman Islands. I send an email, and a few days later we chat via Skype. Tony explains that *Visions of Darkness* was "a really bad vampire movie" with a "really low budget." They worked together as production assistants on a few other B movies: *Skateboard Kid 2* and *Hard Bounty*, where they met Kelly LeBrock. Tony solves another mystery in my brother's Hollywood career. I remember that one of my brother's favorite scripts was almost sold, but something went wrong at the last minute. It was called *Hostage*, a suspense flick about a guy who takes his own family hostage. According to Tony, the script for *Hostage* made its way to "a very big-time producer" who managed to get interest from both Martin Sheen and Laurence Fishburne. My brother didn't like the terms of the deal. As Tony put it, "He thought we should be paid more for the project, whereas I just wanted to make the movie, as I saw it as our break, even offering to give him my paycheck." This is Tony's side of the story, but it fits a pattern I would see again in my brother's life: sabotaging big opportunities over details.

I could blame his upbringing: the absent father. I could blame his personality: the restless dreamer bored with reality. I could blame the woman who stole his youth in ways I still struggle to comprehend. I don't want the story of his career to be reduced to a tragedy. I want to see it as a choice: like embracing the patch or calling himself XL the 1I, a choice to find redemption in the struggle.

MY FAVORITE PICTURE OF US sits atop a bookshelf near our front door. I'm riding on his back, my arms around his neck, my legs across his hips. His arms are out wide. His chest leans forward. We are both beaming.

My two-year-old daughter points to the picture. She wants me to name the two boys, strangers to her eyes. I worry that she will be confused if I tell her that the awkward kid with the buzzed head is her father.

The photo is black and white, shot in front of a car dealership somewhere in the Valley. I'm eight. He's sixteen.

"Papa," I say and point at myself. I use the same title we used for my brother's father. I've never liked the word *Daddy*. It feels right to be Papa to my kids. Still, it seems strange to point at myself, hoisted on my brother's back, and say the word *Papa*.

We're both beaming, but not in the same ways. His smile is broad and wide. His teeth are gleaming. I'm grinning high into my cheeks, but I refuse to open my mouth. Even now, I am too shy to smile with my teeth.

"Papa," I say again. My daughter is incredulous or maybe just bored. She has no idea what this means to me. She is silent as she waits for me to name the next figure, the one whose gleaming face is so close to my own.

"Uncle Peter," I say. "Uncle Peter."

She giggles and points, and my chest tightens. I wish she knew what it felt like to ride on his back, to be safe in his love.

Now, I see a darker side to that photo: there I am, safe and happy, totally unaware that I'm another burden he was made to carry. Long before that night in Santa Monica, my brother had been forced to grow up too fast. Losing his eye shattered what remained of his youth. Most of us transition into adulthood slowly. We have our rites of passage: a bar mitzvah, a quinceañera, a driver's license, turning twenty-one. Such milestones matter because aging is so gradual. For my brother, everything changed overnight. He lost his boyish good looks, his dream of being the next teen heartthrob. No more boy band—he wasn't a boy anymore.

He turned to funk, R&B, and the blues. He started a band called Goliath. They practiced in his garage, performed in bars and nightclubs, and played a lot of covers: Stevie Wonder's "Higher Ground," Lionel Richie's "Hello," George Michael's "Teacher." As with all his projects, my brother had huge dreams for Goliath, dreams I had largely forgotten when a package arrived in August 2016.

I'm opening the mail on the front porch while my son searches a thicket of vines for his favorite berries. The vines grow up the iron railing that surrounds the porch. I know they're weeds and I should cut them, but I won't until my son outgrows his obsession with berries. I open a large manila envelope and find a note from one of my brother's closest friends, along with a promotional flyer for Goliath that must date back to 1998 or 1999. My son exclaims, "Berries!" He shows me his find, then carefully picks the berries, first the green ones, then the yellow, and finally his favorites, the red. I watch him, then turn back to the flyer. The opening sentences speak in my brother's voice so clearly that I begin to cry.

"At first sight, it's clear that comparing GOLIATH to any other band is nearly impossible. At first listen, it becomes unnecessary." That's classic Peter Slate marketing hype: punchy and breathless. He plays up the band's diverse sound: "Call it funk, call it rock, call it Hip-Hop . . . We don't care!" The reference to hip-hop intrigues me. Was he already thinking ahead to his next move? The most interesting detail is how he describes himself: "6'8" front man Peter U." His use of that *U* stuns me: It must have been Uderulu, a name I never heard him use for himself, a name he must have kept his own.

IT'S A HOT NIGHT IN JUNE, and the Blue Saloon is packed. It's a small place on a dreary corner in North Hollywood and might feel dingy if not for the crowd. Every seat is taken. A lot of Peter Slate fans are here, many of them old friends. I would be mortified to play in front of my own friends, but he loves the attention. Toward the end of the show, he calls a young woman onto the stage. It's her birthday, and he asks us to sing to her. After a round of "Happy Birthday," he announces that he's going to sing to her too. Instead of "Happy Birthday," he pulls out the Bill Withers classic "Make Love to Your Mind." I smile watching him fall on his knees next to the embarrassed, slightly drunk young woman. Then, I wonder: is this enough for him?

Now, I feel guilty even asking that question. Who am I to judge his happiness? Siblings aren't supposed to be judges, yet here I am, writing a book about my hero, as if I can understand what he felt, what he should have felt. There is a comparison inherent in such judgment, the presumption that his life should have been more like mine. I worried about his ambition making him unhappy, but in the Blue Saloon, I was the one overlooking the joys of the present, too focused on the uncertainties of the future. I still remember his smile gleam as he belted out the chorus. To worry whether such a moment was enough for him was to look away from the joy on his face. I could frame my concern as an expression of love, but it was also an extension of my need for security and stability. I projected my own craving for control on a man who was always wilder, a man whose life refused to be bounded, whose dreams overflowed in ways I loved and feared.

As my brother formed Goliath, I was applying to college. My application essay was about the night he lost his eye—about his loss and how that loss inspired me to live better. I used a line from one of our favorite songs, "Tennessee." I remember watching the music video with my brother and thinking of our ancestors, the generations of Slates who lived in Tennessee. Some of them must have owned slaves. We've come a long way, I thought. I overlooked the possibility that my brother and I might respond differently to the way the song evoked the history of Jim Crow violence. Sure, we shared a Southern grandfather, a White man from Tennessee, but that didn't mean that a song about racial inheritance would resonate the same for me and for the young Black man who was my brother. I ignored our differences when I quoted "Tennessee" in my application essay. I turned the loss of my brother's eye into the cheapest cliché of the admissions genre: tragedy transformed into opportunity—for me, not for him. His wound became a bridge to my future.

WE ARE WATCHING A TV SPECIAL about James Brown, lying side by side on his giant white couch. It's spring break in my first year of college, and I'm staying with him for a week. When the show goes to commercial, I sit up and ask:

"Are you proud to be Black?"

"No, not exactly," he replies. "I'm not into the whole Black pride thing."

I turn my attention back to the commercials, but he begins again.

"I'm not ashamed to be Black, but I'm not sure *pride* is the right word for how I feel about it."

"What is the right word?"

"*Aware*, maybe, or *determined*."

"Aware?"

"Aware of what it means to be Black, and that not all of it applies to me."

Confused, I stay silent until the show goes to commercial again. Then, I ask the real question that troubles me:

"Does Black pride mean hating White people?"

He laughs.

"Just because you love yourself doesn't mean you have to hate someone else."

MALCOLM X HELPED ME UNDERSTAND my brother's approach to Black pride. After he left the Nation of Islam in 1964, Malcolm discarded the idea that all Whites were enemies and embraced the possibility of collaboration across racial lines. At the Oxford Union in 1964, he called upon "the young generation of Whites, Blacks, Browns, whatever else there is." "I, for one, will join in with anyone," he declared, "I don't care what color you are—as long as you want to change this miserable condition that exists on this earth."

My brother loved Malcolm X. He loved his defiant pride, his commanding style. He didn't have an image of Malcolm on his dorm room wall (like I did), but his voice changed when he talked about him, as if to say that this was a man who deserved our respect. "Malcolm was our manhood," Ossie Davis said, "our living, black manhood." Could he be my manhood too? I wonder whether my brother thought it was strange that I had that Malcolm poster up in my room. The young Malcolm abhorred his White ancestry. He associated racial mixture with the rape of Black women. My brother never rejected his Whiteness. Still, I wonder what he thought when his White little brother put up that poster of Brother Malcolm. Did he smile, or did he cringe?

WHEN I TURNED TWENTY-ONE, I decided to find my father. I asked my brother for help, and he responded with a question that was surprisingly hard to answer:

"How do you spell his last name?"

He's sprawled on his big white couch, his Compaq Presario perched on his lap. I step over the long silver cord that snakes across the floor and into the modem and sit down on the opposite end of the couch. It's breakfast time, and I'm carrying a bowl of Raisin Bran and a coffee mug full of OJ. I place the OJ on the coffee table and lean in to watch my brother typing. It's the spring of 2001. The world survived Y2K, but the Internet still seems miraculous to me.

He asks again, "How do you spell his last name?"

"I don't know. Mom doesn't remember. I can think of at least four different possibilities."

"Well, let's start with one."

"What if this works? What if we type in the right name and get his phone number?"

"That's your call, bro. You're running the show. Whatever you decide to do, we'll make it happen."

I was close enough to reach out and pull him in for a hug or to lay my head down on his shoulder like I always did as a kid. I could feel his love for me. It had a physical quality, like a warmth in my muscles. I yearned to show him that I loved him, too, but instead of moving in for a hug, I sat back and took a bite of cereal.

THE INTERNET FAILED US, but my brother stuck to his word. First, he suggested that we call the telephone directory. When that also failed, he came up with another idea.

"Wasn't he a therapist, your dad?"

"Yeah, at least back then he was."

"Maybe another therapist would know how to find him."

A few days later, I walked into the lobby of the university counseling office, my heart racing with fear and excitement. On duty was a middle-aged man with a red beard and a kind, awkward smile. His big round glasses made him look like a friendly owl. He explained that if my father was still a licensed therapist, his address would be listed in an online database. He offered me a glass of water, and I sipped slowly as he typed the name, the most likely spelling first. No luck. The second try returned an address. He wrote it down on a small yellow sticky note. I slid the note into my pocket, thanked the counselor, and walked back to my car, stopping twice along the way to check that I had not lost the thin square of paper.

The address was in Pasadena, no more than an hour from my brother's house. He and I drove together. Our plan was simple: he'd wait in the car, while I confirmed that it was the right address. As I climbed the stairs, I felt anxious and lightheaded. I stopped at the top of the stairs to take a deep breath and discovered that I was only a few feet from my destination, a plain wooden door. Without a nameplate of any kind, there was no way to confirm that I was in the right place.

I knocked, and a tall skinny man opened the door. I recognized him instantly. After years of staring at old photos, this was a face I knew well. Even his scar was visible, a thin shadow on his cheek. He asked me what I wanted, his voice curt. I replied with a question: "Are you Bill ____?" He started to close the door, mumbling that he was busy, and I blurted out: "I think I may be your son." He opened the door a few inches and stared at my face. "I see," he said. "Why don't you give me your phone number?" I asked for a piece of paper, and he retreated into the room, leaving the door slightly ajar. A large white cat sprawled on a wooden chair, watching me. He returned with a pad of yellow legal paper, and I scrawled my number quickly but carefully. I didn't know what to say, and neither did he. We exchanged silent nods, and the door eased shut.

By the time I made it back to the car, I had an idea. My brother drove us to a nearby bookstore, where I bought some fancy paper, cream in color with an arabesque watermark along the left edge. While my brother perused the shelves, I wrote a letter to my father. I explained that I did not want anything from him. I was not upset with him. I only wanted to talk. When I was done, we drove back to the apartment, and I left the letter in the mailbox. That night, he called. It was a short conversation, and we agreed to meet in person again.

The next time, I drove myself. He had prepared a list of points we should discuss: a lifetime of catching up to do, all laid out in large cursive script on that same yellow legal pad, my phone number scrawled across the first page. The list was daunting: his battles with leukemia, his family history, my hopes for our relationship. We had lunch at Hamburger Hamlet. We sat in a large booth in the corner. The conversation was careful but not cold. At the end of the meal, we agreed to meet again. Twenty-one years was a long time to cover in one conversation.

That night, I told my brother everything. We were sitting in his living room, but we might as well have been back on that bus riding home from my elementary school. There I was, yammering on again. There he was, the big brother listening patiently. He lit tea candles and placed them on his mantle and the windowsill near the deck. He dimmed the lights and brought me a cup of chamomile tea. He listened. When I was done, he leaned in and put his hand on my knee.

"I'm proud of you, bro. It took courage to do what you did."

I thanked him for his help and told him that I loved him. Now, I see that wasn't enough. He had known Bill for years. They had memories of each other. I should have suggested they meet. I should have told my brother that I wanted him to come along for the next meeting.

He must have been curious. He might have been jealous too. Jealous of me for finding my father. Jealous of Bill for stepping into the role my brother had played since the day I was born. His place in my life had already been complicated by my growing up and moving away. Here I was, opening a new chapter of my life without realizing that it was new ground for him too. I was so focused on finding my biological father that I failed to see that I was neglecting the only father I had ever known.

MY BROTHER AND I had been growing apart for years. When did it start—the distance between us? I search my memory for clues, and a half-formed image startles me: a wooden chessboard on our dining room table. We played rummy 500, Monopoly, checkers, Chinese checkers, and every video game we could convince Mom to buy. We never played chess. I learned the game in fourth grade and was pretty good by eighth grade, helped along by a Chessmaster computer program and a few books from the library. I tried to get him to play me. He always found excuses, and I stopped asking. I didn't think much about it, the fact that chess is often considered a benchmark of intelligence, that maybe he worried that I was getting too smart for him. It's a ridiculous idea: he always destroyed me in debates, and neither of us put much stock in the fact that my grades were better than his. We both knew that he didn't care much about school. But the world did not see it that way. In the winter of 1995, for my fifteenth birthday, he bought me a wooden chessboard engraved, "Nico: I will forever be in your shadow, smiling. Love, Peter." I was moved by the gift and the message, but was he always in my shadow?

He craved his own accomplishments. It was a sharp need, born somewhere between his father's failure and our grandfather's success— and, with time, my success. In 1998, the year I left for college, he produced a telling list:

1998
formed Goliath
rewrote hostage
bought house
passed classes

It was a report card of sorts. I wonder what he made of this list. Had he done enough to mark the year a success? To mark himself a success?

The distance between us grew after I left for college, and it kept growing. I spent my junior year in Nepal and Chile, then a year in the UK after graduation. It was hard for us to stay in touch when I was abroad and easy to overlook the awkwardness in our conversations. It was more than physical distance that took a toll on our closeness. We were living different lives now. I came home after three months in the Himalayas with a bushy red beard and a new perspective on everything: my future, my politics, the mundane details of everyday life. He knew it right away—I had changed in ways even I could not see.

He was changing too. It saddens me that some of the most dramatic and difficult moments in his life happened when I was thousands of miles away.

I'M COOKING DINNER with two friends at an apartment in Oxford when he calls my cell.

"How are you, bro?"

"I'm good," I tell him, "good but busy." I want to get back to my new friends, two young women who are smart and funny. He is silent, and the silence feels awkward and heavy. So, I ask, "How are you?"

"I'm all right." Pause. "I'm . . . um . . . she's pregnant." Or did he say, "*was* pregnant"? The connection is choppy, and the word *pregnant* echoes long enough for him to ask, "Are you still there, bro?"

"Yeah, I'm here. I'm here. I . . . I love you. I love you, bro." I don't know what else to say. Had he said *is* or *was*? He and his girlfriend have only been together a year, and their relationship is stormy. The street is quiet, and I can hear the sounds of my friends laughing and cooking. The smell of frying onions drifts out through the open door. I want to ask whether his girlfriend is still pregnant; whether he wants to be a father; whether he knows that the child is his, or was his. All I can think to say is "I love you."

"I love you too, man." He's crying. "I don't know what to do. That was my baby, I know that was my baby. I told her it was her choice what to do. Her parents didn't want her to have the child. I told her she needed to do what was right for her. I should have told her that was my baby too. I should have. . . ." He breaks down again. His cries sound muffled and distant coming through my cheap phone. "That was my baby," he says again and is quiet.

How could this have happened without my knowing? I feel so far away, hearing this story over a bad phone connection on the stoop outside my friend's place, the sound of cooking and laughter escaping the half-open door. When he hangs up, I sit outside and watch the sky darken. Then, I go inside and tell my friends what happened. My admission deepens our conversation, and they open up about their own families, the struggles of lives and worlds far removed. Soon, we're all chopping vegetables and drinking wine, brought closer by the distance between us and those we love.

AFTER HE TOLD ME ABOUT HIS GIRLFRIEND'S ABORTION, I promised him that we would talk again soon. When I call, he's driving the 101 toward Hollywood. I ask him how he's doing, and he says, "Good. All good." I know there's more he could say—perhaps more he wants to say—but I'm busy and eager to get off the phone. I tell myself that it's better not to pry. Maybe if we could take a long walk together in the desert, sit and watch the moon crest the sleeping dragon, maybe he would open up with me. "All right then," I say. "I love you." Silence. A distant siren. Then, "Love you, too, bro," and we both hang up.

I can't make sense of the distance that grew between us without going back to the differences that shaped our childhoods: the fact that he was older and shouldered so many burdens, the fact that his father came and went while mine was gone from the beginning, the fact that he was Black and I was White. Now I see our lives as a microcosm of the larger tragedy that still haunts this country. If racism is everywhere, not only in our brains and our hearts but in our cities, our schools, our prisons, our hospitals, our mortgages, and our bank accounts; if the very word *our* has lost its meaning; if the dignity of human life depends on whether you look like me or like him: how can we live as brothers?

The Stage

My brother became a rapper by accident. It's rare to find an accountant who grew up telling everyone, "That's what I'm going to be when I grow up—an accountant." By contrast, thousands of young Black men grow up dreaming of hip-hop stardom. My brother wasn't one of them. He loved the music from its early days—Grandmaster Flash, Kool Moe Dee, the Sugarhill Gang—but it wasn't his dream, not until he found himself living it.

I can't pinpoint when he became a rapper. Before he joined his own group, Supreme Kourt, before he started hanging out with Cypress Hill, he had already begun to place himself and his music within the aegis of hip-hop. He did not have to reject his other musical interests. Hip-hop has always been eclectic and inclusive, and the groups he hung out with—Cypress Hill, Limp Bizkit, Linkin Park, the Black Eyed Peas—all crossed musical divides. Yet there was something new in his identification as a rapper, something that wasn't just musical but also racial, something that wasn't just about how he saw his art but also about how others saw him. I can't understand how he became a rapper without going back all those years to the night those men took his eye. They shattered his fantasy of boy-band stardom and left him with the scars he needed to be "hard"—or at least to fake it.

It's the spring of 2003, and we're at a recording session with Supreme Kourt. The studio is full of people, mostly Black men. I think back to those haircuts at Styles Ville. For most of my life, it's been rare that I've been the only White guy in the room: a couple of holidays with Jack's family, a party with some guys from my basketball team. Now that my brother is rapping with Supreme Kourt, it's becoming a common experience. Of course, he's spent his whole life being the minority, and not just around White people. At Styles Ville or in a room like this—a room full of Black men—his hair and skin would make him different even if he hadn't brought along his White brother.

My eyes travel the room, from the huge mixing console to the eggshell acoustic foam, then settle on my brother's face. He looks tense—or is that just focus, the way his jaw is tight? I look from his face to the others in the studio, and it strikes me that my brother is lighter-skinned than almost everyone else. I tend to see his skin color as medium-complexioned for a Black man, somewhere between milk chocolate and dark chocolate. In this room, he's fair. A Black man among White folks; mixed among Black folks. We're all mixed, of course, but not like my brother, not like those whose ethnic identity is often in question.

I look back at my brother's face. He's in the sound booth now, about to drop his lines. That's when I notice the patch, how black it is against his brown face, and for the first time, I wonder: Is the patch his passport to racial solidarity? Was it the violence of White men that certified his Blackness?

I'm tempted to link my brother's losses—his father, his childhood, his child, his eye—to his embrace of hip-hop. It makes sense that he would turn toward a musical form born of suffering—like the blues—but one that turns that suffering into dreams of epic success. Tupac was worth some $40 million when he died. Jay-Z grew up in Bed-Stuy and now owns an empire. My brother, XL the 1I, craved that blend of hard-edged reality and fantasy-level fame. If only the fantasy hadn't cost him so much.

He started drinking again. Five years sober, then a warm Corona in a dive bar in San Diego. I was scared for him when he told me but tried to hide my fear. I knew that it wouldn't help if he believed that I was questioning his choices. I was the younger brother, after all, and a teetotaler. What did I know about drinking?

He was a rapper now, spending most of his nights at clubs or bars. Everyone drank. Maybe it wouldn't be a problem. His drinking became bad when he felt hopeless and depressed. Hip-hop gave him a new dream, a new community, and a taste of something he had never experienced—the big stage.

THE FILLMORE. The joy of the spotlight, the rush of the crowd. After the show, we go backstage—my brother and me. We climb a flight of stairs to a VIP lounge where the artists relax on plush red couches, the lights dim, the air warm and smoky. I'm twenty years old and scared that I will embarrass myself. I don't want him to know that I'm nervous. When he looks at me, I try to look away, but our eyes catch, and he smiles. Something in that relaxed grin takes me back to Styles Ville. "He's outing himself again," I think. The young Black man, toting around his little White brother.

No one seems to care what I look like. They welcome us as we are, not because we belong but because no one worries about belonging. At least, that's my hope. Is this the welcoming world my brother has always wanted? Or is everyone just too high to give a damn?

No one seems to care that he's mixed. Does he bear that burden here? He has doubts and insecurities, I know, but they are mostly about his career. I want to believe that no one cares about the color of his skin, not on that stage at the Fillmore, and not backstage with the Cypress Hill crew. Marveling at where he has arrived, I remember the subtitle to Nietzsche's last work: *How One Becomes What One Is*. It remains a mystery to me how hip-hop allowed my brother to be himself while becoming someone entirely new.

I'M UP IN THE HOBBIT ROOM, holding two pictures of him side by side: on my left, the baby-faced heartthrob of Up N' Comin, in jeans and a button-down; on my right, the one-eyed rapper, sporting baggy sweats and the patch and a baseball cap pulled low. It's January 2016 and ten degrees below freezing. I have no reason to be up here. I've been through all my brother's things; there are no more surprises to be found in this tiny, frigid room. But something has drawn me back despite the cold. I breathe in and close my eyes. I can feel the cold air enter my lungs. I breathe out and open my eyes. He looks so different from one image to the next, yet so many of his struggles remained the same. Peter Slate was racially profiled even when he was clean-cut and dressed like an eighties rock star. As XL, he embodied the gangster rapper, the thug.

Ask a hip-hop fan about the difference between the gangster and the thug, and you might elicit strong reactions. For many, the thug is the more authentic figure, a tragic character whose experience on the streets yields a more accurate perspective on the violence and drugs that the gangster celebrates to the point of parody. My brother's evolution toward the thug life happened in stages: losing his eye and embracing the patch, buying a fancy car and changing his wardrobe, embracing pot as a lifestyle. If the thug embodies the authenticity of the streets, XL could never be a true thug. If, on the other hand, the thug is defined by public perception—and especially by the eyes of the police—then XL was the epitome of the thug. Driving his Expedition, the music blaring, his braids pulled back in a ponytail, the ambiguities of race and class became erased. He was Black, and he was a thug.

I put down the photos and pick up one of his notebooks. Its blue plastic cover is chipped and scratched. I pull off my gloves and flip through the pages. Song lyrics, mostly love songs from his boy-band days. I put the notebook down and try one with a black leather cover. Here, the lyrics are from his days as a rapper. I'm not sure whether it's because of his age or the shift in genre, but these lyrics are much darker. They express a tragic resignation toward a world that is simultaneously glamorous and dangerous:

> *Night after night, it's the same damn thing*
> *It's a shame all the pain that the game seems to bring*

Rhyming against the hook "vices seem to be poisoning me," XL turns inward:

Sippin on syrup I drift off to sleep
*Shit I drink would make most n****s weep*
I speak the truth with a soul that's deep
I see the dark side with the eye that can't see

This is the only time I can find that he rapped directly about his eye: "I see the dark side with the eye that can't see." The dark side of human nature or of his nature? Of the world that took his eye or of the man who worried that he deserved it?

The closer I look, the more I see a chain of guilt running through his life. It starts with his father leaving. No matter what Mom said, he must have worried that his father left because of something he had done. Then, there is the molestation. Many kids who are abused blame themselves. His aversion to commitment, his fear of success—did he link them back to his childhood and then forward to the loss of his eye? I don't know whether he brought it all together. I don't know whether I can, whether I should.

I rub my hands together and slip my gloves back on. Then, I pick up the two photos—the young singer and the wounded rapper—and hold them both in the air. I wonder what Peter Slate would have made of XL the 1I, and a memory returns.

The bong is four feet tall and shines like gold. Steam rises from its gilded lips in elaborate arcs, as if tracing the letters of an ancient language. The show has just begun, and the air is already thick with smoke. The audience has come prepared to the debut performance of a new musical collective, aptly named Los Marijuanos. Formed in LA in 2001, Los Marijuanos met every other week for open jam sessions. Their music bridged the divide between rock and rap. Anchored by Cypress Hill, the group included the rapper Everlast, the drummer from Jane's Addiction, guitarists from Deftones and Downset, and the bass player from Methods of Mayhem. The gatherings featured two MCs: Mellow Man Ace, one of the founders of Cypress Hill, who gained fame in 1989 with the hit single "Mentirosa," and my brother, XL the 1I.

Tonight, XL is more than a hype man, more than an MC. He is an artist. He has worked his connections to make his group, Supreme

XL the 1I performing on stage in 2002. (Author's collection.)

Kourt, the opening act for Los Marijuanos. Here is his chance to show the Cypress Hill crew that he can rap.

I show up early and watch the stage being set up. I am sitting on a wooden crate near the door, a shy twenty-one-year-old kid, when he emerges from the back and walks out to center stage alone. Does he know that I'm watching him? He stops in front of the mic, palms it with his right hand, and pauses. For a moment, I think that he might sing one of his old ballads, his good eye closed, his patch a black hat pulled low across his face. Instead, he mumbles, "Mic check. One. Two. Three." He steps back, as if to leave, but then pulls the mic in close: "Ladies and gentleman, we'd like to welcome to the stage the man you've all been waiting for, the poet, philosopher, and world-renowned lady's man, Nico Slate!" I stand up and smile, unsure of whether to bow or applaud, grateful for the love of my brother.

Los Marijuanos. Their name explains what brought together such a diverse range of musicians. Weed was everywhere that night. Not just in the hands and mouths of the performers and the fans, but in the iconography of their clothes, the props they used in their performances, the lyrics of the songs.

My brother came to marijuana at the age of sixteen. Although alcohol was available at our grandparents' house, pot was harder to find. Plus, his friends were more into drinking than smoking. The popular kids went to clubs to drink; the losers stayed home and smoked.

Now, pot was cool. From their earliest hits, Cypress Hill had celebrated the power of cannabis. "Hits from the Bong," for example, samples the hook from Dusty Springfield's "Son of a Preacher Man" and the drums from Lee Dorsey's "Get Out of My Life, Woman," while rolling through rhyme after rhyme celebrating Mary Jane. Cypress Hill's blend of music and pot must have felt familiar to my brother, having grown up listening to our mom's records. From Bob Marley to the Grateful Dead, marijuana shaped many of our mom's favorite artists.

The love of weed was deeply personal, profoundly social, and often political. Smoking up was a rejection of the "war on drugs" that had decimated communities of color and fostered the "new Jim Crow" of mass incarceration. As drug laws put more and more people behind bars for nonviolent offenses, pro-pot musicians rallied to change the culture and the law. No band was more committed than Cypress Hill. In 1998, the group organized a massive outdoor music festival appropriately named the SmokeOut.

XL never joined the political campaign to legalize pot, but he did engage in his own form of quiet civil disobedience. One day, while looking for extra toilet paper, I stumbled upon a row of plants thriving under bright lights. Since when had my brother taken an interest in gardening? A different teenager might have tried some, but I had developed an opposition to pot, an opposition I liked to think of as less prudish than philosophical, but which was really just garden-variety fear of the unknown coupled with a teenage need to feel confident about everything.

HE LIGHTS THE CANDLES SLOWLY, as if in prayer, turns on some Miles Davis, rolls a joint, and asks me: "Do you want to try?" My answer comes out more self-righteous than I intend: "No, thanks. I don't want to depend on an external crutch to find peace." He takes a drag, exhales, and smiles.

"Why separate the inside from the out? What about food or water? Aren't those external?"

"Sure, we can't seal ourselves off from the world, but my physical need for food and water shouldn't become a spiritual crutch."

"That's why I like to smoke pot. To connect my body to my soul."

I had been tired when the conversation started, the rise and fall of *Sketches of Spain* lulling me down. Our debate awakens my competitive spirit and something deeper—a need to prove myself to my older brother, to be different from him and respected by him. My gaze floats around the room—the mantle covered with candles, their tiny flames casting long shadows—before returning to find my brother watching me. He's waiting for my answer. I clear my throat and try to sound casual:

"It's not that I want to separate body and soul. It's that I don't want my soul to be dependent on what I put in my body. That's addiction, when we need something in order to have peace in our soul."

"I'm tired of being afraid of addiction. What if you are addicted to the idea of being free from addiction? It sounds to me like this is all about control for you. Control is the worst kind of addiction—you can never get enough."

"Is not fear of thirst when your well is full the thirst that is unquenchable?"

"You're quoting Gibran to support my point! I'm glad I finally convinced you."

"You've convinced me you can defend your point with all the passion of the true believer."

I want to say "with all the passion of an addict," but it's one thing to tell your brother that he's addicted and something else to tell him that he's an addict.

I wish I hadn't been so cocky, so sure of myself and my take on the world. Maybe he would have been more comfortable sharing his own doubts and fears. We could have learned from each other as we did when we were young. He was right: I was addicted to control. I still am. I get nervous about where my family will be seated in a restaurant, as if the quality of our togetherness depends on getting that corner table by the window. I hate throwing food away, even tiny scraps, and micromanage the dinner table. There is a thin line between frugality and compulsive anxiety, and I cross it all the time. Even my need to tell this story, to put his life down on the page—even this is a way to assert control. Here, at least, I know there are limits to what I can decide. This story will never be what I want. It ends too soon.

I MUST HAVE BEEN AROUND TEN when he told me the story of an ant that was climbing a towering tree. Every time the ant passed a branch, he considered stopping to enjoy the view. Every time, he decided to wait until the next branch to take a break. He kept climbing, branch after branch, without looking down, without savoring how far he had come. "What happened next?" I asked, expecting some kind of dramatic intervention to help the ant realize all he was missing. "That's it," he replied. "The ant died without ever stopping to see how far he had come."

FEBRUARY 2003. Linkin Park and Cypress Hill are playing the Nutter Center in Dayton, Ohio. An old friend from AA lives nearby. He gets her into the show along with her teenage kids: one girl, one boy. He spirits the girl up on stage in front of all her friends. Takes the boy backstage, introduces him to the crew. Then, he peels off his favorite jersey and gives it to the boy. In that moment, handing his sweaty jersey to that ecstatic boy, he has succeeded.

I wish he had seen it that way. Hip-hop brought him close to achieving his dreams, but not close enough. First, there was the money. He was not paid much for his work as an MC or the performances of Supreme Kourt. His notebooks are full of inchoate business plans: a music tour company, a record label, a hip-hop convenience store. These were all just dreams. He was still living off the money he had received for losing his eye.

He decided to gamble on a hip-hop clothing company called Joker. The Joker brand was the brainchild of the renowned tattoo artist Mister Cartoon. Eminem, Dr. Dre, 50 Cent, and Beyoncé all wear Cartoon's art on their skin. Originally a graffiti artist on the streets of Los Angeles, Cartoon was an old friend of B-Real. Together, they founded Joker Brand Clothing in 1995, alongside Estevan Oriol, then known as DJ Scandalous. All three men had strong connections to the hip-hop community. They needed someone to manage the company. XL knew nothing about running a clothing company, but he knew someone who did, an old family friend. By introducing his friend to B-Real and Mr. Cartoon, XL brought together two distant sides of his life. As if investing in his own wholeness, he then bought into the company with $100,000. Overnight, all his clothes became Joker Brand. Sweatpants, headbands, baseball caps, even a leather jacket—all emblazoned with the iconic Joker symbol: the sad clown, tears like diamonds, one on each cheek. It was a fitting symbol, the sad clown, always making others happy, never happy himself.

He began to work as a promoter, giving away free clothes to hip-hop celebrities, hiring an array of young men to work the crowds at music festivals. Now he wasn't just a hype man—he was a businessman. The possibilities were endless. Take those young men he hired, all of whom were poor kids of color, mostly high-school dropouts. He saw them as more than an inexpensive way to spread word about Joker. He dreamed of forming a social movement of the street, a cross between the Nation of Islam and the Avon ladies.

The dream wasn't enough. Working for Joker and producing his own music did not satisfy his ambitions. Nor was he making much money. He needed something else.

Soon after the millennium, he created a business plan for a new radio show, *Channel Zero*, that would bring together rock and hip-hop. I still can't explain how, but he managed to get the show on the air and land himself a position as one of the hosts. Named *Mass Distortion*, the show earned a weekly spot on one of LA's most popular radio stations, Power 106, "where hip-hop lives!" His cohosts, C-Minus and DJ Lethal, were both popular DJs known for stretching the boundaries of hip-hop. C-Minus was a radio veteran, a key player in one of the most celebrated hip-hop shows on the West Coast. DJ Lethal gained fame in the rap metal group Limp Bizkit and the Irish American hip-hop group House of Pain. Compared to C-Minus and Lethal, XL was a rookie, yet he was actively producing the kind of cross-genre music at the heart of *Mass Distortion*, "the show where rock meets hip-hop."

This is the highpoint of my brother's career, and it frustrates me that I still can't explain how it all happened—or what it meant to him. On Facebook, I track down the other artists involved in the show. C-

Minus and DJ Lethal are busy musicians, but both are happy to answer my questions. Chatting with my brother's old partners reminds me of walking the campus of Lincoln University, straining to hear his father's voice. I know what his colleagues thought of *Channel Zero* and *Mass Distortion*. I want to know what he thought—what he felt—about his closest brush with fame.

I consider asking Mom whether any of his things might still be in the desert. I don't want to trouble her, but I need to know that I've exhausted every lead. We're sitting in the backyard, watching my kids blow bubbles. It's late June and hot even in the shade. My three-year-old son is an expert bubble maker, but his younger sister struggles, and I worry that she will grow frustrated, unable to make bubbles like her brother. She's eating bubble juice every time she brings the wand to her mouth. I'm about to intervene when she finds the right angle, and a flock of tiny bubbles erupts in front of her face. It's beautiful, the way they hang in the air, the joy in her eyes. I turn to my mom, who is beaming at my daughter. It's a terrible time to ask, but the question escapes me:

"Is it possible we missed some of his things? Bubba's things? Did we get it all from the desert?"

She stares at me, and her shoulders roll in toward her chest. The joy of being a grandparent is overshadowed by something dark and empty. When she speaks, her voice is quiet, almost a whisper.

"He was going back and forth between the desert and LA. You know that. Most of his important things, he kept in his truck. The rest were in the living room or that storage unit in LA. We got all of that. I don't think there's any more."

The kids are blowing bubbles at each other, and I move between them to protect their eyes from bubble juice. I keep my gaze on my mom, but she looks down at her feet as she continues to whisper.

"I offered to let him move into my room. He refused. He wouldn't stay in your room either. He slept on the couch most of the time. Kept his stuff in the living room. Except. . . ." She pauses, stares up at the sky. "Except, I remember him packing a few boxes. . . . He left them in that old camping trailer, you remember, the one we stayed in that Christmas. Did we get those boxes?"

I can hear my kids laughing, but my mind is racing back to the year before Mom married Jack, the year my brother decided to spend

Christmas with Mom and me in the desert. We didn't know it then, but it would be our last Christmas with just the three of us.

It was very cold, and we huddled in the trailer, playing gin rummy and telling stories. There was an icebox, a real one, but we didn't need it. We left the milk on the stairs to the trailer. Little slivers of ice laced the Frosted Flakes we ate for dessert. After drinking the sugary milk, we unwrapped presents, then sat in a circle and played Monopoly. I bought up all the railroads, but my brother had Boardwalk and Park Place, and after an hour we decided to finish the game in the morning. As usual, I fell asleep first. Curled up in an old blue sleeping bag, the felt lining smooth with age, I listened to the two people I loved most in the world. I don't remember what they were talking about, but what remains in my memory is this: a feeling that they could talk to each other forever, that there was something natural in the flow of what they were saying, in the rhythm of their togetherness, something good and true that required no effort to maintain, like a river running down a steep canyon, something that would last as long as the desert and be just as true.

COULD THAT TRAILER still hold his things?

It's a three-hour drive from LA, through Lancaster, Victorville, Barstow. I am reversing the route we took that night he lost his eye. This time I'm alone, and the stakes aren't so high. That's what I tell myself to calm my nerves. I find it difficult to concentrate on the winding road, the Deathtrap Highway. My mind keeps churning the same questions: Will the boxes still be there? What will they contain? I know it doesn't matter. It's not my brother in a hospital bed wondering whether his brain has been cut with glass, whether his eye will ever see again. Still, it matters to me what I will find—or won't find. It matters enough that I have to force myself to concentrate on the road, to watch that blue pickup swerving into my lane from behind the U-Haul truck.

Then come the Joshua trees. I should keep going if I'm going to arrive before dark, but there is something I have to do here. I pull over to the side of the road, get out of the car, and stare at the wild bristling trees. It's a cloudy October day. The air smells of rain. I walk thirty feet off the road to the largest tree I can find. It must be twenty feet tall. I put my hands on its spines, close my eyes, and wait. I can hear the wind moving between the trees, or is that the sound of drizzle upon the sand? No, I feel nothing on my skin, and when I open my eyes, nothing moves, not even the clouds.

I PULL ONTO THE FAMILIAR RED-GRAVEL DRIVEWAY an hour before sunset. I'll have to hurry; the trailer doesn't have electricity. I pull open its metal door, surprised it gives so easily. No need for locks in the desert. There are two small windows in the trailer, but the sun is low, the clouds are dark, and only an echo of light sifts through the frosted glass. I hesitate to climb in. I'm worried about spiders and scorpions. At least there shouldn't be any snakes. The trailer is three feet off the ground. Can scorpions climb stairs?

I step in, and the smell hits me, a pungent mix of dust and mice poop. The first thing I see is my old flannel sleeping bag, thrown like a tarp over a mound in the center of the trailer. I grab hold of the sleeping bag and fling it into the far corner, revealing a pile of boxes balanced atop old milk crates. A cloud of dust fills the air, and I cough as I pry the top off the first box.

Porn, mostly old copies of *Hustler*. Maybe that's why he stored this stuff out here? The top copy is signed "To Peter, with love." The signature looks like Amanda. Or maybe Mandy. One of his friends had gotten a job for *Playboy* and invited my brother to a few video shoots. Maybe that's where he got this signed.

I move the porn box and start to flip through a milk crate filled with Mom's old LPs: the Stones, John Lennon, Paul Butterfield, Sweet Honey in the Rock. I'll play these for my kids someday. I'll play them his music too. I want them to know his voice and to see him as I see him: as an artist and a dreamer.

I step over the milk crate, open another box, and there it is, right on top: the *Channel Zero* business plan. I step back toward the open door, squint through the gloom, and read what anyone else would see as an overheated exercise in wishful thinking. I hear his voice immediately.

The goal of the company was not just to become a popular radio show but "to become the primary cultural portal for the international youth market." *Channel Zero* would "build an online and offline international membership community through its various resources such as online and offline radio, video streaming and services, event sponsorship, and street team promotion." It would be "the pioneer media source of the emerging rap/rock genre." Reading the document makes me smile. Its combination of bravado and detail is classic Peter Slate.

The rest of box three is less exciting—old business cards, an empty rolodex—and box four is even more disappointing. Then, I find them, at the top of box five: a stack of CDs labeled *Mass Distortion*. They are scratched and chipped, and I tell myself that they probably won't play as I walk back to the rental car, a red Chevy Malibu, and pop the first disk into the CD slot. It's starting to drizzle. I should roll up the windows, turn on the heater, but I can't move as the first show starts. I was in England throughout his time on the air. Even if the CDs play, I have no idea what I will hear.

The intro to the show features a veteran of LA's hip-hop community, Abstract Rude. Against a hard beat, Abstract Rude rhymes about the show and each DJ. His line about my brother reminds me of that night at the Fillmore: "bass boost turns high up for XL, place loses it, turns wild, and raises hell." I listen for my brother's voice, as Radiohead leads into Run-DMC and Rage Against the Machine flows into Biggie Smalls. I'm impressed by the fluid shifts of style and sound. What other show would interview DJ Premier, of the hip-hop duo Gang Starr, and Greg Ginn, the leader of the punk band Black Flag? *Mass Distortion* is the musical equivalent of the racial inclusivity he sought his entire life. He had arrived . . . almost.

As with Cypress Hill, he plays a supporting role. Rather than commenting on the music, he offers short riffs on the words of the other DJs. Even when C-Minus and DJ Lethal go out of town, he still talks less than the guest MC. No one can see him, but he keeps drawing attention to his eye. He introduces himself by saying, "My name is XL, otherwise the One Eye." He jokes, "I am XL, representing everyone who has half a face." They laugh, but I wonder why.

The rain has soaked my left arm by the time I think to roll up the window. My hands are wet and cold. I sit in the car after the last CD finishes, then turn on the headlights, circle the driveway, and pull onto the road.

I catch myself looking over at the empty seat next to me. What would he tell me about those CDs if he were sitting here now? I want

him to feel he had succeeded. He performed at the Fillmore and toured
with Cypress Hill and Linkin Park. He had a regular place on one of
LA's most popular radio stations. He was close to fame, but he was not
famous. He made little money and had to sell his house. He moved in
with Mom in the desert, commuting three hours to get to school at Cal
State Northridge. I want him to not care about the money, to know how
far he had come, to believe in himself like he always believed in me.

What did he see driving this dirt road between clumps of creosote
and sage? The road Jack flew down with him perched on top of that
truck. The road we walked together to climb the sleeping dragon. Where
was it taking him, this old clay track? Where is it taking me now?

A BUSINESS FRIEND, another rapper, has a fish tank full of piranhas. For
entertainment, he feeds live rabbits to the ravenous fish. My brother is
visiting with a bunch of industry guys, mostly rappers or music produc-
ers, people he needs to impress. It's time to feed the piranhas, and a thrill
runs through the group. Bloodlust. The men form a circle, as if at a dog
fight. The rabbit is quick and escapes the hands of death. It's a small
black rabbit, and my brother feels for it as it darts between the legs of
the laughing men, as it cowers in a corner trying to remain unseen, as
it's picked up and carried toward the tank of hungry fish. Piranhas eat
their victims in hundreds of tiny bites. My brother knows what death
will mean for that rabbit, and he decides to speak up in its defense. "He's
escaped too many times to die," he'll say and offer to take the rabbit
home with him. It'll live in the laundry room. He'll feed it lettuce and
stroke its black fur. But he's ashamed to speak up in front of the crowd,
and before he can overcome his shame, the rabbit is in the water.

IN 2002, he landed a small role on *The Osbournes*, a reality TV show
that followed the family of Ozzy Osbourne, the English heavy-metal
star known for biting the head off a bat (he thought it was fake) and two
doves (he was drunk at the time). As the show surged in popularity, the
two Osbourne teenagers, Jack and Kelly, became almost as notorious as
their father. My brother was hired to help with the kids. He described
his role as a cross between a bodyguard and an older brother.

In the same box with those *Mass Distortion* CDs, I find a DVD labeled "*Osbournes*, Viva Ozz Vegas, featuring Peter Slate." I take it back to LA and watch it at the hotel near the airport while Emily bathes the kids. I expect a big role, not just because of the label but also because I remember him talking about that episode. The family had traveled to Vegas to celebrate Kelly's eighteenth birthday. My brother in Vegas with the Osbournes: this sounds, at the very least, intriguing.

As the opening credits roll, I can feel my heart beating, and my mouth runs dry. This is a rare chance to see my brother living his dream. There he is, sitting in the hotel room, watching TV and playing videogames. There he is, in the hallway as one of the Osbourne kids throws a fit. I want to root for him, but it saddens me to watch my brother trying to be liked by these spoiled teenagers. He is an extra—nothing more— an extra in a carnival of emptiness. Is that how he would see it? Or am I projecting my own prudish tastes? I know he had fun living alongside such wealth and fame. Still, I find it hard to watch him on that couch, holding an Xbox handset as if that were all he ever wanted.

The image that stays with me: my brother at the back of a bus crowded with Osbourne groupies. There he is, a Black man with a patch, sitting up, alert, as if he is on an airport shuttle and does not want to miss his stop. I'm saddened by the sheer number of people on that bus, all straining for their fifteen minutes of fame. The camera pans the crowd before returning to the front of the bus, where one of the kids is causing trouble. Would anyone have noticed my brother? It does not matter. To be noticed is easy. A towering Black man with a patch is always noticed. If he were famous, he would no longer be the big Black guy with the patch. He would be Peter Slate or XL. He would be himself, and everyone would know him. The last I see of my brother on that bus, he is turning from the camera to look out the window. I have never seen him look so alone. I want to sit by him, tell him I love him, ask him what he sees outside that window. I pause the video and stare at the screen, a grainy image of a Black man sitting alone on a crowded bus, when my three-year-old son wanders into the room. He is naked, wrapped in a towel, holding a red lollipop in his left hand. He places his treasure on my knee as if it were a plate and pulls himself up onto the couch.

"Who's that, Papa?"

"Your Uncle Peter."

"My name is Peter."

"That's right, your middle name. Just like your uncle."

He retrieves the lollipop from my knee, leaving a sticky trail across the hairs of my leg. We stare at the TV together, then I turn to him and study his face aglow with the light of the screen. He has no idea what he has lost.

ON HIS TWENTY-NINTH BIRTHDAY, my brother performs at the Hard Rock Café in Las Vegas. His group, Supreme Kourt, opens for Cypress Hill. Mom and I arrive early and wait for him in the lobby: neon lights, black marble, a wall of mirrors. He comes around a corner and hugs us both, pulling us into the cool softness of his leather jacket. If anyone is watching, it must seem a surprising reunion: two White tourists embraced by a giant Black man wearing cornrows and an eye patch. He is excited and nervous, like a kid before the prom. As he walks us toward the venue, he keeps spinning around to tell us about the celebrities who are expected at the show. I worry that he will career into a slot machine or a pedestrian, but he is a master at navigating such crowded spaces, even with only one eye. He's had years of practice. Nine years from the flash of that bottle to the Hard Rock Café. Does this feel like redemption? Some kind of payment for all he has lost?

At the door to the music hall, he holds up a badge he is wearing around his neck and gestures for us to follow him. Inside, we skirt the stage, pass through another security checkpoint, and go down a long corridor to a large, well-appointed dressing room. The aroma of pot hits us in the hallway, and I expect the room to be packed like a party. Instead, there are just a few guys sitting on couches. I recognize B-Real immediately. My brother greets everyone and makes introductions. He seems nervous, and I realize that I'm anxious too. When he introduces mom to B-Real, I think about making a joke: something about Mom's love for weed, something silly to break the ice. Then, B-Real gives our mother a big hug, and I relax. "Mama Slate," he rasps, "what a pleasure to finally meet you." I look at my brother's face, hoping to see some kind of satisfaction, but I'm on the side with the patch and have no idea what he's feeling.

I know that being on stage at the Hard Rock Café isn't enough for him. Mom and I have to be here. By inviting us to the show, he strives to be himself, his full self, to prove to the world that XL is Peter Slate is Uderulu Osakwe. He wants to achieve his dreams while remaining true to himself. But he has so many dreams. He is promoting Joker and selling *Mass Distortion*. He is writing screenplays and a mystery novel and working on his stand-up routine. He is taking algebra and preparing for the LSAT. He is living ten lives, as if he knows how short his time will be.

The next morning, we're waiting outside the hotel for the valet to bring his Expedition when a 6'10" Black WWF wrestler arrives on a motorcycle. He's wearing an American flag cape and aviator glasses. As soon as he sees us, he strides up to my brother, grabs him in a big hug, and starts laughing. As we climb into the SUV, my brother explains that the wrestler is a friend who is trying to get him to enter the ring. XL the 1I as a wrestler? Why not, I think, and smile at my brother.

Castor and Pollux

HE EXITS THE FREEWAY just after sunrise, sleepy or hungry or needing to pee. He's driving too fast. The curve is sharper than he expects. His SUV spins out of control, five thousand pounds of steel and glass swinging in a wild circle. He overcompensates, pulls hard right, and swerves back across the off-ramp toward the desert beyond. On July 3 or July 5, his truck would have surfed through the sand, pulled down by its own weight until all its momentum had been stilled. He would have lived. But on July 4, 2003, a tractor trailer sits quietly on the side of the off-ramp at Exit 1 on I-10 eastbound, near Parker, Arizona. The driver is asleep in the cab. If my brother had both eyes, he might have seen the trailer. But without his right eye? By the time the paramedics arrive, he is dead.

The curve of the off-ramp, the glint of the cage on the truck, the bright lights of the gas station against the dark hills. What did he see? The police report tells me that his Expedition "received extensive damage to the entire vehicle with the greatest amount occurring to the entire left side and roof." The driver's side. "There was secondary induced damage to the interior and remaining glass. The force of the impact ripped the roof away from the A and B pillars and forced it in an upward direction. This exposed the entire left side of the interior." Exposed my brother. To the air. To the sky. To flying shards of glass and metal.

The night before, an old friend's wedding. Most of his friends have settled down, and my brother has reached the age when attending a wedding by yourself is painful. Still, he has fun. One photo shows him preparing for the garter toss, his right arm outstretched in the Heisman Trophy pose. Another has him dancing in a circle, his arms around two friends, everyone smiling. I can smell his sweat as he kicks his legs. I can feel his heart beating in his chest, his breath fast and clipped, as he dances and sings.

He leaves the wedding just after midnight. By 2:00 A.M., he's on the road, heading toward his girlfriend in Dallas. Fourteen hundred miles. Twenty hours. No sleep. The idea of such a journey is, as everyone will tell us, "just like him." Spontaneous. Impulsive. Reckless.

Mom is visiting me in Mountain View. I'm in the shower when the phone rings. I don't hear the phone. I hear Mom screaming. My first thought: someone has broken into the apartment. I rush out of the bathroom naked, holding a towel as if it were some kind of weapon. I see her collapsed on the floor, weeping and pointing to the phone.

My strongest memory after the sharp, unyielding cries of our mother is the simple, irrefutable logic that the police officer uses to defeat my denial. *Could this be a mistake? How do you know my brother is dead?* He responds with a question: "Is there any reason to believe someone else would be driving your brother's car with his wallet and phone?"

The wallet undoes my denial. Why would someone else have his wallet? The logic is oppressive, but also reassuring. In the cool, emotionless tone of the officer, I see a way forward. Things need to be done. There are people to tell, arrangements to be made, a broken woman on the floor of my bedroom, wailing and gasping for air. There will be time later to ask why and to feel. Things need to be done. I hold my mother as she cries.

Our mother.

I HANG UP THE PHONE, gather Mom in my arms, and whisper in her ear, "OK, OK, OK." Nothing is OK, but that's what comes out of my lips until she yells, bitter with anger, "No, nothing is OK. Nothing is OK." She's right, but I can't remain silent while she sobs in my arms. I need to say something, if only for myself. So, I switch to a new mantra: "I'm here, I'm here." It's an effort to comfort her and to give her a reason to live. "I'm here, I'm here." You can't go with him. Not yet.

She wanted to die. I knew only a few things in those days, and one was this: She was alive because of me. Not that I did anything or said anything to keep her from killing herself—my presence was enough. She knew that she would hurt me if she took her own life. She knew that I would be even more alone.

I gave her life, and she gave me purpose. She needed to be held, to be heard, to be fed. I made peanut butter banana smoothies, scrambled eggs with extra black pepper, rye toast with strawberry jam.

I had just rented a one-bedroom apartment. I don't remember ever considering whether Mom should move in. There was no other option. The apartment had a balcony that overlooked a bottlebrush plant, its red flowers alive with hummingbirds. One morning, while I prepared a breakfast smoothie, she called to me from the porch. I expected the worst, another round of guilt-infused anger. She would become furious over something insignificant—a commercial on TV or a milk carton that wouldn't open—then all her anger would flood back into her own heart, the guilt of the grieving parent returning like water to the sea. I heard that guilt in her voice as she called me to the balcony.

I stepped outside and found her pointing at a tiny brown bird perched on the edge of the balcony. She and the bird were both completely still. I brought her a slice of whole-wheat bread, the kind with seeds baked into the crust, and she broke off a tiny piece and held it in her outstretched hand.

HER FIRST TRIP outside the apartment is to the market. It's been more than a month since we returned from Arizona, but she is still deep in shock and grief. The supermarket is a three-minute drive, but I worry for her as if she were my child. She manages the drive, the parking, the shopping. Unloading the cart at the checkout counter, she finds a pint of coffee ice cream, his favorite. It was not on her list. She had grabbed it instinctively, a small treat for her child. She watches the ice cream container sweat in her hands. She knows that she needs to finish unloading the cart, but her hands are shaking, her glasses have fogged, and she cannot see. She begins to sob. The checkout clerk notices that she is crying. He is a large man with a metal stud in each eyebrow and large wooden hoops in the lobes of his ears. He moves silently from behind the counter, rounds the half-packed grocery bags, and holds her in his arms.

All of this she tells me later that night, as we eat grilled-cheese sandwiches on the balcony. I find it hard to eat, imagining my mother weeping, clutching that melted ice cream. She finishes her story, and we sit silently, the taste of fried butter on my tongue.

"He was blue when he was born."

"What?"

"He was blue, your brother. They thought he wasn't getting enough air."

I've heard the story before, but it's different now: heavier and more terrifying. Yet she smiles as she takes a piece of crust from her sandwich and places it carefully on the railing for the birds. It's the first time I've seen her smile since the accident.

"They tried to take him away, the nurses. The doctor said, 'Give that baby to his mama.'"

Years later, I would come upon Saint Augustine's response to losing a dear friend: "At this grief my heart was utterly darkened; and whatever I beheld was death." *Whatever I beheld was death.* Yet there is that checkout clerk, whose name I will never know, whose kindness reminds me of my brother—always looking to help a stranger, always there for our mom.

A FEW YEARS BEFORE THE ACCIDENT, Mom's thirtieth high school reunion. She does not want to go. Such things are difficult for her, a shy single woman. She does not want to be judged or pitied. He offers to drive her, to wait outside in case she wants to leave early. She trusts him, and that trust gives her confidence. Still, she feels nauseated as they drive toward the old gymnasium and is tempted to ask him to turn around and head home. He notices her anxiety, reaches out, and holds her hand. When they arrive, he surprises her by offering to come in. They walk in together, proud mother and loving son. He talks with everyone, asks good questions, listens politely, makes people laugh. When the music starts, he asks her to dance.

My brother and our mom at her high school reunion. (Author's collection.)

That's when the picture is taken. Neither of them seems to notice the camera. They are holding hands and dancing. She is looking up at him, beaming. He is wearing a black leather jacket. She is wearing a blue velvet top, her only fancy shirt. They are alone in the shot, surrounded by balloons, blue and purple.

He had decided to name his daughter Elizabeth. Mom's middle name. If he had a daughter.

SHE KEEPS HIS ASHES in a black metal box inside a purple velvet bag. The ashes are the heart of the *lugar santo*, the shrine she created for him, the shrine that becomes the physical embodiment of her grief. Four months after the accident, she begins a journal to him:

Oh Peter it has been almost four months and I still want to die. I cry and I don't know how much my tears are for your loss and how much for mine.

The next day, she writes again:

I'm sorry Peter I need you close Please stay with me. No don't if you need or want to move on then do—but I need you I love you I miss you I can't see the page through my tears.

And then again:

Last night Nico placed/poured the ashes into the opening I was drawn to. Then he placed his forehead against the statue and spoke quietly (maybe the other way around) it was beautiful. I touched Your brother asked for a group hug and I melted We won't ever again I miss your heart beat and your arms and being smothered in your hugs never never again

And again:

I asked Nico how he was tonight and he said "I don't know . . ." I am worried Help him please Pete I miss

And again:

How can you be gone

I FIND MOM'S JOURNAL in a box of things related to his death. Mostly legal forms. Probate, they call it, from the Latin *probare*, to test or to prove.

I hold the journal in my hands, its soft green cover still familiar after all these years. It's July 4, 2014, the eleven-year anniversary of his death, and I'm taking stock of our loss. I hesitate to read the journal without Mom's permission, and so I walk down to her room (she lives with me, my wife, my children). I find her staring at the *lugar santo*, candles burning into pools of melted wax.

Near the center of the shrine, a photo: my brother and me, arm in arm on our old couch. We're both beaming. Had we been wrestling for the channel changer? Or singing "Minnie the Moocher"? I close my eyes and try to remember his voice, the way it made me feel safe and free. I open my eyes and watch the candles burn.

A FEW MONTHS AFTER THE ACCIDENT, Mom and I drive to his old house in LA. As we pull into the driveway, I ask what we should tell the people who live here now.

"Tell them your brother used to live here. That's all. They don't need to know more."

"Should I say he's dead?"

"People are afraid of death, sweetheart."

I climb out of the car and freeze. Yellow safety tape crosses the front door. It looks like a crime scene, but it's just that the house is under construction. I knock on the door, ring the bell, then try the knob. The door swings open.

"Hello!" I yell. "Hello?"

I shouldn't go in; it's trespassing. I peer through the open door, my gaze traveling familiar white walls. The polished wood floor glints in the afternoon light. It was in this room that my brother helped me find my father, that he lit candles and played *Sketches of Spain*. Nothing but silence now. I look back at Mom, then duck under the yellow tape and into what was his dining room.

All of his furniture is gone—the giant white couch, the tea candles he placed across the mantle, the kitchen table where we had breakfast with those girls he met in the strip club. I run my hand over the smooth tile countertop and stare into the living room. The chimney is gone, a giant hole in its place. I walk softly across the room. Like a ghost, I think to myself, and step out onto the back deck. His lounge chairs are still here, the chairs we sat in as he told me to be real with women, to treat them as people—the chairs we sat in ten years later when he told me that he'd been molested.

What am I doing here? I look back through the living room, through the open front door. I can see Mom still waiting in the car. I watch her and a memory returns.

It's the night of the attack. She's sitting behind the wheel of her little white Honda, revving the engine as if the car might die, waiting for me to lock the backdoor so that we can leave for the hospital. It's just before dawn, but the moon still hangs in the sky. I'm hurrying to the car and almost drop the keys as I stuff them into my coat pocket while dancing down the stairs of the porch and into the driveway. Just as I clear the stairs and look up to unlatch the gate, I see her face frozen in the moonlight. She is wounded, blanched by the light, but there is strength in her face. She will get us to the hospital.

IT'S ONE THING to rescue your wounded child—something else to outlive him. I worry that she will kill herself—not out of grief or despair but out of guilt. She blames herself. She awoke early that morning, July 4, 2003. She thought about calling him. It was not uncommon for him to call her in the middle of the night. They were both night owls, and she would always choose a conversation with him over sleep. It was rare for her to call him. She worried that she would be interrupting or that he would be asleep. She had many good reasons to not call her adult son at 2:00 A.M. on the night of July 4. As she sees it, however, she should have known that he was in danger. She should have called. That's what parents do when they lose children: no matter the circumstances, they blame themselves.

She also blamed the state of Arizona. There was nothing illegal about where the truck had parked. There should have been. It should have been illegal for a truck to park on the side of an off-ramp. She never blamed the driver, and neither did I. The only time the driver was mentioned was when we explained to other people that *no one else was hurt*. That was one reason to be grateful. My brother had not killed anyone—other than himself.

A FEW WEEKS BEFORE, the three of us had a long, painful argument about his drinking. Mom and I challenged him to become sober again.

He was furious. He looked at us with scorn and yelled, "You don't know how many dangerous things I've done, how many times I've almost died." He did not need to list the details. We knew enough to form our own catalogs of recklessness: drugs, guns, driving drunk, driving tired, driving too fast. He wanted us to know that he had taken these risks, as if to prove that he was too far gone for us to save.

A FEW YEARS AGO, a giant sign fell from a London building and crushed a pedestrian who happened to be, in those terribly banal words, *in the wrong place at the wrong time*. The day my brother died, a Shia mosque in Quetta, Pakistan, was invaded by religious extremists who killed thirty-two people as they prayed. I cannot make sense of such suffering, but there is one distinction I find helpful: some suffering can be prevented. For years, I put his death in the category of "terrible things that could not be avoided." But what if he had both eyes?

I STARE AT A PHOTO of him and his girlfriend on a busy street somewhere in Europe. His cap is pulled down over one of his eyes. The other eye seems tired and unfocused until I realize that it's his fake eye. Strange, that he would pull the cap over his seeing eye. A bright light shines toward me from behind him, probably the evening sun. It looks as if the heavens are opening behind him, as if he has turned his back on the bright unknown, perhaps the future, perhaps the past.

I DON'T REMEMBER whom I called first. "My brother died in a car accident last night in Arizona." "My brother died last night in a car accident in Arizona." My brother died. In a car accident. In Arizona. Last night. The details mattered. Otherwise, they would ask for them, and the call would go on longer.

His friends were the first ones to visit the scene of the accident. I felt oddly upset that they had arrived before us, jealous that they had searched for what remained of his things, of him.

They found the eye. Strange, that such a small thing would be thrown from the car but not blown away by the wind. Strange, that it would be seen among the wreckage. It was its color that made it visible. A tiny shard of green, it stood out against the slick black pavement. It never was a part of him.

I WALK OUR MOTHER into the chapel, a long rectangular room without windows. The ceiling is low. The casket sits on a raised platform at the far end of the room. We walk down the aisle, arm in arm, as if I am the father of the bride. He is the groom. His face is locked in a grimace, like Han Solo frozen in Carbonite. She touches his hands, his face, his hair. Neither of us cries. Not now. Not here. Neither do we speak. I think that I might cry, but it's more of an idea than a feeling. My only feeling is emptiness and the weight of my mother's hand clinging to my arm.

HE WAS SUPPOSED to do the radio show on July 5. Instead, the show became a memorial—not to Peter Slate but to XL. Jeff Garcia, the guest DJ, called him "the nicest guy on the planet" with "the best heart." DJ Homicide called in to remember his "homie." C-Minus grieved on air: "I lost a brother." Everyone called him part of the family, but it was his high school friends who were distraught. They wept and struggled for words to describe their pain.

I find a recording of the show buried beneath the probate papers. The CD is labeled "Peter Slate Memorial." I assume that it's a recording of the memorial service and pop it into Mom's little yellow boombox, expecting to hear a muffled version of "Amazing Grace." Instead, the familiar intro to *Mass Distortion* rolls across my living room, heavy on the bass, while Abstract Rude raps about each DJ. I close my eyes and remember my brother rushing onto the stage at the Fillmore, his body bouncing like a drum.

His death is announced, and it's like I'm hearing the news for the first time. Shock, then emptiness. One of my brother's old high school friends calls in. As she weeps, I feel that I should cry too. It's been more than a decade now since he died, and I have wanted to cry so many times. How many hours have I held Mom as she shakes and sobs? Still, I feel painfully empty as I listen to caller after caller grieve this man I loved like no other.

Nobody knows how to talk about death. They ramble through a litany of platitudes: "He's in a better place." "He would want us to celebrate his life." "He was such a great guy." "I don't know what to say." Many callers refer to his size. He was "the gentle giant," "an oak tree." Or they celebrate him with vague praise: he was "a living angel," "a powerful being," "one of the greatest dudes that ever walked the face of the earth." One of the few times someone says something that actually reminds me of my brother comes toward the end. An old music business colleague, not someone I expect to say something interesting about my brother, offers this: "You couldn't tell him that something was not possible. He was the person who convinced me that I was going to take over the world." Yes, that is my brother.

They play music in his honor: "They Reminisce over You," by Pete Rock and C. L. Smooth. "If Heaven Was a Mile Away" by NAS. Then Cypress Hill's "Illusions." Cypress Hill is on tour in Europe. They send condolences. Later, B-Real surprises us by attending the memorial. We host two: one for biological family and the other for everyone else. The split audience is necessary to allow our mother a space for her grief. It's impossible for her to grieve in the presence of her mother. And what if that relative shows up, the one who hurt my brother in ways his death could never heal?

I could still talk to her. I could demand an apology, an admission of guilt. Or I could tell her the truth: that I don't feel angry toward her, even if I think that I should. It's been fifteen years now since he died and at least thirty since she molested him. Time has sapped my anger. Or maybe it's that my brother's memories were never clear. Whatever happened remains an abstraction, and it's hard to be angry about an abstraction.

I should be angry. I think of the men who took his eye; I know what they did, even if their motives remain unclear. Why am I not angry at them? I go about my life as if his body had never been brutalized, as if his ashes were not sitting in Mom's *lugar santo*, protected by nothing but that metal box, that purple velvet sack covered with candlewax.

IT'S STRANGE HOW LITTLE I remember of the family memorial: the heavy yellow light that squeezed through the stained-glass windows of the chapel, the dark maroon carpet that sucked at my feet like quicksand, the drone of the organ as I stood to sing. Nothing came from my lips. I mouthed the words to "Amazing Grace," a song I've always loved. Nothing but a stone in my gut.

We held the big memorial, the one for his friends, in the auditorium of my elementary school. I associated that room with joy and light: dancing to "Greensleeves," reciting poems while dressed in a toga, playing "Scarborough Fair" on the recorder. The school's leaders offered us the space on short notice. So, I returned to the glory land of my childhood to eulogize my brother.

The room was packed when I saw him enter: B-Real, hip-hop legend and my brother's last mentor. He was wearing a black Joker sweatshirt and matching cap. I stared at him from the podium as the crowd began to settle and recalled watching him perform at the Fillmore, his fist pumping the air, his trademark voice, that crazy high-pitched twang, soaring above the beat. We still had a few minutes before the program was to start, so I crossed the room to thank him for coming. I had spoken to him backstage at the Fillmore and several times since, but I still found surprising the absence of his stage voice when he asked:

"How you holdin' up?" His voice was raspy but gentle.

"I don't know," I responded. "One day at a time, I guess."

I forced a smile. His face remained serious, and there was kindness in his eyes when he told me, "Your brother loved you very much. He was always talking about you." Everyone had told me that, but it felt different hearing it from B-Real. This man was my brother's last hero. I thanked him, crossed back through the crowd, and stepped up to the stage to do the unthinkable—talk about my brother in the past tense.

LISTENING TO THE RADIO MEMORIAL, I am forced to recognize that my brother's death happened in time, on a particular day and at a particular place. It was the convergence of countless events, any one of which might have saved him. How quickly I made sense of his death, came to see it as inevitable. What if the truck hadn't been there? What if he had slept an extra hour? What if nine years earlier he had chosen not to go to that club in Santa Monica, or had gone and not danced with that girl, or had danced with her but decided not to drink, or had placed his beer on a different table, or had walked away from the guy who started the argument that ended with that bottle crashing against his eye? I think again about that day we shot hoops in the desert, about all those times we talked in the car, his patch a blank wall between us. I think about Steven and his friend, the one whose hand brought the bottle down on my brother's face, and I think about that car carrier, a mountain of cold steel, parked like a dinosaur on the right side of the road, his blindside.

The death certificate comes in the mail, a slim white envelope, too light for all it carries. Asked for his occupation at the funeral home, Mom answered "writer." The certificate says "waiter." It's almost funny. He had worked as a waiter for so many years. It's as if death is laughing at his ambitions, mocking our efforts to recognize his achievements. Mom is furious. She spends months getting a new death certificate. For what? No matter what that paper says, my brother's life will resist the dichotomy between success and failure. Sure, you can frame it as a litany of achievements. Here is a list prepared by one of his friends:

He toured with Limp Bizkit and Cypress Hill. He acted as bodyguard to the Osbournes. He was a partner in a clothing line. He helped spark a musical movement on a local radio station by mixing rap and hard rock styles and getting them to dedicate a weekly show to it. He funded a non-profit organization and had plans for others. He cranked out television and movie scripts like Stephen King cranked out horror novels. He wrote poetry and song lyrics. He dabbled in performing, rap, ballads, whatever he could get his hands on. In all this, Peter still made time for his friends.

I know that this list is meant to pay tribute, but I cannot stomach celebrations of my brother's success. His death is not an opportunity to pay tribute. His death is his death. Yet I keep writing. His loss haunts me, condemns me for even trying to write these words. But I can't stop writing. I miss him too much to dwell alone with my grief. I need these words, if not to bring him back, at least to give voice to all that we lost, all that he lost.

My brother is dead. I will never again see his smile, feel his hands on my shoulders. I will never again ask him a question about my life and watch him lean in toward me, his face focused yet peaceful, and know that whatever he says is going to surprise me and be exactly what I need to hear. I will never again come down the stairs and find him lounging on the couch, as if all is right with the world, and lay my body by his side, the warm light from the window playing across our legs, and hear his quiet breathing, and feel the warmth of his chest, and lie there for a long time, both of us awake and not saying anything, not needing to say anything, and knowing in every part of my body that I am loved.

TWO WEEKS AFTER THE ACCIDENT, Mom and I are still sorting through my brother's things. I find some notes he made about racial terminology during his stand-up comedy phase. I don't find them funny, but I treasure them for what they reveal about his take on the silliness of our "post-racial" politics:

> African Americans made a lot of advances in the last thirty years. We've gone from Negro to Colored to Afro-American to African American. See Negro sounded too much like n****r. So that wasn't gonna work. And colored didn't work cause all y'all colored. Now we was cool with Afro American till Barry Manilow had an afro too. So now we got African American. Which confuses the shit out of me cause they don't have just one type of African. They got South African, North African, West African, and East African, and plus all types of others. Which means you can't just be an African American either you should be a West African North American or a North African South American or an East African West American. Now what kinda shit is that. Fuck it! I just wanna be black!

Would anyone have laughed at these jokes? They would have no idea what those words meant for him: "Fuck it! I just wanna be black!" He wanted to be Black without having to stop being himself. He wanted a Blackness that included rather than excluded.

He was not alone in seeking such an inclusive Blackness. In the book he wrote about his father, Barack Obama echoes the famous description of "double-consciousness" offered by W. E. B. Du Bois in *The*

Souls of Black Folk. When strangers first discover his mixed ancestry, Obama writes, "They no longer know who I am. Privately, they guess at my troubled heart, I suppose—the mixed blood, the divided soul, the ghostly image of the tragic mulatto trapped between two worlds." Almost one hundred years earlier, Du Bois had written, "One ever feels his twoness—an American, a Negro; two souls, two thoughts, two unreconciled strivings; two warring ideals in one dark body, whose dogged strength alone keeps it from being torn asunder." The shared image of a soul divided, and the obvious resonance of Du Bois in Obama's prose, might obscure the very different tensions described by Du Bois and Obama. While Du Bois was torn between being Black and being American, Obama is pulled between being Black and being White.

My brother struggled with both forms of double-consciousness. Black, White, African, and American—he was uncomfortable with all these labels. Black came closest to being right. I wonder whether he would have gone the Obama route—first, claim his Blackness, and then find in the Black community a way to be American.

A young man comes from Africa to America for an education. He plans to return home after a few years. He meets a young White woman at the university, and they fall in love. They have a child who embodies the possibility of a new world, a new hope for the future. This is Obama's story, of course, but also my brother's story. Like Obama, my brother carried in his body the potential for a world beyond racism. It was a heavy burden: the mixed legacy, the foreign name, the absent father.

I wonder what my brother would have made of Obama's speech at the Democratic National Convention in 2004, the speech that climaxed with a triumphant defense of our inherent unity: "There is not a Black America and a White America and Latino America and Asian America. There is the United States of America." Of course there is a Black America and a White America. Just look at our cities, segregated and unequal. I expect that my brother would have excused Obama's optimism. He always admired a winner, and here was a man who was, like my brother, accustomed to being the Black man who knew how to talk to White people. For Obama, that ability to speak across racial borders helped win elections. For my brother, it wasn't enough—to save his eye or his life.

I NEED TO TALK WITH STEVEN—not to demand an apology, not to know his side of the story. I need to tell him what I wish he had known that night. That Peter Slate was a good man. That he was loved, is loved.

I go back to Facebook to search for Steven. I'm sitting on my front porch in my camping chair, waiting for Emily to come home. I like to greet her outside, but it's a cold October day, and my fingers have started to ache. I will have to go in soon. Our children are asleep, and I have two baby monitors perched in the cupholder of the chair. I listen to the hum of the white-noise machines that help my babies sleep and scroll through all the men who share the name on the police report. Could he be one of them? One is from Clovis, New Mexico. Another from Fort Lauderdale, Florida. A third from Ann Arbor, Michigan. None are from LA, where I know that Steven went to high school. One of these men could have grown up somewhere else and moved to LA as a kid. Facebook doesn't tell me where these Stevens went to high school. At first, the single one looks suspicious. The others all have kids. I find myself ruling out the guy who posts lots of cute family photos, as if it were impossible for a man to start a fight with a stranger and then turn out to be a good dad twenty years later.

My son cries out in his sleep, then quiets. A bad dream, perhaps.

That witness, the woman who lied for Steven, never responded to my friend request. I don't blame her. Who am I to her? I look through her posts and find a chain of condolences. Her brother has died. I don't know how. I don't even know his name.

I want to feel for her, but the more I scroll through her page, the more I can't imagine talking to this woman whose lies protected the men who attacked my brother. I don't hate her, but there is something about her that repels me, almost frightens me. Her frozen smile. Her unfocused eyes. Something turns me away. Maybe I'm afraid that I will hate her, or that she will hate me. My shoulders tighten every time I open Facebook and only relax when I confirm that she and I are still not friends.

I DREAM OF MY BROTHER. We're sitting back to back in a room filled with windows but without a floor. My feet slide against bare earth covered with moss. I can feel the cold, wet ground beneath my toes. He's telling me about his handwriting, how his cursive became bad because he didn't want anyone to understand what he was writing. I can't see his face, but I can feel his back against mine, strong and warm. I wake up listening for his voice.

I AM SITTING ON FLAGSTAFF HILL, on the quiet edge of campus, waiting to teach twenty undergrads about the civil rights movement. It's unusually warm for late September, and the air smells of grass browning in the sun. I want my students to see what the movement achieved and what remains to be done. I will ask them to contrast the deaths of Emmett Till and Trayvon Martin, and I'm tempted to include my brother's as well. Three young Black men who died too young.

I hesitate to link my brother to Till and Martin. There's a reason my brother's death inspired no protests. The chain of blame is too long and thin to say that he died because of racism. I can tell my students about the love he shared with me, a Black man who raised his White little brother. But even if they could relive it all with me, know him as I know him, they would still be left with the same questions I have. What role did race play the night my brother lost his eye? What role did race play in his death? I look out on the waving grass. Soon, it will all be covered in snow. A small brown bird lands in front of me and looks up at the sky.

I'M GIVING A LECTURE about the murder of Srinivas Kuchibhotla, an engineer from India who was gunned down in a bar in Kansas in February 2017. The man who killed him was an anti-immigrant zealot who thought that he was killing a Muslim. My audience is a group of high school students gathered for a Model United Nations conference. I want them to see that racism and xenophobia are surging throughout the world, but I don't want them to feel powerless. I look over their earnest faces to an empty chair in the back row. I think of my brother, what he might say. Later, I wonder whether anyone noticed that I ended the lecture talking to that empty chair.

I've been teaching history for a decade. I hated history in high school and failed to take a single history class in college. Losing my brother left me thinking differently about the past. The dead became more than mere names. A few months after my brother died, I applied for Ph.D. programs in history.

Most of the courses I teach concern the struggle against racism. I don't talk about my brother very much, but he comes up whenever a student asks why a blond White guy decided to study race. I point out that White people have a responsibility to study race and racism, to acknowledge the privileges of Whiteness, and to fight against White supremacy in all its forms. Then, I take a deep breath and talk about my brother. I'm never sure whether I should. I don't want my students to think that every White guy who studies race has to have a Black brother. I don't want them to think that it was my brother's Blackness—and not my Whiteness—that drives me to study racism.

On weekends, I teach in a program where teenagers write and record their own hip-hop music. I don't know anything about contemporary hip-hop. I talk with the kids about the larger social and political questions they are facing in their lives and try to leave them with some of the lessons my brother gave me—that their lives matter, that their dreams matter. I wish that my brother were standing before them. Not just because he was a hip-hop artist, not just because he was a Black man, but because he was a genius at believing in people and helping them believe in themselves. He did it for me.

WE'RE HEADING TO THE FOREST, my brother and I, with three of his friends. It's the spring of 1990. I'm ten. He's seventeen. Mark is driving, and we're in the back with Ophir. As the road snakes up a steep curve, my stomach tightens and begins to churn. I worry I'm going to vomit. I lean forward to peek out the window, hoping to see something that will take my mind off the prospect of spewing my breakfast on the white leather seats of the car. The road clings precariously to the side of a mountain, and we are only a few feet—inches, it seems—from a steep cliff. Now, I feel sick and terrified. I whisper to my brother: *I don't feel good. Are we going too fast?* He puts his hand on my brow and leans down so that he can whisper in my ear:

> You're OK. The road will straighten out soon. I know it feels like
> we're driving fast, but Mark is the best driver I know. Notice

how he speeds up into the curves? That keeps the car balanced and safe. Imagine Magic running a fast break. That is Mark behind the wheel of a car.

As he talks, I imagine Mark winning a NASCAR race, waving at the crowd, his helmet in one hand, the trophy in the other. I am relieved and distracted, and ten minutes later, we are running through a forest, laughing and waving long sticks at the endless sky.

Ten years later, he hits a jackrabbit in the desert. He pulls over, calls Mom, and asks what to do. She tells him that there is nothing he can do. These things happen. He drives home. After five minutes at home, he grabs some iceberg lettuce, a bowl, and a bottle of water and drives back. He finds the wounded creature lying motionless in the road. Using an old cardboard box, he moves the rabbit to the side of the road and leaves the lettuce and a bowl full of water. He walks back to the car, gets in, and waits. Twenty minutes later, he walks back to check on the rabbit. The lettuce is gone, and so is the rabbit.

I have hundreds of these stories arrayed in my memory like evidence at a trial. Yes, he slept overnight in a park to hold a picnic table so that a friend could have it for her son's birthday. Yes, he drove two hours to take a homeless man out to breakfast. Ladies and gentlemen of the jury, see my brother, a good man. Set him free.

HENRY JAMES ON THE DEATH of his older brother William: "His extinction changes the face of life for me—besides the mere missing of his inexhaustible company and personality, originality, the whole unspeakably vivid and beautiful presence of him." I feel it on my wedding day: *the whole unspeakably vivid and beautiful presence of him.* I am standing at the altar, waiting for the music to begin and Emily to walk down the aisle. My eyes find an empty chair. Five rows back on the left, next to Aunt Terri and Uncle Chuma. I stare at that chair and begin to cry. I want to say they are joyful tears, but how can one separate joy from the fact that he is not here to share it? A thought strikes me: maybe I should have left an empty chair next to Mom. No, he would not have wanted his absence to cast a shadow on this day. Plus, he wouldn't have needed a chair. He would have been at my side.

MY FIRST CHILD IS BORN on a rainy day in April. Rushing Emily to the hospital, I feel a surge of purpose. The roads are wet, but I will get us to the hospital safely. I will do whatever needs to be done. Yet when the anesthesiologist arrives to give Emily the epidural, I grow weak and dizzy. I have always struggled with needles but did not expect to have trouble. It isn't me, after all, who's going to receive the shot. I try to talk myself through the dizziness, but it grows rapidly. I feel my legs buckling, my body collapsing onto the hard cool floor. Emily, in the middle of a contraction, has to remain totally still while the needle slides into her spine, and now all the nurses are worried about me. Lying on the floor, I think of my brother, of that time I passed out after seeing his bloodied face in a different hospital some twenty years ago. I see his face, the bandage strapped across what had been his eye, and I climb back to my feet and take hold of Emily's hand. Her contraction has passed, and the needle is in. Emily has braved the hardest part alone. She squeezes my hand.

I'M SITTING IN THE HOSPITAL ROOM, finishing Emily's breakfast. I can't bear to see food wasted. It's a problem, my obsession with finishing meals; I often eat too much. It doesn't help that I've always loved hospital food. The tray with its neat pouches, the small bowl of Jell-O, smooth and untouched. I am devouring the remains of a blueberry muffin when a nurse knocks softly and opens the door. I wipe crumbs from my unshaven face, embarrassed. It's time to complete the birth certificate. I take the forms and place them on the tray. Emily looks at me and grins, our son asleep in her arms. Another landmark in our lives, our son's life—the birth certificate. Kai Peter Kimball Slate. We decided on his name months ago, but it still feels thrilling to ink in the letters. As I finish his first name and start in on Peter, my hand begins to shake. I have to stop writing. I look up and breathe in. It's raining outside. I watch drops of water streak across the window. I breathe out. I look down at the form and my eyes begin to mist. My son will never know his Uncle Peter.

That's when the idea strikes me: to write a book about my brother. As a historian, I make a living telling stories about the past, but I've never written about anyone I know personally. I'm anxious that people might not like what I have to say about them, but I can't tell the story of my brother's life without talking about the loss of his eye and all the other wrongs that shaped his life and death.

I look down at my son's birth certificate form and finish writing in his name. The muffin is dry and sweet, and I stand up to get a glass of water. As I cross the room, I place the form on the bed so Emily can see it—his name. Kai Peter Kimball Slate. Only just born, and already he's carrying the weight of the past.

THE IDEA that they have children bothers me—the men who attacked my brother. It's not that I worry for their children. I have no reason to believe that these men are evil, that the anger they felt toward that Black guy on the dance floor would translate to their own kin. It's that I have kids too. Fatherhood and Whiteness—what else do I share with these men?

MY SON IS THREE NOW and still obsessed with picking berries off our neighbor's bushes. It's his meditation, his rosary. He works each berry off the stem, a bright red prayer bead plump with juice. He squeezes the berry, and the juice runs down his hand, stains his skin pink and purple. Then, he throws the crumpled berry and looks for another. It's beautiful: his face, so calm and purposeful. I want my brother here with me. I want him to know my children. And those men, living their lives, raising their kids: I want them to know all that has been lost.

THERE IS A BIG WHITE ROCKING CHAIR in our living room. We bought it when Emily was pregnant. A lamp sits next to the chair. At night, if you turn on the lamp and sit across from the chair, it looks as if someone were just there and has gone into the kitchen to make a cup of tea. Sometimes, I catch myself staring at that chair, waiting for him to return.

FATE RARELY DEALS EQUALLY WITH BROTHERS. Therein lies the test of their love. Take, for example, Castor and Pollux. Their mother, Leda, was seduced by Zeus disguised as a swan. Zeus fathered at least one of her children, but which boy remains a point of contention. In some accounts, both Castor and Pollux are the sons of Zeus and thus immortal. My favorite version has Castor as the mortal son of Leda's husband and Pollux as the divine son of Zeus. In an ambush, Castor is fatally wounded with a spear. Pollux runs to his dying brother and beseeches his father, Zeus, for help. Zeus offers his son a choice: spend all of his time as a god on Mount Olympus or gift half of his immortality to the dying Castor. A good brother, Pollux gives up his chance to live among the gods. In some accounts, the two brothers split their days between Earth and the land of the dead. My favorite ending has the two brothers dwelling among the stars, together transformed into the constellation Gemini.

WHEN SOMEONE DIES YOUNG, are they always that age? I'm forty now. My brother died at thirty. Strange, that I'm the older man. I try to imagine what he would be doing now, perhaps law or journalism—the two paths we talked about toward the end of his life, as he began to realize that hip-hop might not work out for him. I imagine him arguing a case before the Supreme Court or sitting at one of those big news desks on TV, wearing a sharp suit, his hair cut short, his large hands perched on the table. Then, I stop. It hurts too much. I don't even know whether he would wear the patch.

WE'RE WALKING ON A BEACH near Morro Bay, my brother and I, talking about basketball. I'm a sophomore in high school, and my team is about to play in a nearby tournament. As we talk strategy, he picks up little stones, polished smooth by the waves. He looks at each stone, then tosses it into the sea. I'm about to ask him whether he thinks that I'm too slow to play point guard (I am), when I notice that he hasn't thrown the last stone he picked up. Instead, he slides it into the pocket of his sweatpants. We keep walking, and he keeps picking up stones. Most go into the sea, but he pockets at least two more before I take advantage of a break in the conversation to ask, "What's with the rocks? Are you starting a collection?" He smiles at me, the dark blue water of the Pacific behind him. "Here," he says, pulling three stones out of his pocket. "Take a look." I step forward and take the stones into my hand. One is pale blue in color and round like a marble. The second is larger, darker, and more angular, almost a triangle. The third is green and polished in the shape of a heart. Before I can ask him another question, he explains, "The little one is to remind me of our time here today. The heart-shaped one is for Mom." "And the triangle?" "I don't know about that one," he replies. "It's just too beautiful to let go."

I AM DOWN IN MOM'S BEDROOM, closing her windows at the end of a long summer day. I open them every morning, close them every night. The arthritis makes it hard for her to pull the sash, close the latch. One day, I will struggle with such a task. I will grow old, and my children will care for me. That's how it's supposed to work, one generation passing to the next. If only it were promised to us that a parent would never outlive a child.

She has lit the candles already, and the soft light flickers across the purple bag that contains his ashes. Candle wax drips onto the bag, pools, and hardens into clumps. A ring of old photos surrounds the bag. His laptop, its screen shattered by the impact, sits quietly amid the candles and the pictures, filled with words he wrote and never again will say. My eye catches the glimmer of the candlelight against the cracked screen, and an idea strikes me.

Two weeks earlier, my infant son spilled tea over my laptop. The Apple geniuses told me that the guts of the computer were "fried." There was nothing they could do. Enter Debadeepta Dey, a friend and talented computer scientist, with a soft spot for lost causes. In less than an hour, he rescued the data from the tea-soaked hard drive. Could he do it again?

Now, I am sitting in his office, surrounded by computer stuff—cords, drivers, sockets—I don't even know what to call these things. I stare at the elaborate equations scrawled across the giant whiteboard that occupies an entire wall of the office. Like the computers, these intricate equations give me hope. If anyone can get data from a laptop that was shattered in a car accident ten years ago—it's Dey. Two days later, he calls. He has the data. Do I want it all? Yes, I tell him. I want it all.

IT'S A BRIGHT SPRING DAY, and all the windows are open. I'm sitting at the kitchen table, my laptop open before me, Dey's flash drive in the palm of my hand. It feels too light for all it promises. I plug it in and feel suddenly embarrassed, as if I'm once again peeking in Mom's wicker basket.

I open the folder labeled "Peter Slate" and am overwhelmed. Photos, songs, dozens of Word docs. Where should I begin? I scan the list of docs and know as soon as I see it. *Cordoba.* I click on the file labeled "Cordoba."

SIX MONTHS BEFORE THE ACCIDENT, we take a family trip to Europe. We are in Córdoba, an ancient city built by the Romans and made famous by the Moors. A city of secret gardens and curving cobblestone lanes, Córdoba would be an ideal place for a honeymoon. I wonder whether he will ever marry. His girlfriend was with us in Paris, but she decided to meet a friend in Amsterdam when the rest of us took the train through the mountains to Barcelona and then the overnight bus to Córdoba. I wonder whether he misses her, as we walk these romantic alleyways and stumble upon a monument to love. Four marble pillars hold a tile roof above a stone pedestal. Atop the pedestal, at the heart of the monument, two hands are touching. *El Monumento a los Enamorados*, the Monument to the Lovers, celebrates the passionate affair between one of Spain's most revered poets, Ibn Zaydun, and the daughter of the Caliph of Córdoba, Princess Wallada, herself a powerful writer. Inscribed on the pedestal in Arabic and Spanish, verses from Zaydun and Wallada testify to their love. He asks me to translate these lines:

Tu amor me ha hecho célebre entre la gente.
Por ti se preocupan mi corazón y pensamiento.
Cuando tú te ausentas nadie puede consolarme.
Y cuando llegas todo el mundo está presente.

I do my best:

You have made me famous among the people.
My heart, my mind are always with you.
When you leave, no one can console me.
When you arrive, the whole world is present.

Six months later, he would lie dying beside a highway in Arizona, but here we are in Córdoba, startled by a love poem written a thousand years ago:

Cuando te ausentas nadie puede consolarme.
Y cuando llegas todo el mundo está presente.

He wrote out the inscription on a sheet of lined paper. I have it framed on my bedside table. I know that it was meant for his girlfriend, but I cannot share that piece of our past, of his future:

When you leave, no one can console me.
When you arrive, the whole world is present.

AFTER YEARS OF DRIFTING APART, here we are together, walking the streets of Córdoba, without my books, without his cell phone, crossing the Roman bridge that spans the Guadalquivir River. Ahead of us rises the Calahorra Tower, a massive fortified gate. He talks about a screenplay he wants to write, a story about a West African boy who travels north to find fame and fortune among the Moors.

We begin to climb the tower, still talking about the story he will tell. How old is the boy? Is he a poet or a scientist? What are his dreams? We arrive at the top of the tower, out of breath and distracted, our minds sifting a story whose end has yet to be written—will never be written. The river sweeps across our vision. Beyond, the old city unravels toward the horizon. We stand in silence, and I feel the urge to take his hand, as if we were walking from my elementary school to the bus. I don't want to disturb him, his chain of thought, and am about to duck back into the stairwell when he puts his arm around my shoulder and pulls me in. We stand together staring at a city we will never know.

My brother and me at my college graduation. (Author's collection.)

Leaving the tower, we are tired and hungry and decide to take the bus home. We sit across from each other, face to face. Evening has come, and the lights of the city play across his sweat-stained patch, his jaw, his wild black hair. He was sporting cornrows a few days earlier, but he has undone the braids, and his hair flares behind him, a plume of smoke. He is not young anymore, and neither am I.

As the bus moves through unfamiliar streets, we go deeper into the story about the boy and the Moors and miss our stop. The bus rumbles into anonymous suburbs and empty shopping malls lit by strange fluorescent lights. We are traveling forward in time, from the ancient city of Ibn Zaydun and Princess Wallada to the anonymous concrete of our modern lives. While the bus propels us forward, our conversation takes us back into the world of the Moors and of the story he will tell of those days, a story about a boy who goes north to find a new life.

"He needs a brother," he says. "There must be two."

WE WALK THROUGH THE MOSQUE, the *Mezquita,* they call it in Spanish. When Córdoba fell to Christian forces, the great mosque was left standing, but its center was destroyed and replaced by a towering cathedral. Around it the mosque persists, arch after arch. Wikipedia tells me that there are "856 columns of jasper, onyx, marble, and granite." Strange, that I have to consult Wikipedia to trigger my memories. I cannot ask my brother what he remembers. If I google his name, I get a real estate agent in Maui. He seems to be a windsurfer. I go back to Wikipedia, the images of the mosque, but the colors are all wrong. Someone used a glaring flash, and the magic of the place is lost. I close my eyes. I see him walking two steps ahead of me, his wide shoulders parting the crowds of tourists like the prow of a ship. I look up at the curve of the arches: stone made fluid. I look down. He is still two steps ahead of me, and I cannot see his face. I try to catch up, to put a hand on his shoulder, but there are too many people, and they keep getting in my way. We walk toward the old center of the mosque, where the gold of the cathedral glitters. When I reach him and finally get a hand on his shoulder, I am startled by the warmth of his body. How can he be dead and still so warm? I pull on his shoulder, but before he can turn around, I wonder: will he have both eyes?

I ASK ALL HIS FRIENDS whether he wanted to have a child someday. I know the answer already, but I like to hear them talk about how much he loved children, how he always wanted to be a father. It might seem morbid, but it's another way to feel close to him, now that I'm a father, to know that he wanted this too. One of his friends jokes that my brother probably had a child. "Maybe two or three, the way he was with the ladies." I laugh but hold my breath. A child? A little Ude, Peter, XL, running the streets of some city, causing trouble, making people smile? I believe that my brother is here with me, with my children. Not looking down from a cloud: with us, in us, a part of who we are. But maybe there's a little one walking around somewhere, too, another amazing kid with a father he will never know.

Acknowledgments

When I was in first grade, everyone in my class celebrated Thanksgiving by drawing something that made us grateful. I painted my brother as tall as a tree, his head in the sky, his skin black against the brown tree, the blue sky. I tried to render an airplane next to his outstretched hand, but my effort looks more like a flying squirrel that was sliced in two. Below the unfortunate squirrel, I painted myself, light gray in color, half the size of my brother, looking up toward him in awe and gratitude. There is much that might be said about my choices of color—why I chose black for my brother and not brown, why I chose gray for myself and not beige—but my teacher wrote on the painting the central message I wanted to share, the only message I can imagine offering at the beginning of these acknowledgments: "I'm thankful for my brother."

I'm also thankful for my mother—for our mother—for her love and for her courage and for filling our home with books and music. My brother and I always felt loved. Mom likes to create scrapbooks filled with poetry, and I want to share two lines in her honor. Of the family she brought into being: "A thing of beauty is a joy forever." Of her own, fiercely independent life: "Age cannot wither her, nor custom stale her infinite variety."

I'm thankful for my brother. (Author's collection.)

I'm accustomed to beginning acknowledgments with a longish list of academic colleagues, followed by a more personal tribute to friends and family. Those who read this book in draft form defy such categorical divisions. Everyone here is a friend. Everyone is family. So, it is with deep love that I acknowledge the tremendous generosity and wisdom of Mark Barga, Paul Eiss, Rebecca Rainof Mas, Jennifer Miller, Jonathan Nassim, Michael Pisano, Jana Poirier, Joanne Proulx, Walter Robinson, Judith Schachter, Kim Sousa, Wendy Strothman, and Van Tran. I am grateful for all the ways you each improved this book, and I am grateful for the love and kindness that moved you to such generosity.

Special thanks to Keisha Blain, Jasmin Darznik, and Robin D. G. Kelley for offering such kind and beautiful descriptions of the book and for inspiring me with your own work.

I am deeply grateful to Shaun Vigil, my editor at Temple University Press, who believed in this book—and understood it—in a way that made me feel, from our very first meeting, as if we were old friends.

I want to thank all of my brother's childhood friends who took the time to speak with me while I was writing this book—and who shared their love with my brother and with me. Daneh, Eric, Mark, Mike, and Ophir—I thank you, and I love you.

I also want to thank those friends who came to my brother later in life, especially B-Real, Tony Mark, Kelly LeBrock, Mike Olmos, Alonzo Bodden, Rahn Coleman, Rozzell Sykes, and Priscilla Ann Rios. My brother loved you all.

Several family members shared memories that helped guide this book, and I want to especially thank my Uncle Dan and Aunt Susan and my Aunt Terri and Uncle Chuma. Your love shaped this book, just as it shaped my brother and me. I love you.

My brother was—in the deepest sense of the word—my friend, and I am so grateful that several of my closest friends are truly brothers. Afam, Alex, Jonathan, Mark, Matt, and Van: I love you all.

I also want to thank my family in Pittsburgh, especially Ann and Kimball Mohn, Lauren and Matt Mohn, and Casey and Mat Calland. I am so grateful for your love and support and to be able to raise children in such a loving family.

I struggle to find the words to thank my wife and partner, Emily Mohn-Slate, who read every line of this book multiple times, and who overcame my writerly stubbornness in a valiant effort to eliminate many pages of sappy, lazy, or overwritten prose. At every stage of the process, she believed in this book both as it was and as it could be, just as she has always believed in me and loved me both for who I am and for who I want to be. Emily, I love you and thank God that you are my partner and that we are alive in this world together.

I wrote this book for my brother and for my children—that they might know each other in some way. Kai and Lucia, your Uncle Peter always said the same thing on his answering machine—and it was an actual little box back then, the answering machine, a box that you plugged into a phone that you plugged into the wall. He always said, "Please remember to be kind to yourself." I wish you could have known him, your uncle, the man who more than anyone else shaped who I am and who I want to be. I wish I knew what he would say to me, what he would say to you. Here is what I do know: he would love you as I love you. He loves you as I love you. Please remember to be kind to yourself.

Timeline

FALL 1938	Chukwudi Osakwe is born in Ogidi, Nigeria.
FALL 1947	Karen Slate is born in Hollywood, California.
OCTOBER 1, 1948	*Perez v. Sharp* legalizes interracial marriage in California.
FEBRUARY 1, 1960	Four African American college freshmen sit down at a "Whites only" lunch counter in Greensboro, North Carolina; sit-ins spread nationwide.
SEPTEMBER 1960	Chukwudi begins classes at Lincoln University, a historically Black college in rural Pennsylvania.
AUGUST 1965	The Voting Rights Act becomes law; Watts erupts in violence.
FALL 1966	Karen and Chukwudi meet at UCLA.
JUNE 12, 1967	*Loving v. Virginia* legalizes interracial marriage nationwide.
DECEMBER 1967	*Guess Who's Coming to Dinner* opens in theaters.
APRIL 4, 1968	Martin Luther King Jr. is assassinated.
JUNE 6, 1968	Bobby Kennedy is assassinated.
JULY 3, 1969	Karen and Chukwudi are married.

AUGUST 30, 1972	My brother, Uderulu Peter Houston Carl Osakwe, is born.
MAY 1974	Karen and Chukwudi are divorced.
FALL 1976	Karen meets Bill, my father.
FEBRUARY 21, 1977	Chukwudi's sister, Ola, writes Karen, "You took away the child . . . a black man's child is black and his and can never become a white."
SUMMER 1979	Karen becomes pregnant; Bill leaves.
NOVEMBER 1979	California voters reject busing as a way to integrate public schools.
WINTER 1980	I'm born—Nico Isaac Claude Obierulu Osakwe; my brother cuts the umbilical cord and is the first to hold me.
1981	Uderulu Osakwe legally becomes Peter Slate; he is nine years old.
1984	We move to a Mexican and Salvadoran neighborhood in the Valley.
1987	Mom marries Jack.
1989	Peter joins the boy band Up N' Comin.
FALL 1990	Peter starts college at San Diego State.
NOVEMBER 7, 1991	Magic Johnson announces that he is HIV positive.
WINTER 1991	Peter writes his first screenplay, *Big Sis*, about an HIV-positive former basketball player.
APRIL 29, 1992	The police officers who beat Rodney King are acquitted; Los Angeles burns.
SUMMER 1992	Mom and I move to the desert.
SUMMER 1993	Peter auditions for *The Real World*; he turns twenty-one.
MARCH 22, 1994	Peter is attacked at the Renaissance Night Club in Santa Monica, California; he loses his right eye.
JUNE 17, 1994	Peter has surgery to implant a prosthetic eye; in the hospital, we watch the O. J. Simpson car chase.
SUMMER 1994	Peter works as Kelly LeBrock's bodyguard; he joins Alcoholics Anonymous.

Summer 1996	We take a cross-country family trip.
1998	Peter cowrites *Visions of Darkness*; he forms Goliath.
August 16, 2000	Cypress Hill plays the Fillmore; my brother, now known as XL the 1I, hypes the crowd.
Spring 2001	I meet my father for the first time; my brother drives me.
May 2001	XL serves as the MC for Los Marijuanos; his group, Supreme Kourt, opens a show.
August 30, 2001	Supreme Kourt opens for Cypress Hill at the Hard Rock in Las Vegas; XL turns twenty-nine.
Spring 2002	XL is hired to protect the kids of Ozzy Osbourne.
Fall 2002	I am studying in England; my brother calls to tell me that his girlfriend has had an abortion.
December 2002	We take a family trip to Paris, Barcelona, and Córdoba.
February 2003	XL travels with Linkin Park and Cypress Hill.
Spring 2003	XL co-MCs *Mass Distortion*, "where hip-hop meets rock," on Power 106.
July 4, 2003	The accident
Spring 2014	Kai Peter Kimball Slate is born.
Winter 2016	Lucia Ann Iona Slate is born.

References and Further Reading

"He was a large Black man dancing with a young White woman . . ." In my first book, I capitalized *Black* but not *white*. "I have chosen to keep 'white' lowercased," I explained, "in part because the capitalization of 'white' and the de-capitalization of 'Negro' long signified white supremacy and in part to register, albeit in a small way, the many historical differences between being Black and being white." I've changed my mind. One of the biggest lessons I learned while writing this book is the importance of White people recognizing their Whiteness. Although I don't expect that a capital *W* will greatly advance that cause, I've come to agree with the poet Eve Ewing and the philosopher Kwame Anthony Appiah that capitalizing both *Black* and *White* is the best approach in our current historical moment. I have followed convention in not capitalizing *mixed*, even though many people have come to identify primarily as mixed, biracial, or multiracial. For an argument in support of capitalizing *Black* and not *white*, see Mike Lewis, "Why We Capitalize 'Black' (and Not 'White')," *Columbia Journalism Review*, June 16, 2020, https://www.cjr.org /analysis/capital-b-black-styleguide.php. For an argument in support of capitalizing both terms, see Kwame Anthony Appiah, "The Case for Capitalizing the B in Black," *The Atlantic*, June 18, 2020, https://www.theatlantic.com/ideas/archive /2020/06/time-to-capitalize-blackand-white/613159/.

"Let's call him Steven—the one who started the fight . . ." I use a pseudonym for three of the figures in this book: the man I call Steven, the man I call Jack, and the woman I call Ola.

"I'm reading about my brother in *Variety* magazine . . ." Michael Fleming, "High Price for Payday," *Variety* 355, no. 3 (May 9, 1994): 18; *Indiana Gazette*, October 21, 1997.

"The war centered on the fate of Biafra . . ." Richard Bourne, *Nigeria: A New History of a Turbulent Century* (London: Zed Books, 2015); Toyin Falola and Matthew M. Heaton, *A History of Nigeria* (Cambridge: Cambridge University Press, 2008). For a more personal perspective, see Chinua Achebe, *There Was a Country: A Personal History of Biafra* (New York: Penguin, 2012); Chimamanda Ngozi Adichie, *Half of a Yellow Sun* (New York: Knopf, 2006).

"The case was perfectly named: *Loving v. Virginia*." Sheryll Cashin, *Loving: Interracial Intimacy in America and the Threat to White Supremacy* (Boston: Beacon Press, 2017).

"The Black writer Chester Himes said . . ." Chester Himes, *Quality of Hurt* (New York: Thunder's Mouth Press, 1972), 75. Also see Khalil Gibran Muhammad, *The Condemnation of Blackness: Race, Crime, and the Making of Modern Urban America* (Cambridge, MA: Harvard University Press, 2010).

"In the 1940s, the Clarks conducted a series of experiments . . ." Legal Defense Fund, "*Brown v. Board* and the 'Doll Test,'" http://www.naacpldf.org/brown-at-60-the-doll-test.

"Supporters of the new law were sensitive . . ." Position Statement from the American Civil Liberties Union to the Los Angeles City Board of Education, 1973, John Walton Caughey School Integration Collection, http://library.csun.edu/SCA/Peek-in-the-Stacks/DesegregationBusing. On the larger history of busing and school segregation, see J. Anthony Lukas, *Common Ground: A Turbulent Decade in the Lives of Three American Families* (New York: Vintage, 1986); Ansley T. Erickson, *Making the Unequal Metropolis: School Desegregation and Its Limits* (Chicago: University of Chicago Press, 2016).

"In the late 1950s, Emory Holmes . . ." Juan-Paul R. de Guzman, "Race, Community, and Activism in Greater Los Angeles," in *The Nation and Its Peoples: Citizens, Denizens, Migrants*, ed. John Park and Shannon Gleeson (New York: Routledge, 2014), 41.

"Asked in 1999 about the surge in newcomers from Mexico and Central America, Carter told a reporter . . ." Kurt Streeter, "Keeping in Touch with Roots at Styles Ville," *Los Angeles Times*, May 1, 1999.

"Aguilar could not speak English but . . ." *Publications of the Historical Society of Southern California*, Volume IV, 285.

"Most of the homes were sold with racial covenants . . ." David Colker, "Saturday Journal: Building a 'Future' in 1948: A Riddle and a Single House Launched 'American Way of Fife' in Panorama City," *Los Angeles Times*, September 4, 1999, http://articles.latimes.com/print/1999/sep/04/news/mn-6823; Lizabeth Cohen, *A Consumers' Republic: The Politics of Mass Consumption in Postwar America* (New York: Knopf, 2003), 170–173; Ira Katznelson, *When Affirmative Action Was White: An Untold History of Racial Inequality in Twentieth-Century America* (New York: Norton, 2006).

"In 1978, a retired policeman went on local TV . . ." Mike Davis, *City of Quartz: Excavating the Future in Los Angeles* (New York: Verso, 1990), 271–272.

"King became famous, and his fame was telling." Kimberlé Crenshaw and Gary Peller, "Reel Time / Real Justice," in *Reading Rodney King / Reading Urban Uprising*, ed. Robert Gooding-Williams (New York: Routledge, 1993), 56–72; Max Felker-Kantor, *Policing Los Angeles: Race, Resistance, and the Rise of the LAPD* (Chapel Hill: University of North Carolina Press, 2018), 222.

"We may be finding that in some Blacks . . ." "Coast Police Chief Accused of Racism," *New York Times*, May 13, 1982; Patt Morrison, "Daryl F. Gates: Clear Blue, An Interview with the Former Longtime LAPD Chief," *Los Angeles Times*, May 23, 2009, http://articles.latimes.com/2009/may/23/opinion/la-oe-morrison-new23-2009may23.

"Later, we would learn the numbers: more than eight hundred buildings burned to the ground . . ." Min Hyoung Song, *Strange Future: Pessimism and the 1992 Los Angeles Riots* (Durham: Duke University Press, 2005); Michael Omi and Howard Winant, "The L.A. Race Riot and U.S. Politics," in *Reading Rodney King / Reading Urban Uprising*, ed. Robert Gooding-Williams (New York: Routledge, 1993), 97–116; Joao H. Costa Vargas, *Catching Hell in the City of Angels: Life and Meanings of Blackness in South Central Los Angeles* (Minneapolis: University of Minnesota Press, 2006), 14; Jerome G. Miller, *Search and Destroy: African-American Males in the Criminal Justice System* (New York: Cambridge University Press, 1996); Melvin L. Oliver, James H. Johnson Jr., and Walter C. Farrell Jr., "Anatomy of a Rebellion: A Political-Economic Analysis," in *Reading Rodney King / Reading Urban Uprising*, ed. Robert Gooding-Williams (New York: Routledge, 1993), 117–141.

"Writing in the 1880s, one of the city's most famous boosters . . ." Helen Hunt Jackson, "Echoes in the City of the Angels," *The Century* (1883), reprinted in David L. Ulin, *Writing Los Angeles: A Literary Anthology* (New York: Library of America, 2002), 48–49; Joseph P. Widney, *Race Life of the Aryan Peoples* (New York: Funk and Wagnalls, 1907); David Rieff, *Los Angeles: Capital of the Third World* (New York: Simon and Schuster, 1991), 75.

"To protect such a lily-white Eden . . ." Davis, *City of Quartz*, 28, 162.

"In 1924, a professor of chemistry in Los Angeles . . ." Andrew Rotter, *Comrades at Odds: The United States and India, 1947–1964* (Ithaca: Cornell University Press, 2000), 167.

"LA's first Black neighborhood . . ." Arna Bontemps, *God Sends Sunday* (1931), reprinted in Ulin, *Writing Los Angeles*, 89; Walter Mosley, *Devil in a Blue Dress: A Novel* (New York: Norton, 1990), 27.

"The practice of 'redlining' neighborhoods based on their ethnic makeup created a self-fulfilling prophecy." Richard Rothstein, *The Color of Law: A Forgotten History of How Our Government Segregated America* (New York: Liveright, 2017).

"'So far as Negroes are concerned,' Langston Hughes said . . ." Arnold Rampersad, *Life of Langston Hughes, Vol. 1, 1902–1941: I, Too, Sing America* (Oxford: Oxford University Press, 1986), 371.

"In October 1995, a Gallup poll found . . ." Jesse Washington, "A Black and White View of the O.J. Simpson Case 20 Years Later," *Huffington Post*, http://www.huffingtonpost.com/2014/06/08/oj-simpson-trial_n_5468851.html; Kathy Frankovic, "The O.J. Simpson Case and the Public: 20 Years Later," YouGov-America, https://today.yougov.com/news/2014/06/12/oj-simpson-case-and-race-20-years-later/.

"Whiteness has long served as a bridge across the class divide . . ." W. E. B. Du Bois, *Black Reconstruction* (1935), 700–701; David Roediger, *The Wages of Whiteness* (New York: Verso, 1991).

"Alcoholism did not discriminate." Ernest Kurtz, *Not God: A History of Alcoholics Anonymous* (Center City, MN: Hazelden Educational Services, 1979), 148–149; *"Special Composition Groups in A.A.," BareFoots*, http://www.bare footsworld.net/aaspecialgroups.html.

Nico Slate is a Professor in the Department of History at Carnegie Mellon University and the author of four books, including *Lord Cornwallis Is Dead: The Struggle for Democracy in the United States and India* and *Gandhi's Search for the Perfect Diet: Eating with the World in Mind.*